India's Immortal Comic Books

Contemporary Indian Studies

Published in association with the American Institute of Indian Studies

Susan S. Wadley, Chair, Publications Committee/general editor

AIIS Publications Committee/series advisory board:
Susan S. Wadley
John Echeverri-Gent
Brian Hatcher
David Lelyveld
Priti Ramamurthy
Martha Selby

Books in this series are recipients of the *Edward Cameron Dimock, Jr. Prize in the Indian Humanities* and the *Joseph W. Elder Prize in the Indian Social Sciences* awarded by the American Institute of Indian Studies and are published with the Institute's generous support.

A list of titles in this series appears at the back of the book.

India's Immortal Comic Books:
Gods, Kings, and Other Heroes

Karline McLain

Indiana University Press

Bloomington & Indianapolis

This book is a publication of

Indiana University Press
601 North Morton Street
Bloomington, IN 47404-3797 USA

http://iupress.indiana.edu

Telephone orders   800-842-6796
Fax orders   812-855-7931
Orders by e-mail   iuporder@indiana.edu

The paper used in this publication meets the minimum requirements of American
National Standard for Information Sciences—Permanence of Paper for Printed Library
Materials, ANSI Z39.48-1984.

Manufactured in the United States of America
Library of Congress Cataloging-in-Publication Data

McLain, Karline.
  India's immortal comic books : gods, kings, and other heroes / Karline McLain.
    p. cm. — (Contemporary Indian studies)
  Includes bibliographical references and index.
  ISBN 978-0-253-35277-4 (cloth : alk. paper) — ISBN 978-0-253-22052-3 (pbk. :
alk. paper) 1. Amar chitra katha. 2. Comic books, strips, etc.—Social aspects—India.
3. Comic books, strips, etc.—Moral and ethical aspects—India. I. Title.
  PN6790.I4M56 2009
  741.5'954—dc22
                              2008030209

1 2 3 4 5 14 13 12 11 10 09

Contents

Illustrations

Acknowledgments

This book has benefited from the generosity of many people and institutions over the years, and it is my pleasure to acknowledge my multiple debts and offer my sincerest thanks here. First, I thank all of the comic book artists, authors, editors, and readers in India and elsewhere who gave freely of their time and insight, without whom this project would not have been possible. I am particularly grateful to Anant Pai at *Amar Chitra Katha* for his hospitality and wealth of stories. Among the comic book artists and authors at *Amar Chitra Katha, Tinkle,* and *Vivalok,* I must single out the generosity of Yusuf Bangalorewala, Pushpa Bharati, Kamala Chandrakant, Luis Fernandes, Satyavrata Ghosh, Priya Khanna, Savio Mascarenhas, Debrani Mitra, M. L. Mitra, M. Mohandas, Pratap Mulick, Dev Nadkarni, Reena Puri, Rajinder Singh Raj, Chandrakant Rane, Subba Rao, Souren Roy, Margie Sastry, Rukmini Sekhar, Yagya Sharma, and Ram Waeerkar. My research in Bombay was made enjoyable by the hospitality kindly offered by the entire staff at India Book House, Dr. Sunanda Pal in the Literature Department at SNDT Women's University, Rekha and Shanta at the Fulbright office, Zarina Mehta at UTV, and so many friends and acquaintances met along the way.

I am indebted to Janice Leoshko and Martha Selby, who had faith in this project from the very beginning, who have read countless drafts of each chapter, and who have been outstanding academic mentors. I also thank Kathryn Hansen, Syed Akbar Hyder, Patrick Olivelle, and Cynthia Talbot, who served on my dissertation committee at the University of Texas at Austin and provided critical guidance as I worked to transform this research into a book manuscript. Many other academic colleagues have generously read and critiqued this book at various stages of the process, and I am grateful for their comments and support: Maria Antonaccio, Laura Brueck, Alicia DeNicola, Edeltraud Harzer, Steven Lindquist, Paul Macdonald, Eric Michael Mazur, Gail Minault, Herman van Olphen, Lisa Owen, Susan Reed, James Mark Shields, Rivka Ulmer, Kamala Visweswaran, Jarrod Whitaker, and Carol Wayne White. I thank Philip Lutgendorf at the University of Iowa, who loaned me his *Valmiki's Ramayana* comic book when I was an undergraduate, first sparking my interest in Indian comics, and I thank the undergraduate students who have enrolled in my seminars at Bucknell University for their engagement with my research on Indian comic books.

This project has received generous financial support from several institutions over the years, for which I am very grateful. Fulbright-Hays DDRA funded my research in India in 2001 and 2002. A return trip to India in 2007 was supported by grants from the National Endowment for the Humanities and the American Academy of Religion. Writing support was provided by a grant from the Dolores Zohrab Liebmann Foundation from 2002 to 2005 and by the University of Texas at Austin. The American Institute of Indian Studies awarded this manuscript the Edward Cameron Dimock, Jr. Book Prize in the Indian Humanities in 2007 and provided supplemental funds for the publication of this book by Indiana University Press. I thank Susan Wadley and the other members of the publications committee at AIIS, as well as the two anonymous reviewers, for awarding my manuscript with this great honor. Finally, I must acknowledge with gratitude my editor at Indiana University Press, Rebecca Tolen, for her valuable insights, as well as Laura MacLeod, Elaine Durham Otto, and many others who worked behind the scenes at Indiana University Press to transform my manuscript into a publishable book.

Several portions of this book have appeared in earlier versions. A segment of chapter 1 was published as "Lifting the Mountain: Debating the Place of Science and Faith in the Production of a *Krishna* Comic Book," *Journal of Vaishnava Studies* 13.2 (2005): 22–37 (copyright © A. Deepak Publishing, Inc. and the author, 2005; reprinted with permission). An earlier version of chapter 6 was published as "Who Shot the Mahatma? Representing Gandhian Politics in Indian Comic Books," *South Asia Research* 27.1 (2007): 57–77 (copyright © Sage Publications, 2007; reprinted with permission). Finally, an earlier version of chapter 3 was published as "Holy Superheroine: A Comic Book Interpretation of the Hindu *Devi Mahatmya* Scripture," *Bulletin of the School for Oriental and African Studies* 71.2 (2008): 297–322 (copyright © Cambridge University Press, 2008; reprinted with permission). I thank the editors of these journals, as well as the anonymous peer reviewers of each of these articles, for their helpful comments.

I have several people to thank for helping me gather images for this book and for generously granting permission to reprint them here: Padmini Mirchandani, publishing director at India Book House, and Samir Patil, CEO of ACK Media, for granting permission to reprint images from the *Amar Chitra Katha* comic books; Rukmini Sekhar, director of the Viveka Foundation, for granting permission to reprint images from the *Vivalok* comic books; Ganesh V. Shivaswamy for help in locating prints by artist Raja Ravi Varma; and Chandralekha Maitra and others at Osian's Connoisseurs of Art for help in locating images of the paintings by artist A. R. Chughtai.

Finally, sincerest thanks to my parents, Nancy, Gary, and Laurie; my brother, Justin; my nephews and nieces; and members of my extended family who have put up with my sojourns away from home and my comic book fixation with a seemingly endless supply of moral support, patience, and good humor. My husband, Jonathan, has read every word in this book many times over, accompanied me on two research trips to India, and endured my absences on other occasions when I was away conducting research. This book would not have been possible without his love and encouragement.

Transliteration Note

In the interest of readability and accessibility for general readers, the use of diacritics is minimized throughout this book. The titles of Sanskrit texts are printed with diacritics, such as *Rāmāyaṇa* and *Mahābhārata*. However, diacritics are omitted when they are not retained in the titles of modern retellings of classic literature, such as the *Valmiki's Ramayana* comic book or the *Ramayan* TV serial; diacritics are also omitted in direct oral quotes from comic book producers, readers, or other sources. Diacritics have been retained when discussing key technical Hindu religious terms, such as darśan and pūjā.

In Hindi and other modern Indian languages, the final short vowel of Sanskrit-language words is often omitted, thus the name of the Hindu god Rama is often pronounced "Ram" and the *Rāmāyaṇa* text is often pronounced "Ramayan." In the interest of consistency, I have retained the final vowel throughout the manuscript, except when directly quoting comic book producers, readers, or other sources that use the shorter form.

Also in the interest of consistency, I have used the name Bombay rather than Mumbai to refer to the capital city of the Indian state of Maharashtra, except when directly citing sources that use the latter version. In 1995, Bombay was officially renamed Mumbai; however, throughout my interviews with residents they commonly used Bombay in spoken conversations.

Finally, wherever Sanskrit, Hindi, and other terms specific to India appear for the first time (such as *dharma* and *ahimsa*), they are italicized and followed by a brief translation; thereafter such terms are romanized.

Transliteration Note

India's Immortal Comic Books

Introduction: Comic Books
That Radiate a Spiritual Force

The *Rama* comic book (no. 15, 1970) in the Indian series *Amar Chitra Katha* features a muscular, bare-chested, blue-tinged hero on its cover, posed with bow and arrow drawn, aiming at a target in the woods just outside the frame of the image (plate 1). Slightly behind him sits a beautiful, fair-skinned woman with long dark tresses, who watches with wonder as Rama, the hero, takes aim. Within the pages of this comic book, Rama establishes himself as a superhero by battling the demon Tataka and her hordes as a young prince; winning the beautiful Sita's hand in marriage through an athletic contest; surviving fourteen harsh years in exile in the wilderness to fulfill a vow made by his father, King Dasaratha; defeating the ten-headed and twenty-armed demon-king Ravana, who had kidnapped Sita, in an epic battle; and returning victoriously with his wife to the kingdom. In the final panel, Rama and Sita are crowned king and queen of Ayodhya (figure 1). Here they sit together on a grand throne, surrounded by their loyal followers and courtiers, while the narrative text proclaims: "Rama was crowned king in Ayodhya, and he ruled for many years" (32).

American comic books from the 1930s through the 1950s are famous for establishing the archetype of the superhero, which can be defined as someone who manifests six essential features: extraordinary powers, enemies, a strong moral code, a secret identity, a costume, and an origin story that explains how the hero acquired his powers and sets forth his motivations.[1] In *Rama*, the Indian superhero manifests all of these features. He demonstrates his extraordinary powers with his bow and arrow in his battles with his demonic enemies, as when he defeats the seemingly unconquerable Ravana. He demonstrates his strong moral code when he willingly goes into exile for fourteen years just to fulfill a vow his father had perhaps foolishly made, and when he sends a messenger to try to make peace with Ravana before their war begins. He assumes a secret identity during his years spent in exile, when he discards his royal attire and takes on the simple costume of a Hindu renouncer, disguising his true identity as the crown prince of Ayodhya. Finally, he has a unique origin story, which is explained in the introduction to this comic book: "The idea that God fulfills Himself in the best of men is conveyed by the life of Rama and that

Amar Chitra Katha makes an Indian proud of his or her heritage. . . . My eyes become moist thinking of the good that *ACK* has done to India's children. *Amar Chitra Katha* is not just a comic book. It radiates a spiritual force.

A reader

Figure 1. *Rama,* no. 15 [reprint no. 504] (Bombay: India Book House Pvt. Ltd., 1970 [1998]), 32. From *Amar Chitra Katha,* with the permission of the publishers ACK Media, India.

is the story of Ramayana." The *Rāmāyaṇa* is one of India's two great epics, the other being the *Mahābhārata.* Both of these epics were first composed in the Sanskrit language and date roughly to the middle of the first millennium BCE. The *Rāmāyaṇa* tells the story of Rama, who is not just an ideal king but a god-king, for the Hindu epic tradition maintains that the Supreme God has multiple *avatars* or incarnations that descend to earth in times of chaos in order to vanquish demonic forces and restore order. Rama is one of the most popular of these avatars among Hindu devotees, who consider him an incarnation of the Supreme God in human form and an ideal man.[2] Thus although the *Rama* comic book features a superhero that is in many ways akin to American comic book superheroes such as Superman and Captain America, Rama is not your average superhero. Rama is a god in human form, and the *Rama* comic book is therefore not a fictitious tale of the victory of good over evil but a Hindu devotional story told through the comic book medium.

Amar Chitra Katha (or *ACK*) is an English-language series that has dominated the flourishing comic book market in India since it was founded in 1967, with over 440 titles created and sales of more than 90 million issues to date. The two predominant and most distinctive forms of comic books in the world today are those of America and Japan. Structurally, these popular Indian comic books are closer to American comics than to Japanese. Like mainstream American comic books, Indian comic books are approximately 32 pages long, and each page is divided into several sequential panels (typically 3–6 per page) that feature a mixture of visual image, dialogue balloons, and narrative text. Indian comics, like American comics, have far more words than their Japanese counterparts and use far fewer frames and pages to depict an action or thought. Artistically, Indian comic books are also more like American comics in their depiction of the human form, which relies more on the tradition of naturalism than do Japanese comics. The similarities between Indian and American comics derive largely from the fact that *ACK* comics were inspired by the American comics that were available in India in the 1950s and 1960s, especially *Tarzan, Phantom*, and *Mandrake*. However, Indian comic books also diverge from American comic books in a couple of significant and interconnected ways.

First, in addition to being influenced by western artistic and storytelling traditions, these Indian comic books draw upon a long tradition of Indian visual and literary culture, and they have been especially influenced by the nationalist period in the late nineteenth and early twentieth centuries when popular images and texts were employed in India's struggle for independence from British colonial rule. Second, in indigenizing the comic book medium, these Indian comic books combine mythology and history, sacred and secular, in their effort to create a national canon of Indian heroes. *Amar Chitra Katha* means "immortal picture stories," and these comics seek to immortalize India's own heroes—its mythological gods and historical leaders—as their protagonists. The first comics in the series were mythological in nature, recasting classical Sanskrit narratives of Hindu deities like Rama, Krishna, and Shiva in the comic book format. Over the years, the series expanded to include issues on a variety of historical figures as well: celebrated Hindu kings such as Shivaji and Rana Pratap; medieval Hindu devotional poets like Ramdas and Tulsidas; modern Hindu sages like Swami Vivekananda; and colonial-era freedom fighters including Subhas Chandra Bose and Bhagat Singh. The successful *ACK* formula transforms such figures into superheroes who encounter their foes, be they mythological demons or medieval Muslim kings or colonial British officers; engage them in fierce battles; and in the end either emerge victorious or die bravely in the process.

For the reader quoted at the beginning of this chapter, a Hindu woman living in the American Midwest, these comics are not trivial throwaway children's books, nor are they mere collectors' items in a comic book maven's showcase. For her, *ACK* comics are far more: They are a resource that has helped her learn about and take pride in her Indian identity as well as a religious force in her life. And she is not alone. For the past forty years, *Amar Chitra Katha* comics have been an important means by which millions of Hindus have encountered the sacred in their everyday lives and a medium that has helped Indians living in postcolonial India and throughout the world define what it means to be Indian. These Indian comic books, therefore, have a power and a significance that is unique when compared with other comic books in the worldwide commercial industry. They are not considered primarily an entertainment product by their creators or their consumers; instead, they are regarded—often even revered—as foundational texts for the religious and national education of their young readers. Like their readers, we too should take these comics seriously, asking what they have meant to the generations of children who have grown up with them, and how the Hindu religion and Indian identity are constituted within them.

The Route to Your Roots

Bombay (also known as Mumbai), the cosmopolitan coastal capital of India's western state of Maharashtra, is famous for its Bollywood cinema industry, its Bombay Stock Exchange, and its teeming masses dreaming of fame and wealth. Bombay is also the home of India Book House, the publishing company of the *Amar Chitra Katha* comic book series.[3] With the permission of Anant Pai, the founding editor of *ACK*, I arrived at the comic book studio in the fall of 2001 and was immediately shown to an empty desk that they had cleared for me. I spent the next year analyzing the production and the consumption of *ACK*. When at the studio I moved between my desk in the artists' enclave, the glassed-in editorial offices that overlooked the artists' floor, and the studio library, observing the production of these comics and interacting with their creators. In chapter 1 I discuss the history of *Amar Chitra Katha* and provide an overview of the production process; here the focus is on who is reading *ACK*, and why.

My methods for learning about the Indian readers who purchased *ACK* comics were wide-ranging. While at the comic book studio in Bombay, I read the fan mail and subscription letters that were received during that year; I discussed the comics with customers who came to the studio in person to make purchases (usually adult consumers who were shipping the entire series overseas to grandchildren or other relatives); and I was granted access to official fan club membership lists, which I used to contact and interview dozens of *ACK* fan club members in Bombay and other urban centers (including Pune, Delhi, Kolkata, and Chennai), as well as in several smaller cities. I communicated with approximately fifty other former fan club members through mail, questionnaire forms, and e-mail. While in Bombay, I also visited college campuses to speak with students about their former comic book reading habits, and I interviewed several school principals whose schools use *ACK* in the classroom. In addition, I interviewed neighbors in Colaba (an affluent neighborhood where I rented a room in a ladies' hostel for my first few months in Bombay) and Vile Parle (a middle-class neighborhood where I rented a flat for the remainder of my time in the city); I sought out bookstall owners in neighborhood bazaars who sell *ACK*; and I spoke with several of the customers who buy secondhand comics as well.

All of this helped to form a picture of what these comics mean to their readers. But often the most useful information came from readers who were so passionate about *ACK* that they sought me out after learning about my research. On several occasions in 2001–2002 Indian journalists wrote about my ongoing research, and in the summer of 2007 I took part in a press conference held in Bombay in honor of the fortieth anniversary of *Amar Chitra Katha*. On each occasion when news articles about my research were published in Indian newspapers and magazines, my e-mail inbox was swamped with messages from readers who wrote to share their individual impressions of the comics. Here is just one of hundreds of such unsolicited messages, received from an Indian reader in August 2007:

> Dear Prof. McLain: I read a recent magazine article about you and that your Ph.D. was on the *Amar Chitra Katha* mythological comic books published in India. Born into a middle-class south Indian family, these comic books were a monthly staple at our home (one used to be bought every month for my brother and I—I think it cost about Rs. 3 back in the 1970s when I was a school kid). We virtually grew up with them, in addition to more "normal" ones such as *Archie, Dennis the Menace*, a World War II series from the UK, and a cowboy series. So, yes, we had an American inclination, quite normal in middle-class urban homes, and an Indian sensibility nurtured on *ACK* and another kid magazine called *Chandamama*. We were the new generation, born post-independence, and did not know Sanskrit like our parents did and relied on these sources for the stories, mythologies, and the divinity that pervade Indian life.

This message raises several important themes that are prevalent among Indian comic book readers. First, note his self-identification as a member of the "new generation," the first generation to be born into and grow up in a newly independent India, an India that had only attained liberation from British colonial rule in 1947. For the first generation of Indian comic book readers, those growing up in the late 1960s and 1970s, this was a time in which India was seeking its footing on the global stage and formulating its own national identity. Indian independence came at a great cost, for the Indian subcontinent was partitioned into two sovereign nation-states: the secular and democratic Republic of India and the Islamic Republic of Pakistan. The partition erupted into widespread chaos and communal conflict as Muslims migrated into East Pakistan (now Bangladesh) and West Pakistan (now Pakistan), and as Hindus and Sikhs migrated from East and West Pakistan into India. Estimates of the death toll in this massive migration range from hundreds of thousands to a million, and millions became homeless refugees. Those who grew up in the aftermath of partition felt its impact on a familial level, through stories of loved ones who were lost or killed or became impoverished during partition; on a national level, through the lasting legacy of Hindu-Muslim communal tensions in India; and on an international level, through the ongoing dispute over Kashmir and the wars waged between India and Pakistan.[4]

Newly independent India faced a number of challenges, and one of the most pressing was the need for national integration. India is a land of great diversity. In addition to the large population of Hindus that makes up approximately 80 percent of the Indian population, there are also Muslim, Sikh, Jain, Parsi, Christian, Jewish, and Buddhist religious communities. There is a vast linguistic diversity in India as well, with more than twenty languages recognized by the Constitution of India. India also features a great range of geographic, ethnic, and economic distinctiveness. All of this presented a substantial challenge to the first generation of leaders in independent India: how to allow for the expression of religious, linguistic, and regional diversity, and yet simultaneously cultivate a unified national consciousness that would forestall further partitions?

"Unity in diversity" was a motto that this first generation heard frequently. It was reinforced through their education, with textbooks that were designed to educate children about the history of each region; through national holidays, with festivals that showcased the diverse customs, arts, and foods of each region; and through popular culture, including *Amar Chitra Katha* comics. As *ACK* continued to grow in the 1970s, its creators added titles about historical figures from the many regions of India in an effort to promote national integration, and began to market the series as "the route to your roots." For a great many of the Indian readers with whom I spoke, *ACK* was instrumental in helping them learn to appreciate the diversity of India and to locate their own local traditions within the larger national tapestry. One reader in Bombay, who had once been a fan club president, stated that *ACK* brought the nation to her doorstep: "In my opinion *Amar Chitra Katha* does represent all of India. It is a complete union of the integrity and culture of India." Another reader, who grew up in south India in the 1970s but relocated to America as an adult, reflected nostalgically about the impact *ACK* had upon his early impressions of India: "My appreciation of the rich and glorious history and tradition of India and Hinduism has been bolstered primarily by *ACK* comics. I am sure many others of my generation feel the same." And indeed, countless others of his generation do share these sentiments.

A second important theme that is prevalent among comic book readers growing up in India is the emphasis on middle-class identity. In an article on middle-class religion in India, John Stratton Hawley writes, "Since the 1950s Indian society has rapidly transformed itself into a major bastion of the middle class" (2001, 225). This vast and rather amorphous category can be nearly impossible to define, but Hawley notes that the middle class in postcolonial India corresponds to English-language conceptions of the middle class in two ways. First, it is "wedged between the upper and lower echelons of society: moneyed 'aristocracy' on one flank, the urban and rural poor on the other"; and second, it is mobile, aiming to move upward into the class above (218). This is a useful starting place for understanding the middle-class sensibility of these Indian comic book readers, but three key hallmarks should be added here: The middle-class readers of *ACK* comics generally read and speak English, they come from an urban background, and they have a global outlook.

English became the language of administration in India in the nineteenth century, when India was a British colony. In postcolonial India, given the linguistic diversity of the country, English remains the national lingua franca, the de facto language of federal administration and of business. However, government-funded schools throughout India are usually conducted in the regional vernacular. To learn English, one must be able to afford the fees to enroll in a private English-medium school. Thus one dividing line between the working class and the middle class is the ability to read and speak English. A number of the comic book readers who grew up in the 1970s were the first in their family to be enrolled in English-medium schools, as part of their families' efforts to move up in socioeconomic status. Others came from more entrenched middle-class families, with parents and grandparents who had also received English educations. For both English-speaking and non-English-speaking parents, the *ACK* comics—created in English for this English-speaking middle-class market—were viewed as a positive influence, a way for children to practice their English-language skills outside of school. As one reader in Bombay stated, "My mother bought the comics when I was at school as a way to learn English and [Indian] culture at the same time."

The middle-class *ACK* readers also typically come from an urban background and have a global outlook. The reader in the message cited above describes himself as coming from a middle-class family in urban south India, where he was raised with an "American inclination" but nonetheless developed an "Indian sensibility" thanks in large part to *ACK*. He and the other *ACK* readers have little knowledge of or connection to village India. Instead, they have grown up in an urban environment that has seen rapid changes in many realms as independent India underwent globalization: industrial, informational, economic, political, legal, social, cultural, and religious. These readers therefore often feel the need to retain their Indian identity in the face of increasing global homogenization. Many spoke almost wistfully of a certain unique "Indianness" that they felt was being threatened with extinction in the modern world. One reader from south India, for instance, saw *ACK* as a way of reviving Indian culture: "*ACK* was my first comic, and whenever I get a chance I still read them. I am 32, but still I enjoy the illustrations, the stories, and the message. . . . It is the only value-for-money comics which brings our glorious culture, tradition, back to life to normal people." Another reader stated that *ACK* comics were important because they help Indians to embrace globalization without submitting to homogenization. In his words, "India is a country with an equally great past as any European country (National Pride). While it is important to embrace modernity (comics in English) it is important to do so on one's own terms (Indian mythology)." For these readers, *ACK* is perceived as a significant force in helping them develop an "Indian sensibility"; that is, helping them to articulate what it means to be Indian in the modern world.

Finally, a third important theme that is prevalent among Hindu comic book readers is the role that these comics play in their religious education. The reader in the message cited above explained that unlike his parents, he never learned Sanskrit, the sacred language of Hinduism; instead of reading the *Rāmāyaṇa* and other Sanskrit scripture, he relied on the *Amar Chitra Katha* comics to learn Hindu "stories, mythologies, and the divinity that pervade Indian life." Traditionally, high-caste Hindus, especially those born into a Brahmin (priestly) caste, would work with a Brahmin priest to memorize at least a few select verses of Sanskrit scripture as part of adolescent rites of passage; others, of course, would go on to memorize far more from the sacred corpus of Hindu scripture. In addition to the memorization of Sanskrit texts, other sources of religious instruction—and group entertainment—in village India include the recounting of Hindu mythology through oral folk stories, wandering bards, puppet shows, plays, and dances. But as families migrated to urban centers in newly independent India in search of employment and educational opportunities for their children, many left behind the traditional joint family system and resettled as nuclear family units. Thus the generation of readers growing up in urban India in the 1970s often did not have an extended support network: no grandmother to tell them the stories of the Hindu gods at bedtime, no village priest to teach them Sanskrit.

Furthermore, the leaders of newly independent India placed a strong emphasis on secular education, particularly science. India's first prime minister, Jawaharlal Nehru (1889–1964), and the leaders who followed him, including his daughter Indira Gandhi, who served as prime minister from 1966 to 1977 and from 1980 to 1984, had to tackle substantial problems facing independent India, especially poverty and famine. Nehru stressed that India's progress was dependent upon the youth of India, and his administration undertook the establishment of numerous village schools and urban institutes of science, technology, medicine, and management in an effort to modernize and solve the nation's problems. The 1960s saw the Green Revolution, the effort to increase agricultural production in order to help the poor attain self-sufficiency in food production and combat famine; this was followed in 1970 by the White Revolution, the creation of a nationwide milk grid. Other problems were tackled: extending the water supply and energy grid through hydroelectricity and nuclear energy programs; increasing industry; improving infrastructure.[5]

Thus the children growing up in India during the 1960s and 1970s were encouraged to study and work for the development of the country. Religious education, therefore, was secondary for many. Learning Hindu scripture and mythology was relegated to one's spare time: to leisure activities such as attending seasonal festive performances of the epics, watching mythological films, and reading mythological comic books. But this meant that while traditional religious instruction was on the decline, the importance of popular media as the carriers of religious beliefs, practices, and identities was on the incline. One senior citizen who raised two children in Bombay in the 1960s and 1970s explained that he and his wife viewed the *ACK* comic books as "accurate and authentic" products that are "loyal to the original" Hindu scriptures. Therefore, they agreed that the comics were useful tools for their children's moral and religious upbringing: "We as parents raised two children with stories from *Amar Chitra Katha* comics and till this day we reminisce with them about moral stories to see how much impact these stories have had on their upbringing."

The generation of comic book readers growing up in middle-class urban families in India in the 1960s and 1970s, then, saw themselves as the "new generation" who would unite across regional, linguistic, and religious differences to help independent India prosper on the global stage; the generation who would retain their distinctive Indianness while coming to terms with their urban environment and the forces of globalization; the generation raised to value English-language education, science, and secularism. *Amar Chitra Katha* comics helped this generation develop a national consciousness through their focus on historic figures from the various regions of India and from its many religious communities; they encouraged this generation to embrace English-language education, science, and globalization while retaining a uniquely Indian sensibility and identity; and they allowed the Hindus of this generation to maintain some connection with traditional Hindu religious education by recasting classical Sanskrit devotional stories of the Hindu gods in this popular medium.

The next generation of comic book readers, the urban middle-class Indians who grew up in the 1980s and 1990s, lived in a very different context. These decades saw the rapid rise of consumer culture in India, especially following the liberalization of the Indian economy in 1991; the increasingly vocal challenges of lower castes to the upper castes who dominated the middle class, as seen in the contentious Mandal Commission report of 1980, which recommended an affirmative action program for the lower castes and triggered protests throughout the decade; and increasing disillusionment with the long dominant political party, the Congress, in the wake of Indira Gandhi's imposition of martial law with the declaration of a National Emergency in 1975, and allegations of corruption during both

Indira Gandhi's term and the rule of her son, Rajiv Gandhi (1984–89). In *The Great Indian Middle Class,* Pavan Varma calls this period the "end of innocence" and argues that the middle class changed drastically over these decades: "Earlier, in the years after 1947, the middle class had given allegiance to a leadership that had an aura of personal sacrifice, a long association with politics in the struggle for freedom, an unambiguous set of ideological beliefs, a professed disdain for material pursuits, and unquestioned personal integrity. Nehru fitted this bill. Some three decades later . . . the middle class was not only bereft of an ideological framework, it was generally tired of the *deceit* of ideology" (1999, 112–13).

In this period, Hindu nationalism gained prominence among the middle class. Hindu nationalism is an anti-secular movement which asserts that Hinduism is the national religion and culture of India. A foundational definition of *Hindutva,* or "Hinduness," was set forth by V. D. Savarkar in *Hindutva: Who Is a Hindu?* (1923), wherein he argued that a "Hindu" was anyone who regarded India as both their motherland and their holy land. Thus Hindus, Sikhs, Jains, and Buddhists could all be considered "Hindus." But for Savarkar and many other Hindu nationalists, Indian Muslims and Christians, who regard places outside of India as their holy land (such as Mecca or Jerusalem), cannot be "Hindus." Furthermore, according to Savarkar and his followers, India should be recognized as a Hindu land and governed accordingly. Although this ideology had existed since before independence, it was in this post-Nehruvian era that the Hindu nationalist movement moved from the sidelines and into the mainstream in urban India. Discussing Bombay in particular, Rachel Dwyer writes that in the 1980s Hindu nationalism "began to reach beyond the traditional Brahminical membership of the Hindu right to the middle castes and classes, a position it achieved through its anti-secularist stance, arguing that although Hindu culture had long been sidelined, now was the time to reclaim a Hindu identity with pride. Its new definition of modernity and the modern state, with an emphasis on family values and religion, had great appeal" (2000, 76).

The Bharatiya Janata Party (BJP) was formed in 1980 as a conservative Hindu nationalist political party that set out to champion the rights of Hindus and to oppose the Congress Party. The BJP, along with other political, social, and cultural Hindu nationalist groups collectively known as the Sangh Parivar (including the Rashtriya Swayamsevak Sangh or RSS, the Vishva Hindu Parishad or VHP, the Bajrang Dal, and the Shiv Sena), have gained a substantial following among the Indian middle class since 1980, and the BJP won the majority of seats in national elections in 1996, 1998, and 1999, but was defeated by the Congress Party in 2004.[6]

During the 1980s and 1990s as Hindu nationalism was on the rise, debates were ongoing in India about the definition of Hinduism; the place of religious minorities, especially the largest minority—Muslims—within the nation; the place of *Dalits* (commonly known as "untouchables" or "outcastes") and lower castes within Hinduism; the proper roles of modern Indian women; and the definition of secularism. As will be seen in the following chapters, these debates form the background against which the producers of *Amar Chitra Katha* decided who to portray as heroes and who to depict as villains in the comic book series. Interviews with readers who grew up in India during this period demonstrate that this is also the background against which consumers read the comics. One reader who grew up in Bangalore, India, in the 1980s and has since relocated to the United States identified himself as a "very proud Hindu," then stated that *ACK* had taught him "every good value there is," proclaiming:

> I have read . . . all about the Muslim saints and invaders. They have been represented perfectly. It can't get any better than this. I don't think a single finger has been pointed at *Amar Chitra Katha* by any of the religious minorities; on the contrary they have upheld it. This is true secularism. This is truth.

When asked if he could name his favorite issues within this comic book series, this reader continued:

> I won't do justice by choosing just a few. I love and cherish each and every single one of them. From the story of Padmini who sacrificed her life, the tyranny of the Muslim rulers who roughed up ancient and glorious India, great women of India, the heroes of battles, the great saints and pious sages of this great land, . . . the numerous and wonderful stories of ancient Indian mythology, . . . the freedom fighters of India, to the gods and goddesses of India. A single word description to all these is "India," and that's what I love about these books.

Such statements not only demonstrate this reader's lasting devotion to *ACK*; they also illustrate the Hindu nationalist conception of India as a Hindu land, populated by heroic men who battle "invading" Muslims and colonial British officers, heroic women such as the medieval queen Padmini who are willing to sacrifice their lives to save their honor from Muslim "invaders," and pious sages devoted to the Hindu gods and goddesses. But this reader was insistent that these comics do not have a Hindu nationalist agenda. "To think of it as being part of a political agenda is insane!!!" he stated. For this reader and others who share his views, *ACK* are much more than mere comics. They are the "truth" of India, a truth so cherished that it is taboo even to question it.

Another reader replied to the question of whether *ACK* had an underlying Hindu nationalist or other agenda by stating, "Please, please don't ever ask this question. This is the best thing that happened to the children of India. I guess one has to be Indian to understand this. Please let's not get cold calculations and political agendas into the picture." But other Indians who grew up in the 1980s and also encountered *ACK* in the context of rising Hindu nationalism chose to reject the comics outright as "damn Hindutva propaganda, meant to brainwash children," to cite the words of one young man in Bombay, who described himself as a "Hindu, but not a Hindutvadi [proponent of Hindutva]." Whether accepting the comics as an unquestionable and cherished national truth, or rejecting them as a distorted Hindu nationalist picture of India, these impassioned responses to *Amar Chitra Katha* testify to the significance of *ACK* in the lives of middle-class Indians, for neither party sees them as trivial children's books. How did this comic book series acquire this status?

The Pleasures of Reading Comic Books in India

When asked if *Amar Chitra Katha* had an underlying agenda or message, another reader who grew up in south India in the 1980s replied:

> Never really thought about it—maybe they tie in to Hindu nationalism. I was 12–13 when I read 'em, so I didn't pick up on much of that. I just loved the stories of Hanuman picking up mountains, blue-skinned archers, Birbal vexing the king, etc. . . . I definitely feel that *Amar Chitra Katha* contributed a lot to my psyche. I have a murky mythology embedded within.

While *ACK* comic books are read by some adults in India, they target children between the ages of eight and eighteen in an effort to teach them what it means to be Indian—to provide a route to their roots—through a fun, visual medium that children will be drawn to. In thinking about the place of these comics in the lives of their young Indian readers, therefore, we must take note of the many interrelated and often overlapping pleasures associated with reading them. This reader's comment serves as a reminder that children find these comics appealing because they enjoy reading them, and they are often not thinking critically about the larger implications of the comics as they do so. As an adult, he now admits that *ACK* may have embodied some ideology about religion and the nation, but as a child he was drawn to the adventures of India's epic heroes. Others also cited issues featuring the Hindu monkey-god Hanuman, the blue-skinned archer and god-king Rama, and other heroes from the *Rāmāyaṇa* and the *Mahābhārata* as their favorites. A reader in Bombay who listed the issues *Rama* and *Karna* (no. 26, 1972) as her favorites remarked, "I love the epic ones. Only these have an essence of Indianness which is truly worth appreciating. It makes you feel proud about being an Indian." Thus one type of pleasure associated with *ACK* is derived from reading indigenous comic books that feature uniquely Indian heroes and stories. The vast majority of Indian readers were familiar with the western comics (American and European) that are readily available in India, especially *Tarzan, The Phantom,* and *Mandrake the Magician* among the first generation of readers; and *Archie, Asterix,* and *Tintin* among the next generation. Although Indian comic strips had previously appeared in Indian publications—such as

Chandamama, a monthly children's magazine that was founded in 1947 and featured a mix of stories, games, and short comic strips featuring Indian characters—*Amar Chitra Katha* was the first to feature Indian figures and Indian stories in the comic book medium. Indian readers have taken great pride in having their own comic book series, claiming during interviews that "nothing matches up to *ACK*," "*ACK* is the most invaluable comics in human history to date," and other equally lofty proclamations of devotion. Significantly, several readers who made such proclamations identified themselves as Sikh, Parsi, Christian, or members of other non-Hindu religions, and stressed that as Indians, the Indian epics were part of their heritage, too. They credited *ACK* with making that heritage available to them.

A second type of pleasure commonly associated with *ACK* is the patriotism inspired by reading the historical issues that feature medieval kings like *Shivaji* (no. 23, 1971) and colonial-era freedom fighters including *Bhagat Singh* (no. 234, 1981) and *Chandra Shekhar Azad* (no. 142, 1977). Shivaji was praised for his "bravery," and Bhagat Singh and Chandra Shekhar Azad were praised for their "patriotism." In the words of one Indian reader, "All the patriotic ones were my favorites—*Bhagat Singh, Rash Behari Bose, Chandra Shekhar Azad*. I liked them because their stories were true and recent." Another agreed, commenting on the *Chandra Shekhar Azad* issue specifically, "Little was known about this great freedom fighter. The comic gave his entire life in a short and easy manner."

Another type of pleasure associated with *ACK* is the pleasure derived from reading the humorous issues featuring Indian animal fables from the classic *Pañcatantra* and the *Jātakas*, including *Panchatantra: How the Jackal Ate the Elephant and Other Stories* (no. 163, 1978), *Panchatantra: The Brahmin and the Goat and Other Stories* (no. 138, 1977), *Jataka Tales: Jackal Stories* (no. 195, 1970), and *Jataka Tales: Elephant Stories* (no. 126, 1977), as well as issues featuring the ever popular Mughal-era court jester Birbal, such as *Birbal the Witty* (no. 152, 1978) and *Birbal the Clever* (no. 210, 1980). Readers liked these comics for their humor and lightheartedness. One reader explained, "The book of *Panchatantra* is quite big and drab to read. *Amar Chitra Katha* in colored pictures makes the stories of *Panchatantra* attractive and readable."

As some of these comments from readers indicate, a fourth type of pleasure comes from the "short and easy" comic book medium itself, which combines text and image to make mythological and historical stories "attractive and readable." One reader stated that he could "look at each picture for hours and admire the care the artist has taken to lay out all the minor details. Like in a war scene, the way broken arrows are strewn around, chariots are lying around, etc." Other readers also stressed the appeal of the image in addition to the word, stating, "A picture is worth a thousand words, of course," and "We new generation kids find Indian past and thoughts outdated, but these comics beautifully depict our stories, giving us a lot of information!"

Yet another type of pleasure comes from the comfort that is derived from the repetition of the successful *ACK* formula in which a hero encounters foes, battles them, and either emerges victorious in the end or dies bravely. Several scholars who have analyzed the reception of popular western entertainment media have noted the importance of repetition, arguing that consumers take pleasure in predictable narrative patterns. In her discussion of popular romance novels, for instance, Janice Radway comments that stock descriptions and formulaic characterizations permit "the reader to get by with a minimal amount of interpretive work" so that the reader's energy can be reserved "for the more desirable activity of affective reaction rather than prematurely spent on the merely intermediary task of interpretation" (1991, 195–96; also Modleski 1982, 32). Discussing the "Nancy Drew" series of formulaic children's books, Meghan O'Rourke notes that "the 'manufactured' nature of the series was curiously reassuring to kids, who felt that there was an endless supply of goods they knew and liked coming their way. . . . the more books that appeared in any given series, the more children bought them, confident that the supply would not run out" (2004, 128). The readers of *ACK* also take comfort in the seemingly endless supply of Indian comics they know and like, and many reported trying to buy as many issues as they could, like this reader who grew up in north India:

> For the longest time I used to buy these comics off the newsstand. Thus it resulted in a constant struggle with my parents for money. Fed up with my constant demands, the rule was that every Friday I could buy a comic book. It worked for a while. However, I started gaming this system, too. I would plead and buy a comic in advance, forfeiting my Friday one. However, come Friday, I'd beg and plead again. Also, I would take money from both parents and not tell them that the other one had already given me money for these comics. The newsstand guy was my first grown-up friend. I used to go there every day for half an hour, I guess.

With each new issue, this and other loyal readers anticipate an Indian hero who will be instantly likeable in his formulaic characterization and a storyline that will be immediately understandable and reassuring in its formulaic pattern in which good battles evil.

A final source of pleasure in reading *ACK* is unique to the Hindu readers who enjoyed learning more about their religion. In the case of mythological issues like *Rama*, some Hindus already know the story that will be told in the comic before they open it, for even without any formal Sanskrit religious instruction many have been previously exposed to Hindu mythology through rituals and festivals, stories told by parents and grandparents, or the mythological TV serials that began airing in the late 1980s. The pleasure they experience in reading *ACK*, therefore, derives not from the originality of the story or character but in seeing familiar stories and characters depicted in the comic book medium as a reinforcement of their religious knowledge base. As one reader commented, "They [*ACK*] were a big part of my childhood days. Fun to read, and read again. If I already knew the story, I would still look for the way it was represented." Other Hindu readers who were less familiar with Hindu mythology viewed the comics as one key source for their religious education, as did this reader who was "quizzed" on his knowledge of the *Mahābhārata* epic by his grandmother when the *Mahabharat* TV series aired in the late 1980s and who used the comics as a study aid: "Parallel to seeing it on TV, the stories from the *Mahabharat* were good to know. I actually could compete with my grandmother in the story when watching the TV."

Again and again, Hindus who grew up reading these comic books credited them with bringing mythology to life through their visual representations of the Hindu pantheon. Many adults were able to describe in detail specific images that still resonate with them from the pages of the comics they read as children. Several, for instance, recalled the imagery from page 27 of the *Gita* (no. 127, 1977), which depicts the moment in the *Bhagavad Gītā* in which Krishna reveals his true nature to Arjuna, demonstrating that he is no mere human—he is an incarnation of the Supreme God in human form (plate 2). One reader stated, "It was such an awesome image, with the rays of light shooting out from cosmic Krishna in all directions, and Brahma, Shiva, Devi, and the other gods within him. I understood the message of the *Gita* from this image." Another said, "I felt like I was Arjuna, standing on the battlefield looking up at Krishna's *virat roop* [cosmic form]. Today this is still the image of Krishna in my mind whenever I read the *Gita* or think about the meaning of Krishna."

A handful of Hindu readers even confessed that during their *pūjā*, or ritual worship of the Hindu gods, they sometimes envision the god or goddess as he or she was depicted in the pages of the comics they read years ago: "When I pray to Ram and Sita, like at Divali [a Hindu festival], I picture Ram and Sita from the comics—blue-skinned Ram with his bow and arrow, and Sita standing just beside him dressed in her simple forest clothes" (refer to plate 1). Such statements demonstrate the significance of the visual image within Hinduism. For Hindus, as Diana Eck has discussed, *darśan*, the act of seeing the gods, is the focus of ritual activity:

> The central act of Hindu worship, from the point of view of the lay person, is to stand in the presence of the deity and to behold the image with one's own eyes, to see and be seen by the deity. *Darśan* is sometimes translated as the "auspicious sight" of the divine, and its importance in the Hindu ritual complex reminds us that for Hindus "worship" is not only a matter of prayers

and offerings and the devotional disposition of the heart. Since, in the Hindu understanding, the deity is present in the image, the visual apprehension of the image is charged with religious meaning. Beholding the image is an act of worship, and through the eyes one gains the blessings of the divine. (1998, 3)

Hindu temples are regarded as the house of god, and Hindus visit temples in order to "take darśan" of the god or goddess that is housed within the image in the innermost sanctum of the temple, believing that the deity is present therein to see and be seen through this ritual exchange of glances. But the presence of Hindu deities is not limited to the inner sanctums of temples; gods and goddesses inhabit other images in order to bestow their blessings on their devotees. In many Hindu household shrines, small statues of the deities are used for daily darśan, as are the cheap printed images of the gods known as "god posters," "calendar art," and "bazaar art" that first became popular in the late nineteenth century with the arrival of the lithographic press in India. But as recent studies of media and religion in South Asia have shown, the Hindu experience of darśan is not limited to those images in temples and household shrines that have been officially consecrated through a ritual process. For example, Philip Lutgendorf has described the "ritualized public viewings" that took place throughout India when Ramanand Sagar's television series *Ramayan* aired on Sunday mornings from January 1987 to July 1988. Recounting just one such incident of televised darśan during the airing of this epic story of the gods Rama and Sita, Lutgendorf writes:

> [A] Banaras newspaper reported on a sweetshop where a borrowed television was set up each week on a makeshift altar sanctified with cow dung and Ganges water, worshipped with flowers and incense, and watched by a crowd of several hundred neighborhood residents, who then shared in the distribution of 125 kilos of sanctified sweets (*prasād*), which had been placed before the screen during the broadcast. (1995, 224)

Similarly, several other scholars have noted that Hindus have readily embraced television, film, and the internet, viewing all of these new visual media as forums for the ritual exchange of glances between deity and devotee and for religious edification through mythological storytelling.[7]

The *ACK* comic books are not intended to be used for ritual worship. In fact, to forestall this devotional reaction to the comic books, Anant Pai stated that he and the first comic book artists decided that the gods featured on the covers should not gaze directly out at the reader, so that the darśanic ritual exchange of glances between deity and devotee cannot occur. Thus on the cover of *Rama*, the god looks off to the side of the image (refer to plate 1); the cover of *Krishna* (no. 11, 1969) employs the same tactic in order to deny the frontality that is key to Hindu iconicity. Pai stated that he took this precaution because he was aware that in making *ACK*, he and many of his artists were not following the ritual prescriptions that govern the making of Hindu religious images (see Eck 1998), and he did not want to run the risk of offending any orthodox Hindus. Nonetheless, within the pages of *ACK* numerous panels do allow for the darśanic experience to occur. In *Sati and Shiva* (no. 111, 1976), Sati is shown in profile with her hands folded in prayer to Lord Shiva (plate 9). The narrative text at the top of the panel states, "Her whole being was concentrated on Shiva. She knew nothing else" (3). Above Sati a thought balloon floats, with Shiva depicted inside it. Here Shiva faces the reader outside the frame, rather than his devotee within the frame, so that his eyes meet our own.

Another example is found in the *Gita* comic book: When Krishna makes his famous speech to Arjuna in the midst of the battlefield, panels in which Krishna addresses Arjuna are alternated with those in which he addresses his remarks directly to the reader. Just before Krishna reveals his divine form to Arjuna, a close-up shot of Krishna's eyes is featured, with a dialogue balloon in which Krishna appears to speak to the reader directly (figure 2): "It is a form you cannot see with naked eyes. You need divine vision. I bestow it on you" (26). Because of this direct darśanic address to the reader, when Krishna does reveal his divine form in a full-page panel on the next page (refer to plate 2), it is as though he has done so primarily for the pleasure of his Hindu readers' edification. Such images do not derive from the American comic book formula, but are instead part of the "distinct gaze" that belongs to comics and other new media in South Asia that have been influenced by Hindu ritual practices and ways of seeing.[8]

Such iconic panels within the *ACK* comic books, in combination with the visual and textual narrativization of sacred Hindu stories, open up space for their Hindu readers to view them as something sacred, even if they do not ritually worship them. Thus we must take readers seriously when they say that *Amar Chitra Katha* comics are a central part of their religious life, that they "radiate a spiritual force." In recounting his first encounter with god posters in India, Christopher Pinney writes of his discovery of their power:

> After a few months, I purchased a large collection of calendar images of the goddess Kali. The violent allure of these pictures—what villagers called "photos of the gods" (*bhagwan ke photo*)—captivated me. For some time I displayed these on the walls of my house. I then tired of them and replaced them with others, less-demanding. Presently, a villager observing my bundle of Kali images expressed concern about their fate: they were powerful things and I should treat them with caution, he advised, and I should certainly ensure that they were worshipped regularly. (2004, 226)[9]

Although the Hindu gods are not considered to be present in the comic book image, as they are in consecrated Hindu temple statues or god posters, the comics in the *ACK* series are also regarded as something that embodies a powerful, efficacious force within and therefore must be taken

care of. Many Hindu readers, for instance, reported that their mothers made special cardboard binders for their comic books, so that the covers would not be damaged during the reading process. Others reported saving their comic book collections into their adulthood—in their parents' homes, in their attics, or on their own children's bookshelves. Such careful preservation is not due to nostalgia and sentimental attachment alone, but also arises from the belief that *ACK* literally could not be thrown away for fear that the gods might view such an act as a sign of disrespect. A few even spoke of the tangible blessings bestowed by the comics as a testament to their power, as did this reader: "Whenever I used to have a fever as a child or when I was unwell, my parents used to buy about a dozen of these comics and give them to me. I used to happily read them and dream about them and get well soon. I still have a huge collection today."

Thus these Indian comic books are notably different from their American, European, Japanese, and other global counterparts in that they are part of the spectrum of the sacred for many of their Hindu readers. This is most notable, of course, with the mythological issues that recast stories of the Hindu gods in this visual medium, but here there is no easy divide between sacred and profane, mythological and historical. Just as Hindu gods can descend to take on human incarnations like Rama and Krishna, so too can humans like Shivaji and Subhas Chandra Bose be elevated to take on godly aspects. Darśan, therefore, is not limited to the "auspicious sight" of gods and goddesses alone, but encompasses a range of Indian leaders as well. Discussing the ways in which secular Indian political figures take on a sacral charge in bazaar art, Kajri Jain writes:

> [T]he presentation of these figures became more or less conventionalized within the formal terms of a visual economy of devotion where narrative realism gave way to frontal, iconographic depictions, allegorical renderings, and direct address to the viewer. Like deities, leaders came to be assigned well-defined iconographic traits: the rose, *sherwani* coat, and "Nehru" cap for

RAJASTHAN IN WESTERN INDIA WAS THE HOME OF THE VALIANT RAJPUTS.

Figure 3. *Rana Pratap*, no. 24 [reprint no. 563] (Bombay: India Book House Pvt. Ltd., 1971 [1994]), 1. From *Amar Chitra Katha*, with the permission of the publishers ACK Media, India.

Nehru; the round "Gandhi" spectacles, walking stick, moustache, loincloth, and loosely draped shawl for Gandhi; Tagore's beard; the white streak in Indira Gandhi's hair; M. G. Ramachandran's fur hat and sunglasses; and so on. (2007, 278)

In Indian comics, as in bazaar art, mythological gods and historical leaders alike have conventionalized iconographic depictions, as is most apparent in the cover art. The cover of *Subhas Chandra Bose* (no. 77, 1975), for instance, features this founder of the Indian National Army with all of his iconographic traits: standing at attention, wearing his army uniform and round glasses, with the tricolor Indian flag waving in the background behind him. Whereas the eyes of Subhas Chandra Bose, Shivaji, Rana Pratap, and other historical figures featured on the covers of the comic books are diverted to the side, like those of the gods, in order to avoid the darśanic exchange of glances, within the pages of the historical comics such an exchange is once again allowed for. Thus while the cover of *Rana Pratap* (no. 24, 1971) features the medieval Hindu warrior-king in profile on horseback thrusting his spear against the Muslim king Akbar, the first page features Rana Pratap with all his standard iconographic traits—his spear and shield, his curling moustache and beard, and his turban—but also shows him in a frontal position, his eyes looking directly out at the reader (figure 3).

Thus those Hindu comic book readers who are already accustomed to the darśanic exchange of glances can take pleasure not only in the auspicious sight of the Hindu gods in the *Amar Chitra Katha* series but also in the auspicious sight of India's historical leaders. As will be discussed in the chapters to come, this and other instances of slippage between mythology and history can also entail a slippage between the categories "Hindu" and "Indian" that has been greatly contested in postcolonial India amid rising Hindu nationalism. When this equation between Hinduism and Indianness takes place in the comic book medium, an entertaining and attractive medium that is renowned for pitting righteous superheroes against evil villains, it takes on a compelling potency for its young readers.

Comic Books and Indian Identity

The study of media, religion, and culture has recently emerged as a burgeoning field of inquiry as scholars begin to recognize the impact that the various media technologies that we encounter in our daily lives can have on religious traditions, symbols, narratives, beliefs, and practices. Yet much work remains to be done, particularly in considering media and non-Abrahamic religions in nonwestern cultures.[10] Comic books in particular have begun to receive serious study in the West as the fields of media and cultural studies have grown in the past several decades, with recent publications on the art, aesthetics, history, philosophy, marketing, and reception of comics. Yet the study of comics outside of America, Europe, and Japan has only just begun.[11]

With respect to the field of South Asian studies, compelling arguments have been made in recent years that analyses of popular visual culture and other public media are crucial to our understanding of modern South Asia. Sandria Freitag has expressed this sentiment well:

> Powerfully evocative visions of the nation dominated the anti-imperial discourse of late nineteenth- and early twentieth-century British India. In the forms of posters, photographs, statuary, and, especially, live enactments in public spaces, South Asians explored and created a new visual vocabulary to express their alternative understandings of the world they inhabited. Yet historians have been astonishingly slow to theorize beyond the role of print in their efforts to interpret this complex past. They have treated the immensely rich visual primary-source materials simply as accompanying illustration for a narrative drawn solely from textual evidence. (2001, 35)

New studies of Indian cinema, television, and bazaar art demonstrate the continued importance of visual media as forums wherein Indians construct a national past and decide what it means to be Indian today.[12] Yet the category of the religious has been largely neglected in these studies of South Asian media. Few scholars have asked how popular media may transform religious beliefs, symbols, and practices; or considered the history that these media have had in the consolidation of multiple Hindu traditions into one pan-Indian religion; or theorized about the impact of popular media on ongoing debates about religious and national identities.[13] Furthermore, the field of South Asian media and culture is dominated by research on Indian cinema. Yet as Arjun Appadurai and Carol Breckenridge have argued, the contours of the media boom in South Asia are barely understood, and studies of various media are necessary as "each of these media technologies has distinctive capabilities and functions, and each interacts in a different way with older modes of organizing and disseminating information" (1995, 7). To date, however, only a handful of scholars have studied Indian comic books, and then only in brief.[14]

In India today yet another generation is being reared on the *Amar Chitra Katha* comic books. Those who grew up reading *ACK* in previous decades now faithfully pass their love for them on to their children and grandchildren. One thirty-something father who was buying comics at a popular bookstore in Bombay stated, "I grew up with *ACK*. My father used to bring the comics home to my brother and me as birthday gifts or whenever we were unwell. Now that I have a son, I want to share *ACK* with him." But an even more eye-opening statement was made by a woman in Pune in a letter she wrote in 2001 to Anant Pai at the comic book studio: "Recently my husband's uncle passed away. He has donated his entire collection of *Amar Chitra Katha* to his niece in his will. Doesn't it prove what a treasure they are? Thank God for giving you this brilliant idea."

At the conclusion of an interview with one former *ACK* associate editor whom I will call Producer No. 1, he posed this question to me: "You are studying *Amar Chitra Katha* and Indian identity. But do you think these are very important for Indian identity?" I replied that I did. He countered, "I think that if you asked me the top twenty things that make up my Indian identity, *ACK* would probably not be on the list. You see, if you take the whole population of India, and then take the number of those Indians who read *ACK*, you will see that the two numbers are very different." I paused, and then stated that I understood that it was primarily middle-class, English-speaking Indians who read *ACK*. He replied, "Yes, exactly, because only they can find and have the money to purchase these comics. And also the medium itself affects the market. You see, the comics never sold very well in languages other than English, even in Hindi. I think that the medium was weird for those readers. But to kids who knew English and already read other comic books, comics like *Archie* and *Asterix,* they would like this medium, too. So you must keep this in mind when you study identity."

As Producer No. 1 accurately suggests, not everyone in India reads *Amar Chitra Katha.* The majority of the comic book readers over the years have been English-speaking, middle-class, upper-caste Hindu boys and girls. But as the many statements cited from readers throughout this chapter demonstrate, for this substantial segment of the Indian population from the late 1960s to today—a segment that easily numbers in the tens of millions—these comics are not trivial artifacts; they are powerful resources that have been incredibly important to the formation of their identities as Indians and as Hindus. On this note I cite just one final reader:

> Growing up as a kid in India, my memories and knowledge of Indian mythology and history are constructed solely of the numerous *Amar Chitra Katha* books that were my staple diet for reading. One of my treasured memories is my grandmother providing me with a few volumes of these comic books every time I went to visit her in Kerala. She would come to the railway station to see me off and her gift to me would be this wonderful collection of books and I would read them and reread them on the long train journey.

Given the phenomenal importance of *ACK* to so many readers, we must now turn our attention to the comic books themselves. After providing an overview of the making and remaking of the first comic book, *Krishna,* and a description of the production process in chapter 1, I have organized each chapter around a particular comic or group of related comics in order to explore the many facets of Indian heroism that are presented in this series. The principal argument of this book is that *Amar Chitra Katha* comics, as a form of public culture that has reached into the everyday lives of millions of middle-class Indian children over the past four decades, are a crucial site for studying the ways in which dominant ideologies of religion and national identity are actively created and re-created by ongoing debate. I perceive *ACK* as "public culture" in Arjun Appadurai and Carol Breckenridge's sense of the term as describing a zone of cultural debate:

> a set of arenas that have emerged in a variety of historical conditions and that articulate the space between domestic life and the projects of the nation-state—where different social groups (classes, ethnic groups, genders) constitute their identities by their experience of mass-mediated forms in relation to the practices of everyday life. (1995, 4–5)

The following chapters explore the specific historical conditions from which *ACK* emerged and the variety of Indian identities—religious, class- and caste-based, gendered, regional, and national—that are debated and constituted in and through the production and consumption of this popular series. As comic book creators decide which mythological and historical figures to single out and cast as Indian superheroes, and as comic book readers decide which issues to buy and which to bypass, they are actively participating in these debates about Hinduism and Indianness through this genre of popular visual culture. With this book, I hope to provide a good base for further consideration of the relationship between media, religion, and culture in South Asia, allowing the uniqueness of these Indian comic books as a medium for identity formation to be explored so that they may then be located in the wider, intertextual context of public culture, both in India where a wide range of other visual media exist and where new comic book brands have now arisen, and transnationally among other world comic book cultures.

1   The Father of Indian Comic Books

Anant Pai was born into an orthodox Hindu Vaishnava family of the Brahmin caste in 1929 in a small town in the southern Indian state of Kerala.[1] Orphaned at a young age, Pai moved to Bombay as a teenager to live with family, and there he attended Wilson College where he earned a degree in chemical engineering in 1952. Yet despite his background in science, Pai was drawn to the publishing world. In many ways, the story of *Amar Chitra Katha* is Anant Pai's story as well. He founded the comic book series in 1967, and he was still editing it as of this writing. Throughout the past four decades Pai has written many comic book scripts himself and has closely overseen the production of each issue. Because of his prolonged involvement, Anant Pai's own beliefs have had a more substantial impact upon these comics than have any other single person's. This chapter provides an overview of the founding of *ACK*, the production process, and the marketing of this series. It also considers how these comic books chart changing religious beliefs and practices through Anant Pai as a devout Hindu, and how the concept of Indianness presented in these comics has been arrived at through the interaction of the founder with editors, authors, artists, and readers, but is also tempered by dominant discourses about religion and the nation.

A natural storyteller, the tale that Anant Pai tells of the founding moment of the comic book series is this:

> In February 1967, my wife and I were visiting Delhi, and we stopped at Maharaja Lal & Sons bookstore. The TV was on in the bookstore—Bombay did not have TV yet, only Delhi, and only black and white—and the program was a quiz contest featuring five students from St. Stephen's College. When they were asked, the students could not name the mother of Lord Ram. I was disappointed, but I thought, well, that is from a long time ago. But then a question came about Greek gods on Mt. Olympus, and the children could answer that question! This is the trouble with our education system: children are getting alienated from their own culture.

Anant Pai first became acquainted with the comic book medium in the early 1960s, while working at the *Times of India*. In addition to rotary presses, the publisher of the *Times*, Bennet, Coleman & Co., also had sheet-fed presses that remained idle except during the Divali holiday calendar printing season. It was with the idea of keeping these machines busy, recalls Pai, that his boss forwarded several imported *Superman* comic books to him and asked him to look into the possibility of reprinting some such comic under the banner of the *Times*. Pai did some research and then suggested that they begin with a thirty-two-page English-language comic book, with the first half consisting of the *Phantom* tales and the second half of locally produced comic tales that would feature Indian characters and scenarios (Pai 2000, 38). The idea was approved, and *Indrajal Comics* was born. In 1964 the first issue, *The Phantom's Belt*, was released. The first thirty-two issues contained tales from the *Phantom*, and tales about *Mandrake the Magician, Flash Gordon*, and *Buz Sawyer* followed thereafter. *Indrajal Comics* was a success, but the comic books were nonetheless not quite all that Anant Pai had envisioned. The second half of each issue never featured locally produced comics. Instead, the latter halves of the first several *Indrajal* issues were devoted to general knowledge, quizzes, and the like. The comic "half" grew larger and larger while the general knowledge "half" got proportionally smaller until, at issue 29, the *Phantom* took over all thirty-two pages.

The idea of creating comic books featuring Indian characters and scenarios resurfaced while Anant Pai was visiting Delhi in 1967. There, watching the televised quiz show and reflecting on his own nephews' love of American comic books, Pai became convinced that the comic book medium could be an excellent means of teaching Indian themes and values to Indian children being educated in English-medium schools, who he feared were learning western history, mythology, and values at the expense of their own. Upon his return to Bombay, Pai took this idea to several publishers, but none were interested. Finally, he met H. G. Mirchandani, publishing director at India Book House (IBH), who was intrigued by the idea and hired him to be the editor of the new comic book series, which they named *Amar Chitra Katha*. After ten poor-selling Hindi-language translations of western illustrated classics like Cinderella, Snow White, and Red Riding Hood, Pai was finally allowed to publish *Krishna* (no. 11) in 1969 (figure 4). Written by Pai himself, it was published in English, not Hindi, for Pai knew from his experience with *Indrajal Comics* that the market for such comic books was the rapidly growing English-speaking middle classes of urban India. *Krishna* inaugurated the birth of the Indian comic book industry: it was the first indigenous Indian comic book, created in India and featuring an Indian hero and an Indian storyline.

The *Krishna* comic book by *ACK* features several key episodes in the life of the Hindu god Krishna that Anant Pai says are drawn from the classical Sanskrit mythological text, the *Bhāgavata Purāṇa* (although the *Harivaṃśa*

Lifting the Mountain

Figure 4. *Krishna,* no. 11 [reprint no. 501] (Bombay: India Book House Pvt. Ltd., 1969 [1992]), cover. From *Amar Chitra Katha,* with the permission of the publishers ACK Media, India.

also appears to be a source, as do more popular renditions of both texts). The comic establishes the formula for this series by focusing its narrative on one hero who is featured on the cover and whose dramatic action centers the narrative: it tells of Krishna's birth, his victory over the demon Putana as a baby, his various schemes to steal butter as a boy in Gokul, his escapades with the *gopis* (cowgirls) as an adolescent in Vrindavan, and it culminates with his heroic martial feats in Mathura. For Pai, a devotee of Krishna, the decision to make this deity the hero of his first comic book was easy. He explained, "Krishna is the most popular god. You see, Ram, he is the ideal man: he never lies, he is a filial son, a loving brother, etc. But Krishna, he is a real-life character, a human figure—that means he actually lived, and also means he sometimes tells lies, steals butter, etc. He is like us. We can relate to him better than to Ram."

There are many gods in the Hindu pantheon, and Pai wanted to begin his comic book series by focusing on the one deity that was dearest to him and that he believed would most appeal to readers. But it was not as easy to decide exactly how to tell the story. Although he had already decided to base the *Krishna* script on the *Bhāgavata Purāṇa,* he was uncertain how loyal he should be to the Sanskrit text. Should he adapt it as literally as possible for the comic book medium, or update it in accord with modern scientific reasoning? He described his uncertainty in this way:

> With mythology so many things that we read don't seem natural or possible. . . . You know the story of how Krishna lifts the Govardhan Mountain on his one finger? Well, is this possible? Scientifically it is not. So I didn't show this, there was no image of Krishna lifting the mountain. Instead, I just had people talking about it, saying, "Look, Krishna has lifted the mountain to shelter us." That way I didn't show something unscientific, but didn't completely ignore this episode in the story either.

Under the guidance of independent India's first prime minister, Jawaharlal Nehru (1889–1964), throughout the 1950s and early 1960s a heavy emphasis was placed on the role of science, technology, and industry in modernizing India, while religion was deemphasized as a part of traditional, premodern India. Anant Pai was a product of these times, and with his scientific background, he found it difficult to comprehend the emphasis on miracles in the *Bhāgavata Purāṇa* and other mythological narratives of Krishna's life. According to Hindu Vaishnava theology, the Supreme God, Vishnu, has multiple avatars (most commonly ten are enumerated) that descend to earth in times of chaos in order to vanquish demonic forces and restore order. The most popular of these avatars among Vaishnava devotees are Krishna and Rama, each of whom is understood to have been an incarnation of the Supreme God in human form. Pai believed that Krishna had once lived and that he was Vishnu incarnate. But, he wondered, if it was true that Krishna was Vishnu incarnate, then in this human form wouldn't he have been constrained by his human limitations? How could Krishna have been physically capable of lifting a mountain on one finger? Feeling that the belief in miracles like the lifting of the Govardhan Mountain belonged to an earlier, more "superstitious" era than the modern, scientific one, Pai decided the best tactic was to mention all of the key events of the life of Krishna in the comic book, but to refrain from depicting them as miracles. Instead, he worked to minimize the miraculous nature of these events.

After Anant Pai had written the *Krishna* script, he had to find an artist who could illustrate it. But finding capable artists for the illustration and the cover art for this first comic book issue was not an easy task. He recalled this initial difficulty: "When I began, there were no institutes that trained comic book artists. I found artists at advertising agencies, and some fine artists too like Yusuf Bangalorewala and Pratap Mulick. But even the fine artists, they did not know how to work in this art form. It was very new. So in the beginning they had to redraw and redraw and redraw the panels." There simply was no ready pool of talented comic book artists in India at this time, because the medium itself was so novel. The *Krishna* cover was created by artist Yusuf Bangalorewala, and features Krishna as a mischievous child, looking over his shoulder as he digs into the forbidden butter pot. Yusuf is a Muslim artist who has worked in a range of visual media: advertising, book illustration, and website design. He was a fan of the comic book genre, having read imported British and American comics for years, and he was excited about the opportunity to work in this medium: "Always wanting to illustrate comic books, I struck pay dirt when I met Anant Pai. He gave me my first break in comic book illustration."

The illustration for the first issue was done by Ram Waeerkar, a Hindu artist who had previously worked for a prominent advertising agency in Bombay. A longtime fan of *Tarzan* comics, he too was thrilled at the prospect of working on the *Krishna* comic book:

> I did not need any visual models for *Krishna*. Technically, I was studying since childhood that subject. So I did my drawings from memory. I knew the mythology. So the only thing that I was looking for was the opportunity. Generally, I knew the comic style, too, from reading comics as a boy. At that time, say around 1950 and 1960, it was *Tarzan*. I fell in love with *Tarzan*, with that kind of style.

Excited about the opportunity to illustrate *Krishna,* Ram Waeerkar quickly went to work. Waeerkar always took pride in his speed, stating on many occasions that each comic book has "150 frames [panels], and they must be done quickly. . . . I make the drawings very fast. I am the fastest artist." Yet this first issue progressed slowly. Pai had given very specific visual instructions and did not hesitate to ask for revisions. As the very first issue in what Pai hoped would be a successful comic book series with many titles, he felt it was more important to get this issue just right and set the tone for future comic books than it was to meet a strict production schedule. Pai was content with Waeerkar's style, as long as he did not get carried away by the influence of *Tarzan*. In classical Indian texts, Krishna is described as a slim, beautiful, blue-tinged or dark-skinned adolescent, so Pai balked at images of a fair-skinned Krishna with bulging muscles. In this first issue they agreed that Krishna would remain a blue boylike figure, but Waeerkar was given free rein with the other men in the story, so that they often have an overdeveloped musculature, holding their exaggerated upper bodies in postures reminiscent of Tarzan. This agreement was quickly overturned, however, so that later mythological issues feature male heroes with bulging muscles, as on the cover of *Rama* (no. 15, 1970) (refer to plate 1). Aside from ensuring that Krishna retained his adolescent quality, a number of the other revisions Pai asked for had to do with the nature of the medium. For instance, he insisted on a number of active panels and heroic close-ups, visual consistency with the characters for quick recognizability, and a general agreement between text and image. He was also very concerned with the depiction of authentic period costume, architecture, and weaponry. But many of the revisions for this issue had to do specifically with the depiction of events in the life of Krishna that are commonly regarded as miraculous.

Popular myths about the birth of Krishna are usually full of miraculous elements. Here is an abbreviated version of this birth story: Kamsa, the cruel king of Mathura, hears a prophecy that the eighth child born to his cousin Devaki and her husband, Vasudeva, will kill him. He therefore imprisons Devaki and Vasudeva and vows to kill all of their children. But when Krishna is born to them as their eighth child, Vasudeva is able to escape with the infant. He rushes baby Krishna to a house in Gokul where another woman, Yashoda, has just given birth to a stillborn girl. After exchanging the two children, Vasudeva returns safely to his prison chamber with the girl, thereby saving Krishna. During this sequence of events, Vasudeva's chains miraculously break, the prison guards remain asleep and do not awaken during his escape, and the Yamuna River parts for Vasudeva's journey to Gokul.

Struggling with his scientific conscience and the limits of his own faith, Pai walked a fine line between presenting these events as scientifically plausible and as miraculous occurrences in the comic book. The parting of the Yamuna River proved particularly challenging. In this panel, Pai's script called for narrative text at the top stating that the "Yamuna was heavily flooded, but the rains soon stopped." And the dialogue balloon for Vasudeva has him thinking, "Why, it isn't at all deep here. Or is this also a miracle?" (6). Here the text allows for ambivalence: A reader could choose to interpret this incident as a miracle if he or she was so inclined, or else as a fortunate break for poor Vasudeva. Pai wanted the image to be equally ambivalent. He asked Waeerkar to redraw it again and again, until finally the river looked as though it could be parting or could equally just be a low ebb in the current.

Similarly, Pai was intentionally ambivalent in his portrayal of Krishna lifting the mountain. Popular renditions of this beloved episode hold that Krishna, then an adolescent, suggests to the people of Vrindavan that rather than worship the god Indra, they should worship the Govardhan Mountain, for it is what protects the village and provides the villagers with sustenance. The people agree and begin to worship the mountain. As they do, Lord Indra grows increasingly angry and decides to teach them a lesson by showering them with a magnificent storm. But Krishna comes to their rescue by miraculously lifting the mountain on one pinky finger and sheltering the whole village with it for seven days and seven nights, until Indra's fury has waned. Although Waeerkar originally penciled this incident featuring a large panel of Krishna lifting the mountain, Anant Pai was adamant that this should not be shown. Instead, he instructed Waeerkar to do a new pencil sketch with several panels: one showing Krishna leading the villagers toward the mountain in the midst of a downpour; one showing the people looking surprised as boulders began to topple and a rumbling sound was heard, and another depicting the villagers with their mouths gaping as they exclaimed in dialogue balloons, "Govardhana is moving!" and "Look! It's rising!" (21). Only after several pencil sketches was this scene finally approved and inked. Ultimately, the actual lifting of the mountain was not shown, and Anant Pai left it to the reader to infer the miraculous nature of this incident.

Because of these and other retakes, the creation of this first *ACK* issue took significant time. Finally, after nearly two full years of work, it was released in 1969. In the next year, *Krishna* was followed by several other issues featuring mythological heroes and heroines: *Shakuntala* (no. 12, 1970), *Pandava Princes* (no. 13, 1970), *Savitri* (no. 14, 1970), and *Rama* (no. 15, 1970). Now, Pai hoped, every Indian child would read his comics and be able to confidently name the mother of Lord Rama and recount tales of Krishna's bravery—tales that allowed for scientific explanations of events as easily as for miraculous ones. In these issues and in those that followed, the policy of minimizing the miraculous was strictly adopted. In his discussion of the *Mirabai* issue (no. 36, 1972) about the medieval poet-saint who was in love with Krishna, John Stratton Hawley notes that the ending of this comic book has Krishna bending over to receive a swooning Mirabai, rather than the traditional ending of Mirabai being completely absorbed into the statue of Krishna at Dvaraka. This ending, Hawley observes, "does not exactly contradict the traditional story, but it also does not exactly repeat it: the element of miracle has been omitted" (1995, 115).

Sales of *Krishna* were initially a bit slow—less than 20,000 copies sold during the first three years—but Pai persisted. He put out a call for scripts, hired freelance authors and artists, and worked to market his comic book series. Originally, the production goal was to create a new comic book every month, but by 1974 the producers had beaten this goal and were releasing a new issue every two weeks to eager fans. In the 1950s and 1960s, imported American comic books like Lee Falk's *Phantom* and Edgar Rice Burroughs's *Tarzan* were the most popular comics in India. But as sales continued to rise, *Amar Chitra Katha* overtook even the foreign competition. By the end of the 1970s, *ACK* had become the best-selling comic book series in India. Today, *Krishna* is one of the most popular *ACK* titles; it has been reprinted more than sixty times and has easily sold over a million copies.[2]

Significantly, however, this successful *Krishna* title is not the original one that Pai and Waeerkar had worked so laboriously over for two years. As I studied the production and consumption of this comic book series, I only learned of the existence of the original *Krishna* issue as I browsed through used bookstalls in various neighborhood bazaars in Bombay, purchasing old *ACK* titles here and there in order to speak with vendors and learn more about the substantial secondhand market in comic books. In one such bazaar in Bombay's Santa Cruz neighborhood, I came upon a tattered edition of *Krishna* with the cover missing and a lot of children's coloring marks throughout it. As I flipped through this well-used comic book to examine the second layer of artwork added by some child years earlier, wondering who had "defaced" these images of Krishna in this manner, since even comic book images of a deity would be considered sacrosanct by most Hindus, I noticed that this *Krishna* was not, in fact, the same *Krishna* I had expected, although it was clearly an *ACK* comic book and, based on stylistic evidence, it had been illustrated by the same artist, Ram Waeerkar. This *Krishna* did not feature any miraculous events, even the lifting of the mountain! Intrigued, I returned to the comic book studio with a new set of questions.[3]

The *Krishna* reprints that circulate today—the version of *Krishna* that I was familiar with, and that most *ACK* readers are familiar with—do feature Krishna lifting the mountain (figure 5). In a large half-page panel, Krishna lifts the mountain on one finger, while the villagers run to him for shelter and one of them exclaims, "It's a miracle! Krishna is holding the mighty Govardhana on his little finger!" (21). Although I had spent months studying all of the original editions of the *Amar Chitra Katha* titles in the library at India Book House, I learned on that day that the "original" *Krishna* issue in the library's collection was only an original edition of the later, revised version. When asked how this revised version came about, Pai explained that as his company grew and he employed more artists and authors— all of whom studied the first issue like a reference manual—questions repeatedly arose about the portrayal of this episode. Many readers had also written in with questions and criticisms. As he thought about these questions over the years, Anant Pai experienced an epiphany. Ultimately, he decided to release a second, revised version. He commented: "I realized that people look on *ACK* as something sacred, too. . . . So, the *Krishna* that you see today, it is different from the original one. The old records were junked, and the artworks were destroyed. Now *Krishna* shows him lifting the mountain. And it is the most popular issue, too. People want to see Krishna lifting the mountain. This I have learned."

In the tumultuous post-Nehruvian climate of the 1970s and 1980s, religion was once again on the rise in India's public culture. Around 1980, Anant Pai got together with an associate editor, Producer No. 2, and artist

Figure 5. *Krishna,* no. 11 [reprint no. 501] (Bombay: India Book House Pvt. Ltd., 1969 [1992]), 21. From *Amar Chitra Katha,* with the permission of the publishers ACK Media, India.

Ram Waeerkar to redo *Krishna.* In this revised edition, they decided, all ambiguity about Krishna's acts would be dispelled in favor of a clear proclamation of their miraculous nature. A new script was written by Anant Pai with input from Producer No. 2, and completely new illustrations were created for many panels by Ram Waeerkar. The parting of the Yamuna River, for example, was rescripted so that the incident now occupied a full page with four large panels (6). In the first panel, Vasudeva stands on one side of the riverbank, with the basket containing baby Krishna on his head. The river is nearly overflowing its banks. Crossing it seems impossible. In the next panel, however, the river parts, revealing a path through the water that Vasudeva crosses on foot in the third panel (figure 6). In the final panel on this page, Vasudeva stands on the opposite riverbank, having now crossed the river in spate. Unlike the original panel depicting this scene in which Vasudeva wades into a shallow spot in the river, the clear images here of a path through the river that is cresting higher than Vasudeva's head leave no ambiguity that what has taken place is truly a miracle.

In addition to the Govardhan Mountain and Yamuna River episodes, other events are also clearly marked as miracles in this revised edition, so that text and image agree in this presentation of Krishna's mythology. Immediately after Krishna's birth, Vasudeva despairs over his helplessness to rescue Krishna while being held as a prisoner, when suddenly his chains break and the door to his prison cell flies open. He exclaims, "It's a miracle!" and then, grabbing the baby, makes his escape past the sleeping

AS VASUDEVA APPROACHED, HOWEVER, THE WATERS PARTED...

guards (5). When as a boy Krishna uproots trees, the villagers say, "This boy is a marvel!" (15); when he subdues the giant serpent Kaliya they exclaim, "What a boy!" (20); and when Trivakra's humped back suddenly straightens after she touches Krishna's feet, they whisper to one another, "A miracle! He must be our saviour" (25).

These miraculous episodes are all extremely important parts of Krishna's mythology, for they demonstrate his power, the fact that he is something more than human, that he is a god in human form.[4] Whereas this superhuman nature of Krishna is a central tenet of the revised comic book edition, it had to be inferred from the original. For instance, the first edition featured Krishna fighting an elephant in a single close-up panel in which he whacks it with his mace in a one-on-one battle. As far as comics go, this is a pretty realistic scene: Krishna's actions are not superhuman here. But the revised edition draws this battle out into a full-page sequence, showing Krishna swinging the elephant upside down by his trunk in one panel and hurling him into the air in the next, clearly the master of the situation and completely undaunted by the size of the beast, as any comic book superhero—or Hindu god—should be. Through these episodes, Krishna is shown to be not only the master of beasts, but the master of gods as well. This is the very point of the Govardhan Mountain episode. By lifting the mountain on his pinky finger, Krishna demonstrates to the villagers of Vrindavan—and to the comic book readers—that he is not just an adolescent boy who is good at herding cattle and playing the flute; he is capable of inhuman feats of strength, heroic feats that protect those who believe in him and that only a god—or a superhero—could accomplish. By outlasting Indra's storm and sheltering the people under the mountain all the while, he demonstrates that he is more powerful even than Indra, king of the gods. He demonstrates that he is indeed the Supreme God, Vishnu, incarnate in human form, yet significantly not constrained by human limitations.

Figure 6. *Krishna,* no. 11 [reprint no. 501] (Bombay: India Book House Pvt. Ltd., 1969 [1992]), 6. From *Amar Chitra Katha,* with the permission of the publishers ACK Media, India.

For the revised edition of *Krishna,* Pai found that the production process was much faster than it had been for the original edition. Certainly, this was partly due to the years of experience that the creators now had in producing Indian comic books. But they also attribute this ease in producing the revised issue to the synchronicity between text and image that the new script allowed for. Producer No. 2 described how text and image should ideally work together in the comic book medium:

> The text and image should match perfectly. You see, the author gives the visual instructions. If the artist is good, then after the image is drawn some of the text will be deleted by the editor. When I edited the comic books I would delete some of the text if the text and image said the same thing, if the image could stand on its own. But if it is a weak image, then the copy is necessary. And often the script itself must be changed before an image can even be made.

In the original *Krishna* issue, many of the images were what she calls "weak," unable to stand on their own and requiring some textual explanation. The most prominent example of this is the Govardhan Mountain scene, in which Krishna is not shown lifting the mountain. Here the reader is uncertain from the images about the events taking place: The only certainty the reader has from these panels is that the villagers are in awe, as their startled faces and gaping mouths demonstrate. It is to the text that the reader must turn for an explanation, and only from the dialogue balloons does the reader learn that Krishna is lifting the mountain. In the revised *Krishna* edition, however, there was no concern to maintain a sense of ambiguity about the miraculous events associated with Krishna, so there was no need for such "weak" images. Instead, "strong" images could be used, images that could be understood on their own. The Govardhan Mountain scene in this edition is such a "strong" image. The reader can look at it and see Krishna lifting the mountain and can discern that this is truly a miraculous act without the aid of any text. Here, the text serves only to complement the image, not to explain it.

Producing the revised *Krishna* edition was a mere matter of months, not years. The script was rewritten in about one month, and artist Ram Waeerkar was able to complete the penciling and inking in just under another month, far faster than his work had progressed for the original edition. For Waeerkar, a Vaishnava himself and devotee of Krishna, the new visual instructions were much more "natural" because he had been exposed to such imagery his whole life: "I know what Krishna looks like lifting the mountain, I know what Krishna looks like stealing the butter, or dancing on the hood of Kaliya, or in the middle of the battlefield. These images are natural for me."

When asked about his change of heart regarding the depiction of miracles, Anant Pai explained how he came to realize that people regard these mythological comic books as something "sacred":

This was in 1975, when there was a Ramayan Mela [festival] here in Bombay. People came from all over the world for this. There was a query: Who is the mother of the villain, Ravan? And a man said, "*ACK* says it is Kaikesi, so it must be so." This made me realize that I must be accurate, that people think the *ACK*s are a legitimate source of these sacred stories.

So how does Anant Pai now reconcile his faith with his scientific background? When asked this question, he replied, "Now I don't tamper with mythology; I present it as it is, because mythology is sacred. This I have learned. I was a student of science, you know. But sometimes science must be kept aside, separate."

When Anant Pai created the original *Krishna* comic book, he elected to tell the story of Krishna not only in a new medium—the comic book format—but also in a new, more modern way: a way that allowed for either a scientific explanation of "miraculous" events or for a more faith-based acceptance of the miracles associated with Krishna. Yet over the years, Pai began to feel more of a sense of responsibility toward textual authority and less freedom for poetic license with Hindu mythological narratives. He has come to the realization that many of the miraculous events in mythological narratives need not be understood literally; rather, they can be understood as containing deeper, symbolic meanings. For this reason, he now believes, the belief in miracles need not conflict with a rational scientific outlook. Thus the stories of these miracles have a place in modern India and in these modern Indian comic books. He explained, citing an example of the famous Hindu cosmogonic story in which the gods and the demons together churn the cosmic ocean in their quest for the nectar of immortality:

> The Ocean of Milk, it is churned in search of nectar, but first poison comes out, not the nectar. This is symbolic. It means that daring to doubt your faith brings you uncertainty and unhappiness also. This is the poison. But if you keep churning, then all your doubts eventually become clear, and you receive the *amrit*—the nectar—finally.

In the end, daring to doubt his faith has indeed resulted in nectar for Anant Pai. Not only does he feel he has a better understanding of his own Hindu faith and of the god Krishna because of his effort to "keep churning" through his spiritual questions; he has also made a very successful venture of his comic book series, which is now loved by millions of loyal Hindu readers for its depiction of the miraculous tales of the Hindu gods.

Producing *Amar Chitra Katha*

As the popularity of the *ACK* comic book series was growing, and issues began to be sold at bookstores, street bookstalls, and in train stations across India, the creators decided to add issues featuring historical heroes to the corpus. These new historical heroes were premodern martial figures at first, with modern figures of national stature following several years later.

The first historical titles were *Shivaji* (no. 23, 1971), *Rana Pratap* (no. 24, 1971), *Prithviraj Chauhan* (no. 25, 1971), and *Guru Gobind Singh* (no. 32, 1972). Thus both historical and mythological Indian figures are "immortalized" as heroes in this popular comic book series, and due to the formulaic template employed in the production process, the line between the two categories—the mythological and the historical—is often blurred.

Each new *Amar Chitra Katha* issue, whether mythological or historical, begins with an idea for a story that revolves around a central character—the hero. Typically, a freelance author is assigned a hero or given a choice of several heroes that the editors have already decided would make good protagonists. The author must then conduct a significant amount of research before they can write the story. Because the heroes of these comic books are mythological or historical figures, the authors must become familiar with the classical mythological tales or the biographical details of the historical leaders. One scriptwriter, M. L. Mitra, put it this way: "You see, writing a comic is not original writing here, as it is with *Phantom* or *Mandrake*—it is myth or biography—and they are the original, those Sanskrit stories and other sources, not your writing." As previously mentioned, Anant Pai became more of a stickler for accurate textual and visual details after he realized that some readers view these comic books as authentic—even sacred—renderings. Producer No. 2, the associate editor of *ACK* from 1971 to 1986 and the author of dozens of scripts, recalled, "Mr. Anant Pai was very knowledgeable about period costume, hairstyles, headgear, weapons, and architecture, and scrutinizing the artworks for authenticity in these areas was entirely taken care of by him." Anant Pai agreed that he did scrutinize the visual details of the comic books:

> In the *Mahabharat* and the *Ramayan,* references are given. For example, usually chariots were shown with four wheels. But there should only be two wheels on a chariot. There is a passage in the *Mahabharat* where a god is asked to protect a chariot's right wheel in battle, and another god is asked to protect the left wheel. Not the right wheels and left wheels. So there were only two wheels. Things like this we would tell the artist.

Producer No. 1 recalled that the majority of the visual references came from books, due to budget limitations. However, the concern with verisimilitude was so great that he and other members of the staff would often go out of their way to acquire visual reference material by visiting important historical and religious sites, like the ruins of the Vijayanagara Empire at Hampi and the Hindu cave-temples on Elephanta Island:

> For something like *Elephanta* [no. 149, 1977], that issue is different. Elephanta is near [Bombay], so we could go, snap photos, and so the art for that one is different, more detailed, accurate. But for many issues we cannot do that. The *Krishnadeva Raya* [no. 151, 1978] issue, that one is also accurate. I went to

Hampi, because it is near my [ancestral] place—I went on my budget, not on *ACK's*—and I took some snaps. So in the comic there is that path between the two rocks that is shown—that is still there today.

The panel in the *Krishnadeva Raya* issue (no. 151, 1978) featuring troops marching out of Vijayanagara across a detailed landscape on page 25 is evidence of the use of visual references in the making of this historical comic book issue about a sixteenth-century king.

Producer No. 2's concern, on the other hand, was with textual accuracy and authenticity. She did a lot of research before writing or editing a script, and she maintains that "more than 70 percent of the titles in the *ACK* series were born out of the dusty, crumbling volumes, mostly the works of Bengali and European scholars, in the Royal Asiatic Society's library." In the following chapters I will explore the impact of these sources upon the comic book narratives and the issue of the comics' proclaimed accuracy; here I limit my concern to the production process. The historical *Jahangir* (no. 221, 1980) issue about the Mughal emperor Jahangir (1569–1627), for instance, was researched and written by Producer No. 2 over the course of seven months. She describes the process in this way: "I looked at the *Akbarnama*. This took me about six months to read, to get clues to Jahangir's personality and character. Then after I had completed the research I reduced all the information into the equivalent of three comic book scripts. Then I had to reduce that down to thirty-two pages!"

For Producer No. 2, a good script is one that has a good story, follows a chronological order, and has some positive value to impart. Ultimately, she feels, "it should arouse the curiosity of the reader enough to make her or him want to delve into the originals." To enable the reader to more easily turn to those "original sources"—as well as to stress the authenticity of the comic books—a short introduction to each issue, the majority of which were written by Purushottam Nedungadi, was placed just inside the front cover and told the reader who the hero or heroine was and what sources his or her story was drawn from. The introduction to *Jahangir* therefore begins in this way: "It is tough to be a famous junior, and more so when the senior happens to be Akbar, the Mughal-e-Azam. This was the tragedy of Jahangir." It concludes with this note: "The events described here are based on the memoirs of Akbar and Jahangir and other historical records."

Once the research and writing are complete, the story is submitted to the editors at the *ACK* studio. Next, the editorial staff scripts the story. This involves deleting any excess verbiage, dividing the text into sequential panels, and clearly marking the narrative text and the dialogue balloons. The editor must also transform lengthy descriptive statements into visual instructions for the artist, specifying what the artist should depict in each panel. M. L. Mitra described the process in this way:

Figure 7. *Durgesh Nandini* script, 1. From *Amar Chitra Katha,* with the permission of the publishers ACK Media, India. Courtesy of M. L. Mitra, Navi Mumbai.

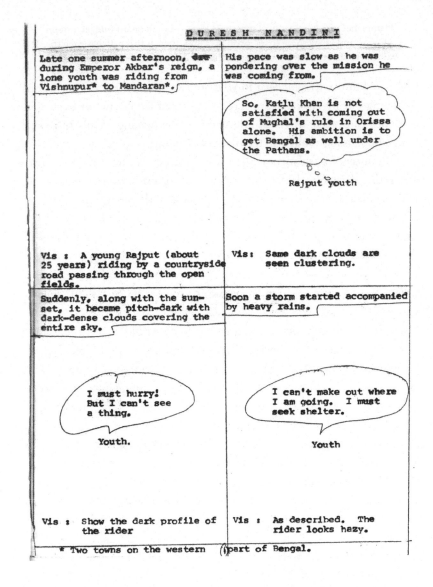

Any writer visualizes everything he writes, from the beginning to the end. So you must tell the artist what you visualize. Sometimes artists themselves may decide, if they have read the original story, but it is always better for the scriptwriter to direct the visuals as well. . . . You must tell the artist the appropriate details—for instance, the right dress, architecture, that sort of thing.

The *Durgesh Nandini* (no. 294, 1983) issue, for instance, is an abridged version of Bankimchandra Chatterjee's 1865 novel of the same name. After the comic book story was written by Debrani Mitra and Meera Ugra, M. L. Mitra then scripted it in the comic book format, dividing the story into panels (figure 7). In the first page of the script the narrative text and the dialogue are clearly delineated, the former appearing in a box at the top of each panel and the latter appearing in balloons in the middle of the panels. The visual instructions are also provided, directing the artist to depict a

Figure 8. *Durgesh Nandini,* no. 294 (Bombay: India Book House Pvt. Ltd., 1983), 1. From *Amar Chitra Katha,* with the permission of the publishers ACK Media, India.

twenty-five-year-old Rajput man on horseback in the countryside in the first panel, dark clouds gathering in the second panel, and the profile of the Rajput in the third panel. Mitra stated that there are three things that must be understood about scriptwriting: "The first thing, there can't be too much description—only speech and thought balloons. The second thing, there is a thirty-two-page limit; you must limit the story to that. The third thing, you must make the story suitable for children; that is, you must think you are a child while you are writing. I used to write the scripts for my own children. They were quite young then, so I would read the stories to them, see where they got confused, and change it."

After the script is complete, it is given to the artist, who first does a pencil dummy and then inks the panels. The editorial department proofs both the dummy and the inking, and requests any necessary corrections.

At this point in the process Producer No. 2 would compare the visuals with the text, making sure the words and images flowed together: "Often when I was editing scripts from the outside—that is, freelance scripts—I would have to take one frame and make it into three frames, or vice versa. Many freelance writers try to make the comic book panel into an illustrated text. This should be avoided for the most part. You see, the narration panel tells one thing, while the balloons or dialogue carry the story forward. The ideal is to pack as much into the panel as possible."

The final *Durgesh Nandini* comic book evidences some of the editorial and artistic changes that were made during the production process (figure 8). The first page has been split into five panels, rather than the four that were originally called for in the script. In the process, the text in the panels of the script has been significantly reduced in the final version. For instance, the narrative text in the second panel of the script has been completely deleted, as it was redundant after the image was created: the reader need not be told that the Rajput man's pace was slow or that he was pondering his mission, for this is now evident from the image and the thought balloons.

Artists, of course, have their own opinions on the production process. One artist who preferred to remain anonymous explained why he felt that some scripts are better than others:

> I always like the scripts that [name of a particular author] writes. I ask to work on those scripts. They are the best, because she gives just the minimum visual instructions. So I can be much more creative with those scripts. Also, if I have a good rapport with the scriptwriter . . . then I can be innovative and approach her with suggestions. But it all depends on the author-artist relationship.

However, due to the freelance set-up of much of the writing and illustration for this comic book series, this level of communication and collaboration between authors and artists is rare.

After the synchronization of text and image has been achieved and the dialogue altered as needed, the comic book moves on to the letterer, who inks in the final text. Then the comic book returns to the editorial department for proofing. Once approved, it is photocopied and reduced to 8½″ × 11″ standard size, and is then hand-colored. When the editor has okayed the color selections, the comic book is sent to Anant Pai for his final approval. Next, the comic book is manually prepared for a version of the four-color process that allows the printing of twenty-six specific colors. Finally, a black-and-white negative is prepared and sent to the printer along with a color guide. The whole process is still manual, due to the prohibitive cost of computerizing it, although the company was investing in more computer technology at the time of my most recent visit to the studio in 2007. Although the first issues took many months to create, after the process was streamlined the majority of the comic books were produced in just one month.

Originally, the *ACK* comic book series was marketed as children's leisure literature. Early ads targeted middle-class school-age readers, telling them to "prepare for the summer holidays" by buying new comic books. However, the producers of *ACK* quickly realized the potential in marketing their comic books to adults. Producer No. 2 recalls:

> I was bent on making *ACK* family reading. . . . I knew that in those days children read what adults chose for them and any decent, well-produced reading material that appealed to parents and grandparents would reach the children. Besides, there were many adults who had never come across the stories gleaned from dusty, crumbling, literal translations, which made tedious reading unless one was a researcher! Any good story, well told, would appeal to all age groups was my firm belief, and it proved true!

Whereas comic books (*manga*) in Japan are widely accepted and read by children and adults alike, comic books in India in the 1960s and 1970s initially faced many of the same criticisms as comic books in America in the 1940s and 1950s concerning their presumed audience of gullible children: that they discourage the reading of "serious" literature, they promote violence, and they objectify women.[5] In America these concerns led to the implementation in 1948 of a self-regulatory or self-censoring code under the oversight of the Association of Comics Magazine Publishers, which stated, among other things, that sexy, wanton comics should not be published; crime should not be presented in such a way as to throw sympathy against law and justice or to inspire others with the desire for imitation; vulgar and obscene language should never be used; and ridicule or attack on any religious or racial group is never permissible (Nyberg 1998, 165).[6]

Amy Kiste Nyberg has written that another "solution to the comic book 'problem' came from the publishers themselves, in the form of educational comics" (1998, 6). New series like *True Comics, Classics Illustrated, Picture Stories from the Bible,* and *Topix Comics* were all started in the 1940s in the effort to use the comic book medium in a responsible way for the religious and secular education of children. In the first five years of production, *Classics Illustrated* alone sold 100 million copies, and more than 20,000 schools purchased the comics for their libraries and classrooms (Nyberg 1998, 7–8). The producers of *Amar Chitra Katha* were well aware of not only the ways in which American companies had attempted to combat criticisms and fears of the comic medium, but also the success of *Classics Illustrated* in marketing its product to American parents and educators. They recognized that in order to make a success of *ACK,* they would have to overcome the common prejudice that comics were intellectually inferior products that at best were a waste of time and money and at worst could seriously hamper an Indian child's moral and intellectual development by diverting them from their studies and introducing "western values" in place of traditional Indian ones.

In the effort to overcome Indian parents' resistance to the comic book medium, *ACK* producers began to actively market the series as an educational product to parents, grandparents, aunts and uncles. One clever full-page ad that ran in these comics in the 1970s reverses the traditional grandparent-grandchild relationship by suggesting that a child who reads these comic books will be able to tell his grandmother bedtime stories from the *Mahābhārata*, rather than vice versa. This was meant to be especially appealing to parents in urban cities like Bombay where nuclear families were beginning to replace the traditional joint family structure. Ads like this suggested that if no grandmother was available to tell a bedtime story for the religious edification of the child, mothers should not fear—*Amar Chitra Katha* could do the job! Another ad from the mid-1970s pitched *ACK* comics as the ideal birthday present that was both fun and educational for distant aunts, uncles, and grandparents to buy for girls and boys alike.

The producers also decided to work at marketing their product to educators. In February 1978, therefore, India Book House organized a seminar on "The Role of Chitra Katha in School Education." Many urban school principals attended, and the Union minister of education, Dr. Pratap Chandra Chunder, was the chief guest. In his preliminary remarks, Baldev Mahajan, acting commissioner of the prestigious Kendriya Vidyalaya Sanghatan School in New Delhi, stated that because the term *comics* had come to acquire a foreign and derogatory meaning, *chitra katha* (picture story) is a more comprehensive and culturally appropriate term that should therefore be applied to this literature. When Anant Pai addressed the crowd, he tried to persuade the teachers gathered there that comic books—or chitra kathas—could indeed be useful educational tools. Defining a chitra katha as "a series of pictures, telling a story, developing a situation, or presenting the same character in varied circumstances," he argued that it is a medium that captures children's interest by combining visual images with the world of words. He then named several of the most popular fears about comic books: that children who read comics will ignore their studies and lose interest in literature, that comics provide too much exposure to violence, and that children acquire prejudiced values by imitating comic book heroes. Dismissing all of these fears, Pai argued that the appeal of comics could be harnessed to promote intellectual growth, that he guards against gratuitous violence in his chitra kathas, and that he ensures that only those people are depicted as heroes in his series who cherish the values that sustain society, while those who repudiate those values are depicted as villains. Anant Pai concluded his speech with this impassioned plea: "If there are bad comics, let us oppose them as we oppose bad books or bad movies, but let us not frown on comics as a medium of education" (*Role of Chitra Katha in School Education* 1978, 2–4).

Additional speeches were given by M. C. Joshi, superintending archae-ologist of the Archaeological Survey of India, on "Chitra Katha through the Ages"; by V. P. Dwivedi, the assistant keeper of the National Museum in New Delhi, on "The Role of Chitra Katha in Promoting Cultural Aware-ness"; by Subba Rao, former teacher and associate editor of *ACK*, on "The Use of Chitra Katha in Teaching History"; and by Dr. K. R. Mitra, language officer of the Kendriya Vidyalaya Sanghatan, on "Language Development through the Ages." The Union minister of education, Dr. Chunder, also gave a speech in which he dismissed the notion that comic books were a western medium by pointing out India's long history of the combined use of text and image to tell stories. Referring to the Ajanta cave murals (ca. fifth century) accompanied by verses and to medieval Indian illuminated manuscripts and scroll paintings, he explained that chitra kathas were a truly Indian medium and could be used to disseminate Indian culture. He further stated that he felt *Amar Chitra Katha* comics, in particular, should be used in India's schools because "there are biographies of great men from different parts of the country; there are tales from Sanskrit; classics and folktales of various regions—all of which could help in promoting national integration" (*Role of Chitra Katha in School Education* 1978, 2). Together these illustrious speakers reassured their audience that Indian comics—chitra kathas—are an authentic Indian medium and that they promote authentic Indian values.

But what was perhaps most persuasive to the assembled teachers was the discussion of a recent experiment in teaching history and the printed write-up that was passed out to all present. In this experiment, thirty schools in New Delhi split their Class VII and VIII history students into two groups. The first group read an *ACK* comic on a historical figure; the second read the standard textbook. Those who read the comic, it was reported (complete with graphs and charts), not only received higher marks but also thoroughly enjoyed learning the lesson (*Role of Chitra Katha in School Education* 1978, 10). After the seminar concluded and the results of this experiment were publicized, sales soared as English-medium schools across the nation ordered *ACK* for their libraries and classrooms. Now advertised as "the only comics welcomed in schools," "endorsed by educationists," and "the route to your roots," the scholarly accuracy and Indianness of these comic books was highlighted in an effort to appeal to more parents, educators, and potential advertisers. Among the usual "Yip-pee It's Dipy's!" and "Campa Cola" ads, new school-themed ads began to appear in the pages of the comics at the close of the 1970s, encouraging kids to "put Parle on your school books—and in your lunchbox, too!" and to purchase school supplies such as Omega Glory mathematical instruments and Ekco sketch pens.[7]

At this time, the creators of *Amar Chitra Katha* also decided to translate some of their most popular issues into various regional Indian languages in an effort to capture the non-English-speaking market. Previously, they had targeted urban, English-speaking, comfortably middle-class children, but Anant Pai and the other producers realized a potential audience existed in the growing number of upwardly mobile families with children enrolled in vernacular schools throughout India in the 1970s. Using the original artwork, new lettering was applied in order to make issues like *Krishna* available in Hindi and various other regional languages including Bengali, Malayalam, Kannada, and Assamese. By the late 1970s the comic books could be found everywhere: in posh urban bookstores and busy streetside stalls, on train station platforms alongside soda and snack vendors, and even at dusty roadside stands in tiny villages. They were also mailed out to subscribers—to individuals throughout the country as well as an increasing number of school libraries—who anticipated the arrival of each new comic book.

In 1980, seeking to capture younger readers—those eight years old and younger who would grow into *ACK*—a new comic book series called *Tinkle* was created. Featuring several short, easy-to-read fictive comic stories and a recurring cast of comical Indian characters in each issue, this monthly comic "from the house of *Amar Chitra Katha*" has proven to be quite successful. Many of the stories featured in *Tinkle* are written and submitted by the readers, who eagerly await each issue to see if their story will appear. In 2001, the associate editor of *Tinkle* reported receiving as many as 6,000 mail entries per month. Significantly, the vast majority of these fans didn't stop reading *Tinkle* when they were old enough to read *ACK*—they subscribed to both!

Fan clubs sprouted up in the early 1980s and were noticed and encouraged by the producers, who asked the presidents of such clubs to mail in reports of their members and activities. In no time, the *ACK* staff had created an official "Amar Vikas" monthly newsletter that they mailed out to these fan clubs—at no charge, initially, although a small fee was eventually instituted. The newsletters typically featured a short story with a cover image on the first page. Within the pages various puzzles, word finds, jokes, and quizzes were included alongside several short fiction and nonfiction pieces that were mailed in by loyal readers. On the back cover of the newsletter an "Around Amar-Tinkle Clubs" roundup was featured, listing the latest activities of the various fan clubs (such as starting a comic book lending library or holding quiz contests to test knowledge of the comics). Those who wrote in to the newsletter did so with great hopes that their name and story might be published or that they might win one of the prizes—always comic book issues—that were mailed to the first ten responders who correctly answered the quizzes. By 1985 there were over

200 of these fan clubs, mailing in more than 4,000 letters and contributions to the *ACK* office per month; by the end of the decade the number of fan clubs had risen to over 450.[8]

Due to such marketing strategies, sales continued to rise, reaching 50 million copies sold by 1986. Although monthly sales figures are hard to come by, several sources have reported that by the mid-1980s monthly *ACK* sales had reached "around 60,000 copies in English, 25,000 in Hindi, 8,000 Assamese, and 6,000 each in Kannada and Bengali, every month. At the same time, a cheaper, digest-sized Malayalam version, printed as a franchise by the Malayala Manorama group, sold almost 140,000 copies" (Doctor 1997, 38). Additionally, further comic book sales occurred through foreign editions that were printed as joint ventures for Indians living abroad in such languages as Bahasa, French, German, Japanese, Serbo-Croat, Spanish, and Swahili. Furthermore, sales figures fail to capture the true circulation statistics of these comic books. The readers I spoke with stated that they regularly traded around comic issues with their circle of friends. One reader, for instance, commented that he purchased *ACK* "in bookstores, or sometimes in used book sales. Also we used to read them in libraries. If I owned one, I would always share it." Comics, like many magazines in developing countries, often reach a larger audience than is realized, as they are usually shared with friends and siblings, borrowed from lending libraries by numerous readers, and resold in secondhand bazaars. In my browsings of secondhand bazaars in Bombay, I noticed that working-class children often purchased used comic books for just a rupee apiece, far cheaper than the retail value for new editions.

But by 1991, with the release of *Jawaharlal Nehru* (no. 436, 1991), a biographical issue about independent India's first prime minister, sales had dropped so low that the creators decided to stop making new *ACK* comic books. Only 24,000 copies of *Jawaharlal Nehru* sold during 1991—nowhere close to the breakeven mark of 40,000 copies (Doctor 1997, 38). This was disheartening for the comic book producers, especially given the tremendous resources that went into the making of *Jawaharlal Nehru*—it had involved an unprecedented amount of research in order to write the script, and the artwork took several years to complete. Both the author, Producer No. 3, and the artist, Yusuf Bangalorewala, stated that they were committed to producing a responsible, authentic biography of the great leader in the comic book format. So what happened between the mid-1980s and 1991 to cause sales to decline so dramatically? Anant Pai chalks it up to the rising popularity of a competing medium—television:

> Overall TV popularity has hurt all print media here, including *Amar Chitra Katha*. You know, we used to sell five lakh [500,000] copies every month. Now we reprint only 6,000 to 12,000 every month. Sales are much lower because of the TV. . . . That is why we stopped making new issues—because sales were

down. The youth today is interested in watching TV, in the internet, in all of this new technology. So they read much less now.

Doordarshan, the Indian government-run television network, was first introduced in 1959, but it was not until the mid-1980s that it reached into the average home. As Purnima Mankekar notes, the mid-1980s and early 1990s witnessed "a dramatic expansion of television in different parts of India, with the number of transmitters increasing from 26 in 1982 to 523 in 1991" (1999, 5). In 1984, the first televised entertainment serial was introduced, enthralling the audience, and other tremendously successful serials quickly followed. From January 1987 to July 1988, Ramanand Sagar's *Ramayan* serial aired, captivating viewers across the nation in an unprecedented way. Philip Lutgendorf reports that conservative estimates of Doordarshan's daily viewership during this period range from 40 to 60 million, with the most popular episodes being viewed by anywhere from 80 to 100 million people (1995, 223).[9] *Amar Chitra Katha* and Doordarshan were competing for the same audience, and Doordarshan appeared to be winning. Not only was Doordarshan's core target audience the urban middle class, but its regular viewers were women and children—the very audience that had previously been such loyal purchasers of the comic books.

In 1985, prior to any of the televised epics, the comic book producers had decided to serialize the great Indian *Mahābhārata* epic. Beginning with *Mahabharata 1: Ved Vyasa* (no. 329, 1985), they released a new title in this series each month (a new historical title was also released each month, in keeping with the bimonthly release schedule). This serialization of the epic went on for four years, until the final issue was released in 1989: *Mahabharata 42: The Celestial Reunion* (no. 411). When B. R. Chopra's *Mahabharat* television serial aired on Doordarshan from September 1988 to July 1990, this spelled big trouble for the comic book series. Some fans took great pleasure in encountering the epic in both mediums, as did the reader cited in the introduction who gleefully commented that it was because of the *ACK* comics on the *Mahābhārata* that he could compete with his grandmother's knowledge of the epic when they watched the episodes together on TV. However, many others grew bored with the repetition. One former *ACK* fan who cancelled his subscription after Doordarshan's arrival expressed strong feelings on this matter: "Uncle Pai lost me as a reader when he introduced his never-ending *Mahabharat* series. That is when I stopped reading *ACK* and stopped my subscription, too. The best part about *ACK* was the unpredictability of what was coming next! There was *Mahabharat* on TV and now *Mahabharat* in *ACK*—that, too, in excruciating detail. I wish he had never done that. I would have continued to buy *ACK*."

It was not just *Amar Chitra Katha* that suffered under the changing market in these years. Comic book series and children's magazines featuring comic strips including *Indrajal, Chandamama, Parag,* and *Balarama* all experienced declining sales. Indian business analyst Ajay Sharma put it this way: "The eighties were grim for the publishers of children's magazines and comics. The market shrank by 50 percent every year, and several old favourites had to close shop as the young set got hooked to television" (1994, A4). Analysts M. Anand and M. Rajshekhar assessed the situation in a similar way in their discussion of *Chandamama* and *ACK:* "Both magazines reached their zenith in the eighties—boasting of monthly sales of nine lakh and five lakh copies respectively. And then, sales began to slip. It was the nineties, and cable television was pushing print out of fashion. Kids glued to the idiot box hardly had the time or the inclination to read. Many thought that the two magazines would die" (2000, 52).

During the 1990s, the producers of *ACK* made several attempts to recapture the market. In 1994, India Book House decided to relaunch the comic book series by releasing "deluxe editions" of more than two hundred of the earlier titles—those that could be salvaged after a fire destroyed much of the original artwork and negatives. For these deluxe editions the old covers were replaced with glossy covers made from thicker, laminated paper stock. The old cover artwork was resized to fit within a brightly colored border, and the titles were redone in a brighter, more eye-catching format. Accompanying the release of these deluxe editions, various release parties were held in urban centers throughout India. For instance, "Amar Chitra Katha Week" was held in Bangalore (April 23–29, 1995), featuring fancy dress contests in which children dressed up as their favorite *ACK* characters, contests in which children colored masks of characters from the comic books, and quiz contests presided over by Anant Pai himself (Kavitha K. 1995). These new deluxe editions also came with a new price tag: the first comic books sold for 1.25 rupees apiece; in the late 1970s the price was raised to 3.50 rupees; in the mid-1980s the price was upped again to 10 rupees. The new deluxe edition issues were sold at a whopping 25 rupees apiece in the mid-1990s, and the latest price tag is 30 rupees per issue.

In the late 1990s the producers of *Amar Chitra Katha* also branched out into several new media in an effort to recapture the market, beginning with the production of audiocassette recordings of the comic book tales. In 1998, in association with Bangalore-based Phoenix Global Solutions, they released CD-ROM versions of the comics (priced at Rs. 599). Also in 1998, a television show produced by Universal Television in Bombay (UTV) and based on the *ACK* comics began to be aired on Doordarshan-1.[10] Zarina Mehta, director of UTV, stated that she originally wanted to produce an animated show, but found the cost too prohibitive. She therefore decided to create a live-action version of the comic books, using the original scripts as her guide for the storylines of episodes including

"Krishna," "Ganesh," "Shakuntala," and "Tansen." Like the scriptwriters for the TV show, the costume and set designers also relied on *ACK* for their visual inspiration.

The comic book creators have tried a variety of other tactics to keep their product in circulation. Although new bimonthly titles officially ceased being written in 1991, when India Book House decided to focus on reprinting previous best-sellers, some new *ACK* issues have occasionally been released. "Bumper issues," comics ranging from seventy-two to ninety-six pages in length rather than the standard thirty-two, began to be released in 1992, beginning with *Valmiki's Ramayana* (no. 10001). Some of these bumper issues were reprints of earlier special issues that were now being reissued in the new "deluxe edition" format with new covers, such as *Dasha Avatar* (no. 10002) and *Jesus Christ* (no. 10003); others were completely new creations, like *Valmiki's Ramayana*; while still others combined three earlier single issues under one new cover, such as *Tales from the Panchatantra* (no. 10004) and *Tales from the Jatakas* (no. 10005). Other special releases have included a fourteen-volume *Mahabharata* set (based on the forty-two single titles released between 1985 and 1989), which was released in 1989 and was so popular, despite its high price of Rs. 980, that the initial press run sold out immediately and anxious fans wrote to the publisher to request that their names be placed on a waiting list for the next press run. Hardbound collections of five similarly themed single issues, called "Pancharatna" (five gems), have also proven popular, especially as gift items.

Finally, a few commissioned issues have recently been released. The first was *G. D. Birla* (no. 382, 1987), a biographical issue about a prominent Indian industrialist who died in 1983. Discussing this issue, which was commissioned by the Birla Foundation, author Yagya Sharma described how it differed from the usual *ACK* comic book formula: "We didn't try to build Birla into more than what he was. He was a great industrialist, a very important man in that way. But . . . for a hero it takes conflict to carry the story forward. There must be a conflict, a climax, and then some sort of resolution that features the hero in a positive light. . . . We did not try to do this sort of a story with Birla. . . . It is a biography about his life; it is meant to educate."

Another commissioned biography is *Swami Pranavananda* (no. 679, 1998), which was sponsored by Bharat Sevashram Sangha, the organization that was founded in 1917 by the Hindu guru Swami Pranavananda. In 2001, while I was conducting my field research, *Swami Chinmayananda* (no. 732) was released. Breaking with the standard narrative formula, this issue also does not present the Hindu guru Swami Chinmayananda (1916–93), founder of the Chinmaya Mission that sponsored this issue, as a hero in the typical comic book fashion. Rather, it provides a biographical account of this spiritual leader's life from a follower's perspective. The cover art also breaks with the standard formula, featuring a photograph of the Swami. But the comic book producers had little concern that such changes to the successful narrative and visual formula would harm sales, for the sponsors of commissioned issues agree in advance to buy a guaranteed number of issues and fund the initial print run. The fact that these prominent organizations sought to include their founders in the canon of Indian heroes established by *Amar Chitra Katha* is a noteworthy testament to the high regard that they have for this comic book series. Anant Pai recalled Swami Chinmayananda's fondness for the series: "Swami Chinmayananda always spoke about 'teaching Hinduism to Hindus.' And for that reason he was a great fan of *ACK*. He wrote the introduction to the *Gita* issue [no. 127, 1977], and from this time on he had the desire for an issue on himself." So far, the *Swami Chinmayananda* issue has sold well. Just four months after the initial press run of 30,000 issues, a second, nonsponsored run was printed to appease the public demand for this title.

Most recently, the producers of *Amar Chitra Katha* have realized the value of the internet in marketing their comic books, and in conjunction with the creation of their website in 2004, they decided to go back into a limited production schedule for new issues. The website features a brief history of *ACK* and a catalog of available deluxe edition reprints. Also featured is a shopping-cart system for online purchases, which can be shipped within India or abroad, making the comics now easily available to a global market. Along with the launch of the new website, *ACK* also celebrated the release of a new issue: *JRD Tata: The Quiet Conqueror* (no. 735, 2004), the story of one of India's leading industrialists, Jehangir Ratanji Dadabhoy Tata. As of this writing, the latest new issue to be released was *Kalpana Chawla* (no. 736, 2005), a biographical issue about the Indian-born NASA astronaut who died in 2003 when the space shuttle *Columbia* exploded during its reentry into the earth's atmosphere. And the latest news reports indicate that *ACK* has just been purchased by the start-up ACK Media, which plans to explore opportunities to move *ACK* and *Tinkle* into digital animation, toys, and other media (Saptharishi 2007).

In 2000, *Amar Chitra Katha* released its lengthiest bumper issue yet: a 272-page tome about the life and deeds of Krishna, called *Bhagawat: The Krishna Avatar* (not numbered). In this issue, when Krishna is shown lifting the Govardhan Mountain (plate 3), the scale is even grander than it was in the revised *Krishna* edition, so that Krishna appears as a miniscule figure lifting a magnificent mountain so big that its peak extends beyond the panel's frame. Here it is most apparent that Anant Pai's newfound appreciation for the miraculous in mythological narratives of the Hindu

**Conclusion:
The God of All of India**

deities—an appreciation that grew out of his interaction with comic book producers and readers—has caused him to reformulate the comic book template so as to incorporate miracles. Between the remaking of *Krishna* and the release of *Bhagawat,* many other issues about Krishna have also been released which prominently feature miracles. When asked to comment on the abundance of Krishna-themed comic books in the *ACK* series, Pai stated:

> Yes, there are a lot of comic books on Krishna especially. You see, he is the most popular god in India—in the north and the south, everywhere. Even the chief minister of Kerala, he is against religion, an atheist, but even he goes to a Krishna temple on important days. And there is a Muslim poet in Karnataka, he is still living today, Nissar Ahmed, who has written many poems to Krishna. Beautiful poems. And in Bengal roadside singers sing Krishna's glory from village to village. Their songs are called "baul" songs. Krishna is the god of all of India.

This statement that Krishna is "the god of all of India" demonstrates how Pai's own understanding of what it means to be a modern Hindu aligns with dominant discourses about religion and nation in two ways. First, this statement positions Vaishnavism as the dominant form of Hinduism. As a religion, Hinduism is difficult to define: there is no single historical founder, no single text that all Hindus hold sacred, and no single system of belief. Instead, it is characterized by an array of regional and sectarian gods, scriptures, beliefs, and rituals. This diversity has led several scholars to claim one can only speak of Hinduism in the plural, of many "Hindu traditions."[11] However, beginning in the late nineteenth century, leading Hindu figures such as Swami Vivekananda and Bharatendu Harishchandra set out to define Hinduism as a unified and systematic religion on par with other world religions. In this process, the *Rāmāyaṇa* and *Mahābhārata* epics were often drawn upon due to their immense popularity throughout India to set forth a shared body of literature that could unite Hindus from multiple regions. Furthermore, the *Bhagavad Gītā* in particular (the sixth book of the *Mahābhārata*) was drawn upon to set forth a monistic and monotheistic doctrine to undergird Hinduism by claiming that the Supreme God (in all of His many manifestations) is the ultimate reality. The effect of this was to privilege devotionalism to Krishna and Rama, the central gods of the Indian epics who are both considered incarnations of the Supreme God Vishnu in Vaishnava theology. This equation between Vaishnavism and Hinduism has been contested by some for ignoring the beliefs and practices of a great many Hindus, including Shaiva sects devoted to the god Shiva and Shakta sects devoted to various goddesses, as well as those who are devoted to regional and lower-caste deities that are not found in Sanskrit scripture.[12]

Second, this statement that Krishna is "the god of all of India" positions Hinduism as the national religion of India. Not only does Anant Pai believe that Krishna's mythology should be familiar to all Hindus, but he also believes that Krishna's mythology should be familiar to all Indians, no matter their personal religious beliefs. This sentiment was shared by other *ACK* producers, including artist Pratap Mulick, who emphasized that artists must believe that the epics had happened, that they were ancient Indian history, in order to accurately draw epic scenes. When asked if one therefore had to be Hindu to draw such images, he replied: "No, no. Whether a Hindu, Jain, etc., a person can create such images. It is not a question of being Hindu; it is a question of being Indian and knowing India's history." However, the combination of historical and mythological issues in this comic book series has been particularly appealing to Hindu nationalist leaders who seek to make Hinduism the national religion of India, and a number of prominent Hindu nationalist politicians have endorsed the series. In August 1997, when India was celebrating its fiftieth year of independence, *The Story of the Freedom Struggle* (bumper issue no. 10) was released. This seventy-two-page issue begins with the arrival of western merchants in India, recaps the rise of the British colonial regime and the beginnings of the struggle for independence, and ends with Jawaharlal Nehru hoisting independent India's tricolor flag atop the Red Fort on August 15, 1947. Created by stitching together a few new transitional panels with panels and storylines from several previous issues—primarily *March to Freedom 1: Birth of the Indian National Congress* (no. 348, 1986), *March to Freedom 2: A Nation Awakes* (no. 356, 1986), and *March to Freedom 3: Saga of Indian Revolutionaries* (no. 360, 1986)—this bumper issue received a tremendous sales boost when Atal Bihari Vajpayee, India's eleventh prime minister and a leading member of the BJP, agreed to officially release it as part of the nation's ceremonies. When *Bhagawat: The Krishna Avatar* was released in August 2000, Dr. Murli Manohar Joshi, India's Union human resources development minister and also a leading member of the BJP, presided over the official release ceremony. Holding aloft this issue, Dr. Joshi endorsed *Bhagawat: The Krishna Avatar* in particular before the crowd and lauded the educational value of the entire comic book series more generally, stating that the "future generation should know [our] country's rich heritage and culture and our education system should encourage ways and means to achieve this" ("Future Generation Should Know" 2000). With this proclamation Joshi not only echoed Dr. Chunder's statement from more than twenty years previously about the educational value of this Indian comic book series; he also made it clear that he believed that both historical and mythological issues should be used in schools to help Indian children connect with their roots.

This release party for *Bhagawat: The Krishna Avatar* occurred shortly after the 1999 general elections, when the BJP was reelected with Atal Bihari Vajpayee as the prime minister. In 2000, Joshi, Vajpayee, and other BJP officials were working to fulfill their campaign pledge to "Indianize, nationalize, and spiritualize" the school curriculum. As they commissioned Hindu nationalist historians to rewrite the NCERT (National Council of Educational Research and Training) history textbooks, a bitter controversy erupted between right-wing politicians and left-leaning historians. While I was conducting field research, the nation remained embroiled in heated disputes over competing visions of the national past.[13] For Dr. Joshi, however, these debates were moot: he had already decided that these mythological and historical comic books provided exactly the kind of narrative of Indianness that he would have educators and parents instill in the youth of India.

Now hailed as the "Father of Indian Comics" and as "Uncle Pai" by several generations of readers, Anant Pai's vision has clearly struck a chord. *Amar Chitra Katha* has weathered the lean years, and the comic books appear well on their way to achieving an immortal presence as the latest generation of Indian readers passes their love for them down to their own children. From a floundering product line that was initially viewed with suspicion and skepticism by many parents and educators, these comics are now viewed as an authoritative source on the Hindu religion and Indian culture by millions of Indian readers—a genuine route to their roots. But whose roots do these comic book issues really provide a route to? Certainly, they are a window into Anant Pai's own beliefs about what it means to be Hindu and Indian. Yet, as we have seen, the concepts of Hinduism and Indianness that are presented in this comic book series have ultimately been arrived at through the interaction of the founder with editors, authors, artists, and readers, and are also tempered by dominant discourses about religion and the nation. In this way, these comic books act as a crucial site for ongoing discussion about what it means to be a modern Hindu and what it means to be Indian. In the following chapters we will further explore the mythological and historical heroes of this comic book series, examining the ways in which, like Krishna, they have acted as a locus for debate about who deserves to be commemorated as Indian heroes and how their stories should be told.

Long-Suffering Wives and
Self-Sacrificing Queens

2

American psychologist William Moulton Marston (under the pseudonym of Charles Moulton) turned to Greek mythology to develop Wonder Woman, a superheroine he envisioned who would appeal to "America's woman of tomorrow" by defeating her opponents not through the use of brute force but through her "loving, tender, maternal, and feminine" virtues (Danna 2005, 73). When Wonder Woman first appeared in 1941, mainstream American comic books were dominated by superheroes like Superman and Captain America who engaged in amazing feats of strength as they fought for the American way and who gained a predominantly male readership. Marston believed that a new female archetype was needed, one that would appeal to girls and would help them develop the strengths unique to their sex: their greater capacity for love and their sex appeal—strengths that, once fully developed, would ultimately lead to world peace under the governance of women. Essentialist and utopist though his vision was, Wonder Woman caught on, although the readership of such comics remained predominantly male. Over the decades she has proven to be a perennial American icon, inspiring a range of other superheroines and continuing to appear in comic books.[1]

Anant Pai was determined from the outset to market *Amar Chitra Katha* comics to all Indian children, boys and girls alike, and to do so he wanted to develop a cast of male and female archetypal Indian heroes and heroines. Rejecting Greek mythology and American superheroes and heroines who wore star-spangled costumes and fought for the American way, Pai turned instead to classical Indian sources to teach children mythology and reinforce Indian values. *Shakuntala* (no. 12, 1970) was the second *ACK* comic book to be printed, following *Krishna* (no. 11, 1969), and was the first issue in the series to feature a female protagonist (figure 9). Shakuntala is a mythological character whose story is first told in the *Mahābhārata* epic, although the classical Sanskrit play *Abhijñāna-śākuntalam* (ca. fourth–fifth century CE), written by the poet Kalidasa, is the best-known version of the story.[2]

What does it take to be the first Indian comic book heroine? What virtues did Shakuntala possess that marked her for this exalted position?

You know the term *Bharatvarsha?* It is an original name for India. It means the land of Bharat. The comic book ends when Bharat is just a boy, because it is about Shakuntala. But the story goes on. Bharat grows up, ascends Dushyant's throne, and brings all of India under his rule. So Shakuntala is very important, because she is the mother of Bharat. She is the mother of Bharat, the emperor, but also the foremother of all Indians.

Anant Pai, personal interview

Figure 9. *Shakuntala,* no. 12 [reprint no. 530] (Bombay: India Book House Pvt. Ltd., 1970 [2001]), cover. From *Amar Chitra Katha,* with the permission of the publishers ACK Media, India.

This chapter considers the wide range of late nineteenth- and early twentieth-century visual and textual antecedents of the *Shakuntala* comic book. From the latter half of the nineteenth century forward, the female figure was vital to the process of envisioning the emerging nation of India in both colonial and nationalist discourses. In the discussions that ensued between Orientalists (colonial scholars and officers) and Indian nationalists about the status of women past and present, the epic heroine Shakuntala emerged as the epitome of the Indian woman, although the interpretation of her significance varied greatly from one party to the next. Whereas debates around the making and remaking of the *Krishna* comic book centered on the question of the relevance of miracles in the postcolonial era, debates around the making of *Shakuntala* and later issues featuring female heroines centered on the question of the appropriateness of Shakuntala and the virtues she embodied for postcolonial Indian women. After considering Shakuntala's significance as the ideal Indian woman within the context of colonial modernity, this chapter also discusses an alternative feminine Indian archetype that arose in the *ACK* series as a result of such debates.

The core of the Shakuntala story, in both the *Mahābhārata* epic and Kalidasa's play *Abhijñāna-śākuntalam,* is the relationship between Shakuntala, a maiden raised in a forest hermitage, and King Dushyanta. While hunting in the forest one day, King Dushyanta meets Shakuntala and falls immediately in love. The two are joined in a hasty marriage. Dushyanta then returns to the city, leaving Shakuntala behind with the promise that he will send for her. Time passes, but Shakuntala—now pregnant with the king's son—receives no word from Dushyanta. She eventually sets out for the city on her own, but upon arriving at the king's court she is stunned when Dushyanta claims to have no memory of her. In both versions of the story, Shakuntala and Dushyanta are happily reunited in the end, but the reasons for Dushyanta's forgetfulness are quite different, as is Shakuntala's response to it. Indeed, such significant alterations were made to the heroine's character that Stephanie Jamison has commented, "Though Kalidasa's Shakuntala is practically catatonic in her languor, the epic heroine is by contrast a shrewd bargainer and learned in the law" (1996, 249). It is Kalidasa's Shakuntala—the modest, long-suffering, submissive version of the heroine—who has been remembered and celebrated over time, and it is this Shakuntala who is featured as the first heroine of the *Amar Chitra Katha* series.

The comic book begins with Shakuntala's adoption by the Hindu renouncer Sage Kanva, who finds her when she is just a baby, abandoned near his hermitage by her mother, the heavenly nymph Menaka (plate 5). Shakuntala grows up in this remote environment, surrounded by her animal companions and a couple of girlfriends. When King Dushyanta bursts into this idyllic setting one afternoon, pursuing a stag, the sage's disciples halt him, telling him that he cannot hunt on this sacred ground. Learning of Sage Kanva's presence there, the king decides to go seek the blessings of this holy man, but stops en route when he sees Shakuntala—now a lovely young woman—and the two are love struck. In side-by-side panels, Dushyanta is shown on the left side looking to the right panel and thinking, "Oh! How beautiful she is!" while Shakuntala is shown on the right side looking to the left panel and thinking, "What a handsome man he is!" (6). The king happily agrees to help the disciples by destroying the pesky demons that haunt the woods and always interfere with Hindu prayers, and on this pretense he stays at the hermitage for several days while Sage Kanva is away.

Figure 10. *Shakuntala,* no. 12 [reprint no. 530] (Bombay: India Book House Pvt. Ltd., 1970 [2001]), 8. From *Amar Chitra Katha,* with the permission of the publishers ACK Media, India.

One day, as King Dushyanta is patrolling the woods for demons, he hears the voices of Shakuntala and her girlfriends. He pauses to listen, secretly watching the young women from behind a tree (figures 10 and 11). Here Shakuntala reveals to her girlfriends her desire to marry the king. Shy and therefore unable to approach Dushyanta about this desire, Shakuntala instead writes her feelings down on a lotus leaf, which her girlfriends then convey to the king, thereby bringing about the *gāndharva* marriage on the bottom of page 9. According to classical Hindu legal texts such as the *Manusmṛti,* a gāndharva marriage is the seventh of eight recognized types of marriage transactions, described as the "fruitful union by desire of a maiden and the bridegroom" that is "devoted to sexual intercourse and arising from lust" (Jamison 1996, 211). Whereas the *Manusmṛti* regards

Figure 11. *Shakuntala,* no. 12 [reprint no. 530] (Bombay: India Book House Pvt. Ltd., 1970 [2001]), 9. From *Amar Chitra Katha,* with the permission of the publishers ACK Media, India.

this lustful transaction as one of the lower and least respectable forms of marriage because it does not involve the bride's father or other relatives, the comic book subtly suggests through its insertion of the word *love* in the vows the couple makes before exchanging garlands that, although arranged marriages have long been the norm in Indian society, love marriages—which have grown increasingly popular in urban India during the past several decades—are not a western fad, but have always had a place in Indian society.

A few days later, King Dushyanta returns to his kingdom after slipping his ring onto Shakuntala's finger and promising to send for her. Shakuntala is so lost in thoughts of her absent husband that she fails to notice a visiting holy man, Durvasa, and does not attend to him with the traditional hospitality rites that are his due. Sage Durvasa curses Shakuntala for this slight of duty, stating that the person she is thinking of will forget all about her until such time as he sees an object he has given to her. Shakuntala is so sunk in her gloom that she is unaware of this curse. Sage Kanva returns and learns of both the marriage and the curse. He realizes that he must send Shakuntala—with the ring—to the king, and offers her some advice: "Don't let riches make you proud, and be a good and faithful wife." Shakuntala, shown kneeling before him with her hands folded, her head bent, and her veil draped over her head, replies, "I shall do all that you say, dear father" (15). In this panel, text and image work together to emphasize Shakuntala's transformation from a carefree young maiden into a long-suffering wife.

From this point on, Shakuntala patiently and without complaint endures one hardship after another. After losing the king's ring, she is publicly rejected by her husband, who claims to have no memory of her; she is kicked out of Dushyanta's royal court; she is left behind by Sage Kanva's disciples, who harshly proclaim that they cannot return with her because "a wife's place is with her husband" (21); and she is abandoned in the forest, alone and pregnant. Fortunately, another holy man, Sage Maricha, takes her in and allows her to raise her son at his hermitage. After several years have passed, Dushyanta's ring is found in the city and returned to him, triggering his memory of his marriage to Shakuntala. Finally, the two are reunited. Shakuntala—who still has no knowledge of Durvasa's curse— neither scolds nor rebukes her husband when he suddenly appears; rather, she greets him with a smile, tells him that she is happy to see him after all these years, and informs her son that this man is his father.

The comic book ends after this happy reunion, with a final blessing that is bestowed on the couple by Sage Maricha: "Always work hard for the happiness of your people. Your son Bharat will one day become a great emperor, and our country will be called Bharat after him" (32). This ending parallels the introduction to the comic book, wherein the reader is informed of the national importance of both the story and its heroine: "And it is claimed that it was their son, Bharat, a direct ancestor of the Pandava and Kaurava princes, who gave our country its name—BHARAT." Like many Hindus, Anant Pai believes that the Indian epics and other mythological sources preserve the stories of figures who lived on the Indian subcontinent during the prehistoric era, both gods like Krishna and Rama, who were incarnations of the Supreme God in human form, and legendary ancestors. Thus one of the reasons that Shakuntala was chosen to be the first heroine of the *ACK* series is that she is one such ancestor, the woman who gave birth to Bharat, who would grow up to become the legendary emperor from whom India would derive its Sanskrit name (Bhārata). In Pai's words, she is the "foremother of all Indians"; she is not just symbolically, but quite literally also, Mother India (Bharat Mata).

Pai also considered Shakuntala to be the ideal embodiment of virtues that are understood to be both feminine and Indian. In the first comic, Krishna embodies male heroic qualities such as strength and bravery as he encounters his demonic foes, engages them in fierce yet playful battles, and emerges victorious. But in this second comic, Shakuntala embodies a different set of heroic qualities, foremost of which are her constant devotion to her husband and her fortitude during all her travails. Other early comic books in the *ACK* series featuring mythological heroines include *Savitri* (no. 14, 1970), who was so devoted to her husband that Yama, the Hindu god of death, restored his life; *Nala Damayanti* (no. 16, 1971), about Damayanti's long search for her missing husband, Nala; and *Shiva Parvati* (no. 29, 1972), about goddess Parvati, who performs prolonged austerities in order to win the god Shiva's love. Shortly thereafter, historical heroines were introduced, like *Padmini* (no. 44, 1973), a Hindu Rajput queen who committed *sati* (self-immolation) in the year 1303 in order to free her husband to fight on the battlefield without worry that, should he be defeated, she would be forced to succumb to the advances of the invading Muslim king. On the cover of this issue (figure 12), Padmini is depicted in a frozen narrative moment, posed in a way that allows our eyes to linger on her body. She stands before the great fire, preparing to immolate herself. Her eyes are downcast as she calmly offers a tray of flowers and incense to Agni, the Hindu god of fire. She is a fair-skinned, voluptuous woman wearing a gorgeous, revealing outfit and an abundance of jewelry. Here the reader is encouraged to appreciate the beauty of Padmini's form, while simultaneously taking comfort in her purity and virtuosity.[3]

On the cover of *Shakuntala* (figure 9) and throughout the comic book, Shakuntala is depicted in static poses that allow our eyes to linger upon her body. As a fair-skinned, voluptuous woman, she is also marked as an idealized Indian woman through her posture and gestures, her jewelry and ornamentation, and her sari draping and hairstyle. This image illustrates how central the "male gaze" is to the definition of this feminine ideal. In her essay on visual pleasure in the cinematic context, Laura Mulvey argued that viewing pleasure in classic Hollywood films is traditionally split between the active/male and the passive/female, and that the woman's passive presence in a film functions on two levels: "as erotic object for the characters within the screen story, and as erotic object for the spectator within the auditorium." Whereas the man's active presence is what the spectator identifies with and what moves the plot forward, the woman's passive presence causes the narrative to halt, "to freeze the flow of action in moments of erotic contemplation" (Mulvey 1975; also Guha-Thakurta 1991, WS-94). This "male gaze" is not limited to the cinema, but can be found in other visual media as well, including Indian comic books. The

Figure 12. *Padmini,* no. 44
[reprint no. 605] (Bombay:
India Book House Pvt. Ltd.,
1973 [1999]), cover. From
Amar Chitra Katha, with the
permission of the publishers
ACK Media, India.

Shakuntala cover presents a frozen narrative moment that reflects the active/passive gendered divide of the male gaze. Here Shakuntala sits quietly in the forest, bidding farewell to her animal companions before traveling to the city. Unbeknownst to her, she is watched by Sage Kanva and one of her girlfriends. As they gaze on Shakuntala from within the image, we gaze on her from the perspective of her absent male lover, whose gaze we spectators are meant to identify with. It is by viewing Shakuntala through Dushyanta's eyes that she becomes an erotic, desired object.

This male gaze is employed further throughout the narrative of the comic book, as can be seen in the love-letter episode on pages 8 and 9 (figures 10 and 11). This narrative sequence is framed by the male lover, who secretly watches Shakuntala from behind a tree while she pines for him at the top of page 8 and who marries her at the bottom of page 9. The male lover's gaze is thus the pivotal point of reference in this two-page spread, for it is his (hidden) gaze that casts Shakuntala as a desired, sensual ideal, just as it is his (revealed) gaze that causes Shakuntala to bend her head, lower her eyes, and veil herself in submission before him once he makes his presence known. The reader, like the male lover, is encouraged to appreciate the beauty of Shakuntala's form, to linger on her full hips and downcast eyes while simultaneously taking comfort in her virtue.

Shakuntala, Padmini, Savitri, Damayanti, Parvati: These heroines' stories come from a variety of sources within the vast corpus of Indian mythology, history, and legend. Yet all of these heroines are long-suffering, dutiful wives who are depicted in a similar manner—they are voluptuous, fair-skinned, bedecked in golden ornaments, and draped in revealing silken cloths, with their eyes downcast and their heads bent in submission. How did such dutiful wives come to be the ideal Indian woman? To answer this question, to understand how Shakuntala came to epitomize qualities that are widely understood as being both distinctly feminine and distinctly Indian, we must investigate the archetype of the modern Indian woman that was constructed within the context of colonial modernity.

Orientalists had been enamored with the story of Shakuntala since 1789, when the Sanskrit scholar Sir William Jones made available the first English translation of Kalidasa's play, called *Sacontala, or The Fatal Ring.* Jones's English translation of the play was quickly translated into French, Italian, and German, and inspired new editions and translations throughout the nineteenth century.[4] In 1855 another Sanskritist, Sir Monier Monier-Williams, published another English translation of Kalidasa's play, this one in free verse, titled *Sakoontala, or The Lost Ring.* He viewed the play as a product of "the golden age" of Indian civilization, calling it "the most celebrated drama of the great Indian Shakspere [*sic*]," Kalidasa. Discussing the merits of this and other classical Indian plays, Monier-Williams wrote:

> [W]hen to the antiquity of these productions is added their extreme beauty and excellence as literary compositions, and when we also take into account their value as representations of the early condition of Hindu society—which, not withstanding the lapse of 2,000 years, has in many particulars obeyed the law of unchangeableness ever stamped on the manners and customs of the East—we are led to wonder that the study of the Indian drama has not commended itself in a greater degree to the attention of Europeans, and especially of Englishmen. The English student, at least, is bound by considerations of duty, as well as curiosity, to make himself acquainted with a subject which illustrates and explains the condition of the millions of Hindus who owe allegiance to his own Sovereign and are governed by English laws. (1855, vii)

Monier-Williams felt that his new translation of the classical play *Abhijñāna-śākuntalam* would help the British to better understand their

Visions of the Modern Indian Woman

present subjects and thereby better rule them. However, as Orientalists increasingly felt the need to justify the colonial presence in the latter half of the nineteenth century, the notion of a timeless India—an India ever obedient to "the law of unchangeableness"—was steadily replaced in colonial discourse with a new emphasis on the degeneracy of contemporary Indian society in contrast with the glory of ancient Indian civilization as found in the epics and other classical texts, and the status of Indian women, past and present, was central to this contrast. *Purdah* (the seclusion and/ or veiling of women), child marriage, polygamy, and sati were among the customs commonly cited as evidence of the abject status of women in modern India, while epic heroines such as Shakuntala, Savitri, and Damayanti were held up as examples of what Indian women had once been in an earlier golden age: educated, cultured, and spiritual wives and mothers (Chakravarti 1990, esp. 46; also Mani 1990 and O'Hanlon 1992).

At this same time, the racial notion of the "Aryan" was gaining prominence in Orientalist scholarship, including the work of the Sanskritists Jones and Monier-Williams, resulting in the consolidation of the idea of the golden age of Indian civilization, so that it became not just a Hindu golden age but an Aryan one as well (Trautmann 1997). In this discourse, Shakuntala and other classical Indian heroines were recast as Aryan women (Chakravarti 1990, 61). Romila Thapar has argued that as enthusiasm for Romanticism faded in the second half of the nineteenth century and "race science" grew, a new interpretation of Shakuntala arose. She was no longer seen as the child of nature but as the "rustic maiden" who embodied the female virtues of modesty, chastity, self-sacrifice, devotion, and patience— all proper Victorian virtues that Aryan women of modern Europe and classical India held in common, but that the racially inferior native women of contemporary India no longer did (Thapar 2000, 17–20).[5]

The qualities associated with the term *Aryan* in Orientalist scholarship—not just race, but also such positive attributes as culture, spirituality, and freedom—appealed to Indian nationalists as well. Thus in the debates between Indian liberals and conservatives on the status of women in modern India, both sides generally accepted the Orientalist location of ideal Indian womanhood within the past golden age of Hinduism and agreed that Hindu women had fallen to occupy a degraded position in contemporary society; their conflict arose over the question of how best to achieve the resumption of women's former glory and over the interpretation of what that glory actually entailed. Hence while conservatives held up Shakuntala and Savitri as traditional role models of chaste, spiritual Hindu women who performed their wifely duties within the realm of the household, liberal reformers held up the same figures as modern role models of educated women who chose their own partners in marriage as adults (Chakravarti 1990; Tharu 1990). Eventually Shakuntala came into such prominence as an ideal Indian woman—albeit variously interpreted—that she was contrasted not only with contemporary Indian women but with the women of other nations as well. The poet and nationalist Rabindranath Tagore, for instance, favorably compared Kalidasa's Shakuntala with Shakespeare's Miranda of *The Tempest,* arguing in the *Modern Review* that the Indian model of femininity was better than the western one, for whereas Miranda's purity is based on ignorance and inexperience, Shakuntala's purity has ripened through experience and restraint and delivered her into wifehood and motherhood (1907).

In the midst of this discourse about golden age Hindu women and the degraded status of modern Indian women, the Indian artist Raja Ravi Varma (1848–1906) shot into prominence. Varma is widely acclaimed to be the first modern Indian painter, and art historian Tapati Guha-Thakurta has described him as the "last of a dying breed of court artists" who became the first artist of modern India to emerge "at the head of a trend of Westernization in Indian painting" (1986, 166). Varma began his career as a self-trained portrait artist in the southern Indian Maratha court of Travancore, but ultimately earned his fame for his narrative paintings of Indian mythological and historical subjects. Working in the new medium of oil and experimenting with the western academic techniques of shadow, perspective, and depth, Varma sought to create the same simulation of reality in his paintings that was then being created with the camera. Yet he simultaneously infused his paintings with idealism and thereby developed what Geeta Kapur has termed a mode of "surrogate realism" (G. Kapur 2000, 150). Varma's paintings in this mode of realism were immensely popular, appealing to colonial officials and other Orientalists, Indian nationalists, and the growing middle classes in India.[6]

Orientalists praised Ravi Varma as the non-European who had successfully applied the western academic style of painting to Indian themes. In the 1870s, when Varma first began to create narrative paintings, he drew on India's classical heritage as it was then being defined—the epics, the *Purāṇas* (mythological accounts of the Hindu gods), and the plays of Kalidasa—for his inspiration. The first of these paintings was *Shakuntala Patralekhan (Shakuntala Writing a Love Letter to Dushyanta),* which he painted for the 1876 Madras exhibition (figure 13). It depicted Shakuntala lying on the forest floor, draped in a yellow sari and dreamily writing her love letter on a lotus leaf, surrounded by her girlfriends and animal companions. It won a gold medal and brought Varma widespread recognition for his unique combination of western academic style and traditional Indian subject matter. The Duke of Buckingham, then governor of Madras, purchased the painting immediately upon viewing it at the exhibition. (The location of the original is unknown; however, this painting was widely reproduced in books, including the 1903 book *Ravi Varma: The Indian Artist,* and was made available as a lithograph as well.) Due to the widespread interest in the story of Shakuntala in colonial circles at the time, Varma was urged to create additional versions. One of his later paintings of Shakuntala was used by Monier-Williams as the frontispiece to the fifth edition of his translation of Kalidasa's play when it was printed in 1887; other Shakuntala paintings by Varma include *Shakuntala* (ca. 1888, Maharaja Fatehsingh Museum Trust, Laxmi Vilas Palace, Baroda); *Shakuntala* (1898, Government Museum, Madras); and *Shakuntala Looks Back in Love* (1898, Shri Chitra Art Gallery, Trivandrum).

Varma's paintings of Shakuntala and other Indian epic heroes and heroines were as well received by Indian nationalists as by Orientalists. Balendranath Tagore wrote in the journal *Sadhana* (1891–92) that the vivid "word pictures" evoked in the passages of Kalidasa's *Abhijñāna-śākuntalam* seemed to be waiting to be translated into pictorial form and that Ravi Varma's unique success was due to the fact that he had succeeded in giving the "right" visual form to these classical literary subjects (Guha-Thakurta 1995, 18–19). In 1888 and again in 1894, Varma toured India, filling up sketchbooks in an effort to study the basic unity that he was convinced underpinned the diversity of India. He was particularly concerned to identify an Indian female type from among this variety in terms of costume, style, and physiognomy. The result of the tours was that Varma chose the sari as the best dress in which to drape his heroines, rejected the earlier Indian traditions of miniature and Kalighat painting in favor of a western academic style, and assumed an Aryan basis for his heroines' physiognomy. His painting *Ravana Slaying Jatayu* (1906) provides a good illustration of this point. Sita is the fair-skinned, sari-draped epic heroine who is modeled on the women in contemporary European prints, while her abductor, Ravana, is clearly marked as the villain by his dark skin, among other features.[7] Together, these were some of the elements that, in Balendranath's words, gave the "right" visual form to Shakuntala and other heroines.

In a 1907 tribute to Ravi Varma after his death in 1906, Ramananda Chatterjee wrote in the *Modern Review:*

> With the exception of his style, every thing else in his pictures is Indian. But his foreign style, as far as we have been able to observe, does not detract from the usefulness of his paintings as sources of enjoyment and instruction or as an influence that makes for nationality. From the Himalayas to Cape Camorin, however much our languages, dress, manners and customs may differ, the social organisation and national character are much the same everywhere. This is due to no small extent to the influence of our national epics, the *Ramayana* and the *Mahabharata*. Ravi Varma's pictures taken from these epics appeal to all Hindus, at any rate, throughout India. (1907, 146)

Indeed, Ravi Varma's paintings were tremendously appealing to the growing Hindu middle classes in Bombay and throughout urban India. In 1890,

after Varma had finished a series of fourteen paintings on epic themes that were commissioned by the Gaekwad of Baroda, the paintings were displayed so that the public could view them. Describing this exhibition, an anonymous biographer of Ravi Varma wrote in 1903:

Figure 13. *Shakuntala Patralekhan,* lithograph print by Raja Ravi Varma. Courtesy of Ganesh V. Shivaswamy, Bangalore.

> They were publicly exposed for some days and immense crowds of people assembled from all parts of the Bombay Presidency to see the paintings. They produced quite a sensation for a period, for it was the first time that subjects from the great Indian epics had been depicted on canvas so truthfully and touchingly. Hundreds and thousands of their photographs were sold all over India. (*Ravi Varma: The Indian Artist* 1903, 10–11)

There was such a demand for Varma's "truthful and touching" images of Indian deities and epic heroes and heroines among the middle classes that Varma, together with his brother C. Raja Raja Varma, founded the Ravi Varma Lithographic Press in 1894. Ten years earlier, Sir T. Madhava Rao had first planted the seed for the press when he encouraged Varma to send some of his works to Europe to have them oleographed in order to better meet the demand for them, writing to him: "You will thereby not only extend your reputation, but will be doing a real service to the country" (Venniyoor 1981, 24). Varma's interest in lithography grew, as did his belief that the act of founding his own lithographic press was a patriotic one. The lithographs that were most popular with the middle classes were images— "god posters"—of the Hindu deities that could be used for ritual darśan in their private pūjā rooms. Describing these lithographs, Ravi Varma's biographer E. M. J. Venniyoor writes:

> The first picture to come out of the Ravi Varma press was *The Birth of Shakuntala*. The choice of subject to mark the birth of the press would seem to have symbolic overtones, the promise of the finest concepts in India's heritage, its religion, mythology and traditions. *Saraswati* and *Mahalakshmi* followed, and these found their way into the *puja* rooms of Hindu households immediately. ... To meet the demands of every Hindu sect, Ravi Varma painted every one of their gods—Krishna, Vishnu, Shiva, Ganapati, Gouri, Kali, the various *avatars* or incarnations of Vishnu. (1981, 38–39)

In 1895, Varma's first lithograph, *The Birth of Shakuntala,* won the "best lithograph" prize at the Bombay Art Society's annual exhibition. Like Venniyoor, I too am inclined to view the choice of this subject for the first lithographic print as a highly symbolic one. By 1895, Shakuntala had come to symbolize for both Orientalists and Indian nationalists all that the Indian woman had once been in the former golden age of Hinduism. When understood in this context of colonial modernity, the image of her birth takes on increasing significance. It is not just a depiction of the birth of the ancestral matriarch of India. It also represents the rebirth of that idealized woman and all of the archetypal virtues she had come to symbolize in the new woman of modern India.

Yet Ravi Varma's vision of the ideal Indian woman did not go uncontested. Varma had looked to western realist paintings as well as western popular imagery—including dramatic photographs and lithographic prints of the tableaux vivant genre—for the stylistic inspiration behind his Indian-themed paintings, thereby forging a "modern" Indian aesthetic. But at the dawn of the twentieth century, a group of art scholars and artists began a new movement known as the Bengal School of Art and publicly denounced Varma's modernity in favor of a "traditional" Indian aesthetic that called upon the East, rather than the West, for both its style and its content.[8] Ananda Coomaraswamy, a leading Indian art scholar, wrote that Varma's paintings were just not Indian enough: "Theatrical conceptions, want of imagination, and lack of Indian feeling in the treatment of sacred and epic Indian subjects, are Ravi Varma's fatal faults. No offence can be greater than the treatment of serious or epic subjects without dignity; and Ravi Varma's gods and heroes are men cast in a very common mould, who find themselves in situations for which they have not a proper capacity" (1907).

In a similar vein, E. B. Havell, principal of the Government School of Art in Calcutta from 1896 until 1905, critiqued Varma's application of western "common realistic trickery" to Indian subjects, which he felt demonstrated "a most painful lack of the poetic faculty in illustrating the most imaginative Indian poetry and allegory" (1980: 252). Interested in locating a plane of "high" Indian art that was distinct from both western art and "low" art forms in India, Coomaraswamy and Havell were also particularly disturbed by Varma's use of the modern technology of lithography, for they felt that it contributed to the withering of the aura of the unique work of art by delivering it to the masses.[9] Coomaraswamy alleged that, by their association with the real-life models that Varma used (especially "unsavory" sorts like actresses and singers) and by their ready availability to the urban middle-class masses in the form of god posters, Varma's Hindu gods and goddesses had fallen from their divine status.

Sister Nivedita, another proponent of the Bengal School of Art, criticized Varma's *Shakuntala Patralekhan* painting in particular for portraying this mythological heroine as a common woman and an ill-bred one at that: "Not every scene is fit for a picture. And this truth needs emphasising in modern India especially, because here an erroneous conception of fashion has gone far to play havoc with the taste of the people. In a country in which that posture is held to be ill-bred every home contains a picture of a fat young woman lying full length on the floor writing a letter on a lotus leaf! As if a sight that would outrage decorum in actuality could be beautiful in imagination!" (1907).

Here we see that Nivedita, like Coomaraswamy, expresses concern not only over Varma's "realistic" presentation of Shakuntala, which she feels degrades the foremother of all Indians, but also over the popularity of this lithograph of Shakuntala, which she states can be found in every Indian home. However, as art historian Partha Mitter notes, it was precisely this concrete presentation of Shakuntala—the depiction of her as "a pretty young Kerala girl lying on the ground, writing a love letter"—that was so appealing to so many, because it was such a break from the "generalized emotion" of traditional painting (1994, 202). Orientalists, nationalists, middle-class masses—all were drawn to Varma's images because they brought to life Indian gods and heroes in a way that the highly stylized Kalighat and miniature painting traditions in India previously had not.

Thus despite such criticism by these proponents of the Bengal School and the virtual dismissal of Ravi Varma in high art circles ever since 1900, Varma's paintings and lithographs have had a lasting impact on India's visual culture, from calendar art and god posters to films and cinema billboards to comic books. Indeed, Erwin Neumayer and Christine Schelberger write that Varma "laid the foundations of a pan-Indian 'Hindu' iconography" through his popular god posters: "These cheap, mass-produced icons were the models for the pictorial aesthetics of a new India—the religious as well as the profane. Any other visual medium that followed had to adhere to the canons set by them" (2003, 1–2). The *Shakuntala* comic book evidences Varma's canonical influence in its depiction of the heroine as an idealized yet realistic or "concrete" girl (figure 10): a beautiful but shy woman who lounges against a tree in the forest, writing a love letter to a king who she fears will never notice her since she is "only a poor village girl" (8). Here this sequence of panels recalls Varma's *Shakuntala Patralekhan* painting (figure 13) in the way that Shakuntala reclines against a tree in the midst of an idyllic forest complete with pet deer, flowers, and her two girlfriends in the middle panels, and then sits up to dreamily write her love letter on a lotus leaf.

Although many of the artists working in the *ACK* studio were familiar with Ravi Varma's work, the creators of *ACK* did not have to look directly to Varma's paintings for their visual inspiration in creating *Shakuntala*, for this vision of the ideal Indian woman has infused popular culture in India throughout the twentieth century. For instance, Varma's impact on the visual culture of modern India can be witnessed in the career of the actor Bal Gandharva (a.k.a. Narayan Shripad Rajhans, 1888–1967). Bal Gandharva played female roles in the Marathi theater due to the proscription of actresses that lasted into the mid-twentieth century.[10] Gandharva joined the Kirloskar Drama Company in Bombay in 1905 and made his debut in the title role in the Marathi staging of Kalidasa's *Shakuntala*. Immensely successful as a female impersonator, he was regarded as the standard of beauty, elegance, and refinement during his day, and he set the fashions for middle-class women's dress and behavior. Dnyaneshwar Nadkarni notes that contemporary middle-class women imitated Gandharva even down to the strings of flowers with which they adorned their hair and the gossamer handkerchiefs they carried in their hands (1988, 59). Photographs of Bal Gandharva in character as Shakuntala reveal the overlap between the actor's impersonation and Varma's feminine ideal: Gandharva's body is turned coquettishly away from the actor playing Dushyanta, with his head bent in submission, while his hand reaches out to the hero in a gesture of partial restraint and partial encouragement. The folds of his sari, his bejeweled ears and neck, and the flowers in his hair all appear to be closely modeled on the epic heroines as they had been envisioned by Varma.[11] Similarly, the Shakuntala on the cover of the *ACK* comic book (figure 9) shares the same bent head and downcast eyes, the same bejeweled ears and neck, and the same flowers in her hair. Within the pages of the comic, Shakuntala also exhibits the same coquettish posture of partial restraint and partial encouragement when in the presence of the king.

In addition to shared costumes, gestures, and stances, Ravi Varma's paintings of heroines and Bal Gandharva's impersonations of those heroines were alike in their combination of narrative and iconic elements. Like the western tableaux vivant photographs that inspired him, Varma's paintings of mythological women are narratives that have been frozen at a dramatic moment, a moment chosen so as to allow the male gaze to linger on the feminine image. Discussing Varma's painting *Shakuntala Looks Back at Dushyanta,* in which Shakuntala glances back at her lover under the pretext of picking a thorn from her foot, art historian Tapati Guha-Thakurta writes:

> [T]his very gesture—the twist and turn of head and body—draws the viewer into the narrative, inviting one to place this scene within an imagined sequence of images and events. On its own, the painting stands like a frozen tableau (like a still from a moving film), plucked out of an on-running spectacle of episodes. These paintings also reflect the centrality of the "male gaze" in defining the feminine image. Though absent from the pictorial frame, the male lover forms a pivotal point of reference, his gaze transfixes Shakuntala, as also Damayanti, into "desired" images, casting them as lyrical and sensual ideals. (1991, WS94)

Such images simultaneously cast the woman as a mythological heroine and a sensuous ideal, encompassing both the sacred and the secular. To repeat an oft-cited quote, in these paintings "goddesses are luscious women, and luscious women goddesses" (Uberoi 1990, WS44). This technique of the frozen moment was also used in the theater. Bal Gandharva and other actors would pause the continuous story while striking a pose onstage at particularly dramatic points in order to allow the audience time for a double take. In this way the narrative was regularly interrupted with iconic, frontal presentations (Kapur 1993b, 92–93). This technique was employed in early Indian cinema as well, incorporated by the first Indian film director, D. G. Phalke.

Dhundiraj Govind "Dadasaheb" Phalke (1870–1944) is famous as the creator of the first Indian feature film, *Raja Harishchandra* (1913). Prior to producing films, however, Phalke dabbled in other newly available visual media technologies. As a student at the Kala Bhavan art school in Baroda he bought his first still-life camera in 1890. He then went to Ratlam where he learned the three-color blockmaking, photolithography, and darkroom printing techniques. He painted set designs for the theater, ran his own portrait photography studio, and even became a trained magician. In 1905, Phalke went to Lonavala (near Bombay) where he made photolitho transfers of Varma's oleographs for the Ravi Varma Press. He was so successful that he was awarded a medal at a Bombay exhibition and then established his own company, Phalke's Engraving and Printing Works, later called the Laxmi Arts Printing Press (Saklani 1998). Phalke first became interested in film in 1910–11 after he saw *Life of Christ* at the America-India Picture Palace in Bombay. It was this film which inspired Phalke to use this new technology to bring images of the Hindu gods to life: "While the life of Christ was rolling fast before my eyes I was mentally visualising the Gods, Shri Krishna, Shri Ramchandra [Rama], their Gokul and Ayodhya. . . . Could we, the sons of India, ever be able to see Indian images on the screen?" (Rajadhyaksha 1993, 49).

Like Varma, Phalke worked with the mythological genre in order to define "Indianness." Despite using the new medium of film, a technology recently arrived from the West, he located this Indianness in both the production process and the images he created, claiming: "My films are *swadeshi* [Indian] in the sense that the ownership, employees, and stories are *swadeshi*" (Rajadhyaksha 1993, 66). The images that Phalke created were heavily influenced by Varma's narrative paintings and the technique of the frozen moment used in theater. Ashish Rajadhyaksha has argued that in *Shri Krishna Janma* (1918) and other mythological films, Phalke realized a distinct gaze, one that mediated the opposition between "Indian images" and "industrial technology" and their pressures toward static and mobilized images, respectively, by repeatedly alternating frontal, iconic shots of Krishna with action shots, to the extent that strict dramatic continuity was sacrificed (1993, 68–74).

Phalke made more than 40 silent films between 1913 and 1937. Unfortunately, only 13 of over 1,000 silent films made in India have survived (Nair 1980), and very little footage remains of Phalke's work, hence it is difficult to examine Phalke's portrayal of the feminine ideal in depth. Yet through newspaper advertisements placed by Phalke we know that he sought "handsome faces" for films and that he was disappointed when only "ugly, lacklustre or deformed" persons from the red-light district turned up for the female roles; he once reportedly exclaimed: "Imagine their vulgar mannerisms, half exposed breasts, and swaying hips as Sita or Draupadi!" Although he appealed to "inwardly beautiful" women from "good families," few volunteered (Dharap and Shahane 1980, 18; S. Chakravarty 1993, 39; Saklani 1998, 12). Phalke's wife and daughter acted in some of his early films, and he resorted to female impersonators for the female roles in many others.[12]

Further evidence of the spread of the Varma aesthetic into Indian cinema through the films of Phalke and others can be found in the new medium of film posters and booklets that began to emerge in the 1920s. Discussing these new advertisements, Rachel Dwyer and Divia Patel state, "The starting point for this new ocular era was the imagery created by Phalke in his films produced between 1913 and 1937, projecting a strong visual aesthetic that was to have a lasting influence on Indian cinema and was itself subject to many influences, the most significant of which was the painter Ravi Varma" (2002, 104–5).

This shared aesthetic can be seen when the booklet cover for Phalke's film *Setu-Bandhan* (*Bridging the Ocean*, 1932) is compared with Varma's painting *Sethubandhanam* (*Rama Humbling the Seas*, 1906). Both of these images of the Hindu god Rama break with earlier two-dimensional, iconic images of Rama in which he is depicted according to traditional iconographic standards in *tribhanga* pose (contrapposto, with "three bends"), flanked by Sita on his right, Lakshmana on his left, and Hanuman kneeling in the foreground. Varma's and Phalke's uses of realism and narrative in their depictions of Rama lend the deity a new substance through his muscle, weaponry, and emotion and by making the deity so tangible, so real, they deliver the mythical past into the present (see Kapur 1993a).

But the visualization of the female form remains the site where Ravi Varma made the greatest impact. Varma's images of Indian women were so popular that during his own lifetime they were plagiarized by the owners of other lithographic presses. His images were also featured in advertising in India and abroad—one English company even used *The Birth of Shakuntala* to advertise its baby food. In the 1940s and 1950s, the Indian film industry was rapidly expanding. As it did so, the feminine ideal envisioned by Varma thrived through the actresses who now starred in the films and the billboards that were created to advertise the films. Dwyer and Patel have demonstrated that artists like S. M. Pandit, who designed posters for films like *Draupadi* (1940) and *Barsaat* (1949), emphasized the physicality of the female form in such a way that they too transferred a sense of unearthly divinity to film stars and an earthly physicality to mythological subjects (2002, 110).

The fair, voluptuous, sari-draped, and ornamented heroines of Ravi Varma's oil paintings were thus disseminated to the public through lithographs, theater, film, film hoardings, popular advertisements, and other forms of visual culture. Through these various media a publicly visible image of the ideal Indian woman was constructed, one that complemented the ideal Indian woman being constructed by male novelists and socio-religious reformers in various textual media from the late nineteenth century forward. This ideal Indian woman could be identified through such external markers of femininity as her gestures and posture, jewelry and ornamentation, sari draping, and hairstyle. And these external markers of femininity, once equated with the new visual template of mythological heroines such as Shakuntala, became equated with more internal markers of femininity: purity, spirituality, and a long-suffering nature. The significance of this equation is that these external markers of Indian femininity allowed the internal qualities of women to be publicly recognized, so that they could then enter into the modern public realm.[13]

From the *Amar Chitra Katha* covers, it is evident that the statement first made of Ravi Varma's paintings—that "goddesses are luscious women, and luscious women goddesses"—applies equally to these comics. Varma's lasting influence is apparent not only in the style of these images—such as the combination of realism and idealism and the use of the narrative mode—but also in the very content of the comic books. Varma was instrumental in establishing the visual canon of modern Hinduism. The gods and goddesses and epic heroes and heroines that were painted and printed by

The Indian Feminine Ideal in *Amar Chitra Katha*

Varma—including Shakuntala, Rama and Sita, Nala and Damayanti—are the very gods and goddesses and epic heroes and heroines that have been featured in the *Amar Chitra Katha* corpus. And many of the historical Indian figures that Varma painted are also featured in this comic book series as historical heroes. However, in making *Shakuntala* and later titles featuring heroines in the *ACK* series, the creators debated the appropriateness of Shakuntala as a role model for postcolonial Indian women, focusing on several key issues: her costume, the virtues she embodied, and the need for an alternative archetypal feminine ideal.

Visually, the heroines of the *ACK* comic books have much in common with the heroines of Varma's paintings, but one significant point of deviation is that of costume: Whereas Varma had chosen the sari as the best dress to drape his heroines in, the heroines of the comics are consciously clad in far less. While on one of his tours of India to study and devise a national costume, Varma and his brother had visited the Karle caves near Pune. Varma was curious about the scanty clothing of the Buddhist figures there, but decided that such dress was not appropriate for his "proper" heroines from Sanskrit literature (Mitter 1994, 201–2). Familiar with Varma's sari-clad heroines and with Wonder Woman and other popular American superheroines who were costumed in the scanty equivalent of strapless bathing suits, Pai wanted to strike a happy medium by finding a costume that would appeal to youthful readers with its revealing and glamorous nature, yet would still be Indian. Thus a century later, when Anant Pai "toured" classical Indian literature in search of references to costume, he came up with something other than the sari as the garment of choice for his comic book heroines:

> In the classical period men and women wore a lower garment, the *antariya*. Women wore an upper garment, the *uttariya,* too. And rich people wore a waist garment with details, colors. It is like what Bharat Natyam dancers wear today. This was called a *prapata*, and on top of it the very rich would wear a *rasna*, a golden chain. And women also wore an unstitched garment. You know, to cover themselves on top. And there was also the *ushnisha,* which was worn on the head when they went out. Men wore this, too.

When asked how he knew that this is what was worn in ancient India, Anant Pai responded: "From the texts, the *Mahabharat* and the *Ramayan.* For instance, we know from the *Mahabharat* that Draupadi said, 'I am only in one garment—how can I go before the assembly like this?' From such things we know how they dressed back then."

Others involved in the production of these comic books also brought up the subject of costume. When asked about accuracy in his artwork, artist Pratap Mulick commented:

We must stick to certain conclusions that Mr. Pai has reached, based on his reading of the Sanskrit texts. For instance, women's dress. Pai has researched and knows that women only wore a brassiere for their upper garment. Then they had a single lower piece, with a belt over it, and a small covering garment. And ornaments, lots of ornaments, including the belt. And men wore a *dhoti* [loincloth], with no upper garment, and lots of ornaments too.

Producer No. 1 stated that because Pai was so particular about the accuracy of costume, the artists and editors at the comic book studio always referred to a book on ancient Indian dress by the art historian Moti Chandra that was kept in their research library. In this book, *Costumes, Textiles, Cosmetics, and Coiffure in Ancient and Mediaeval India* (1973), Chandra surveys sculpture, coins, and texts from the Vedic period (circa 1500 to 600 BCE) through the twelfth century CE in an effort to appreciate the development of Indian costume over time. Summarizing the Vedic period, Chandra writes:

> The Vedic Indians wore three garments: *nivi* or loin-cloth sometimes having long and unwoven fringe, a garment *(vasas)* and an overgarment *(upavasana, adhivasa)* generally consisting of a wrapper or sometimes consisting of a jacket, bodice or cloak like *pratidhi, drapi* or *atka. Pesas* was worn by dancing girls and was the forefather of modern *peshwaz.* The *ushnisha* or turban is met in later Vedic literature and was worn by the Rajas and Vratyas and also sometimes by women. (1973, 23)

This passage is similar to Pai's discussion of clothing, although some of the terminology differs. But whereas Chandra speaks of a variety of clothing styles according to period and region, one style of women's clothing—purported to be from the Vedic period—has been used in the comics from the classical period through the medieval period and for mythological and historical heroines alike. Thus, less impaired by Victorian sensibilities than Ravi Varma, Anant Pai envisioned a modified costume for Indian women, one which was draped from the hips down much like the sari on Varma's heroines, but which revealed the comic book heroines' voluptuous curves even more, yet remained in his opinion authentically Indian, distinguished from the western bathing suit and other costumes worn by American superheroines.

This sartorial choice has received some criticism. For instance, Indian journalists Sanjay Joshi and Rajni Bakshi wrote in the *Telegraph:*

> [W]hat is decidedly peculiar is their pictorial depiction of women. Considering that the main consumers of these comics are children, there seems little need for the many scantily clad and voluptuously drawn female figures which adorn their pages. In such a context this type of artwork appears obscene, to say the least. We have seen such sexism in films, advertising—but now children's comics! (1983, 8)

However, most readers responded positively to the depiction of women, and many of them commented on the "accuracy" of their clothing in particular. When asked what he thought of the representation of women in *ACK* comics, a man in his midtwenties immediately turned to the issue of women's clothing, stating:

> On a relative scale, I've seen women dressed up like eye-candy more often right now than I did back when I was a kid, but that wasn't the kind of fantasy I was interested in escaping to back then! Seriously enough, they were drawn well, often better than their male counterparts, and dressed pretty accurately to the period they were in. As far as virtue went, they were either straight or crooked, and the complex moral-ambiguity type personas were most often seen in the males.

In response to the same question, another male reader (the same one who identified himself in the introduction as "a very proud Hindu") stated:

> This aspect of representing women in India should be glorified as much as possible. The Indian lady was so open in her dress code back in the good olden days. It was only after the unfortunate series of invasions that women started to cover themselves more and more. Through *Amar Chitra Katha* I began to feel a sense of pride about Indian women, and this is just one of the values I cherish among all the others that *Amar Chitra Katha* has given me. And today the West talks about women being discriminated against in India. If only they take a look at our culture and if only they look at themselves and the kind of lives they lead. *Amar Chitra Katha* has built in me a pride about my race, my culture, my history, and my India.

Most female readers also responded positively to the depiction of women, stating that they found the female characters very pretty and appealing when they read these comics as children. During a group interview with a dozen postgraduate students in Bombay, one recalled, "The men are so muscular, and the women are so pretty." Several others nodded in agreement, and one said, "I remember thinking that their dress, their ornaments are just so amazing. Sometimes I would even try to paint the women after reading the comics." Then the woman next to her paused, flipped through the *Shakuntala* comic book, and countered: "Actually, they are only perpetuating stereotypes in the *Amar Chitra Katha*. In all these pictures the characters are romanticized. They have those curvaceous women revealing everything in fanciful dresses and exotic jewelry and all that. I mean, look how they show the women as being so coy, yet showing everything, even their navels!"

Apart from the occasional criticism, however, the depiction of women and their clothing in *ACK* has been overwhelmingly perceived as both positive and accurate. This general acceptance of a single, revealing costume for all Indian women from the Vedic through the medieval period—not to mention a single, voluptuous feminine figure—as "authentic" and "accurate" demonstrates how dominant the late nineteenth-century image of the ideal Indian woman has become.

In fact, the perceived authenticity of these comic books is so great that they have been used as reference material by the producers of films and television serials set in premodern India. Zarina Mehta, a producer at United Television (UTV) in Bombay, commented that these comics are used by costume and set designers. When Mehta produced a live-action series based on the *ACK* comics that aired on Doordarshan (DD1) in 1998, she used the comic books as the visual guide for the costumes, sets, and narrative flow. In making their "Shakuntala" episodes, therefore, the actress was costumed and coiffed just like the *ACK* heroine. In fact, Mehta stated that the only major deviation was in the opening that they used:

> In the television medium, the first two minutes of a show are very important— that is when you must hook the audience. The *ACKs* can be very slow in the beginning. We would never start with a "once upon a time" slow sort of open- ing. We started with a big event, with action, to lure the children in. The rest of the story and the endings we often told in the same way as they were told in the comics, but it was important to change the beginning.

Mehta felt that the first few pages of the *Shakuntala* comic book, in par- ticular, were far too slow. Beginning with Shakuntala's birth and adop- tion (plate 5), the story does not begin to depict the interaction between Shakuntala and Dushyanta until the fourth page. The television serial begins with Dushyanta's first glimpse of Shakuntala in the forest. Here in the first scene of the televised "Shakuntala" series—as on the cover of the *Shakuntala* comic book—the "male gaze" that we have become accustomed to viewing Shakuntala through dominates.

In the *Amar Chitra Katha* comics, it is not just Shakuntala who is de- picted in this frozen dramatic moment which allows the gaze to linger on her form, so that readers can take in the external markers of her femininity, including her costume, jewelry, hairstyle, and posture, while also reflecting on the more internal markers of her femininity, including her modesty, spirituality, and long-suffering nature. In the comics, this one visual style is employed to depict a range of Indian women from throughout the vast corpus of myth, history, and legend—mythological heroines like Shakun- tala, Hindu goddesses like Sati, and historical queens like Padmini—for all of these women demonstrate how an ordinary woman can be transformed into a goddess through unswerving adherence to the code of *strīdharma* (woman's duty), the normative code of behavior for Hindu women, ac- cording to which the wife is to worship her husband as her lord. This feminine ideal of the orthodox Hindu tradition is expounded in a range of religious texts, both old and new, assumed in most of the ancient myths and epic stories, and widely upheld by both women and men throughout India today (Leslie 1994). Such a woman is known as a *pativratā* (one who takes a vow to worship her husband as her lord) and is characterized by her modest, chaste, long-suffering nature. Shakuntala, who patiently and without complaint endured one hardship after another while waiting for her husband to come to his senses, is one pativratā; another is the Hindu goddess Sati, who was so devoted to her husband, Shiva, that when her father insulted him by refusing to invite him to a ritual sacrifice, she immolated herself in protest; a third is the historical queen Padmini, who committed sati in order to escape the advances of the invading Muslim king and to free her husband to fight and die on the battlefield. Whereas the appropriateness and authenticity of Shakuntala's costume was discussed by the creators of *ACK*, a second issue that generated considerable discussion among both creators and readers was the relevancy of the virtues that Shakuntala and other pativratā heroines embodied for postcolonial Indian women.

In Hindu mythology, *tapas* refers to the spiritual austerities that a male devotee, or *tapasvin*, voluntarily suffers through his devotion to a god or goddess, such as standing in prayer on one leg for years or sitting in daily meditation surrounded by five fires. Legends abound of tapasvins who have achieved great worldly powers by pleasing the gods with such tapas and of others who have obtained *moksha*, spiritual liberation, through tapas. Female *tapasvinīs*, however, are focused not on demonstrating their devotion to the gods in the quest for powers or liberation, but instead are intent on demonstrating their ultimate devotion to their husband. Often the gods are pleased with such displays of wifely devotion and grant such pativratās a special boon; thus Savitri, through her ascetic penance, is able to regain her husband's life from the god of death. Kathryn Hansen argues that the tapasvinī exemplifies a heroics of masochism and that the woman who commits sati is glorified because her action is the most public and final way in which a faithful wife can demonstrate her heroic endurance: "The sati is deified because her acts—like those of Parvati, Sita, Savitri, and other goddesses—represent the normative achievement of self-sacrifice carried to an heroic extreme" (1992, 17–18). The woman who commits sati therefore belongs on the same ideological continuum with other pativratās, a continuum that incorporates history and myth, mortality and immortality, the secular and the sacred.

In the *Padmini* comic book, Padmini is upheld as an idealized heroine, "a perfect model of ideal Indian womanhood," for her willingness to sacrifice herself by committing sati (inside front cover). At the end of this issue, a sequence of panels features a large fire pit, into which Padmini leads the other Rajput women, while heroically proclaiming, "No sacrifice is too big to save one's honour!" (29). The depiction of sati in this and other issues has generated substantial criticism and debate. In 1977, just a few years after the publication of *Padmini*, the Indian Federation of University Women's Associations (IFUWA) surveyed over sixty *Amar Chitra Katha* titles to determine whether there was a sexist bias to the comic books, and concluded that there was, citing the emphasis on the "pre-eminent presence and role of men, on women as appendages, on the emphasis on the 'home syndrome' and value of 'self-sacrifice,' obedient wives, a high premium on fertility" (Lent 2004, 67). Several Indian journalists and activists have also accused the producers of glorifying sati (Kumar 1983), and a number of female readers came to the same conclusion, as did this woman in Bombay who had read these comics as a girl and was reviewing a stack of them during my interview with her:

> I have been looking through this *Padmini* comic book. This comic, especially the ending, really does glorify sati. This is quite evident from the ending. This is where the mediation comes into the telling of history. Of course it is a fact that this practice existed, but that is not enough to justify its presence here in this format. And here it is glorified as a personal choice, a heroic choice. Look at this cover picture. It is told as if she wished herself to do this. But its social context, that is not told. Did Padmini really have a choice?

Anant Pai is familiar with this criticism, and he had an explanation for the heroic depiction of Padmini ready when I raised the subject with him:

> I am always asked, wherever I go, about sati, about why I depicted Padmini burning herself. But it happened. I cannot change that. And the Rajputs saw it as an act of bravery. You know, this is the explanation I always give: "That which is done for the good of others, even at the cost of the self, is good; that which is done to benefit the self, at the cost of another, is a sin." . . . This is how I decide what should be depicted and what shouldn't be.

Here Pai stresses that sati should be understood as a heroic act because it is self-sacrificing and done for a greater good. Yagya Sharma, author of the *Padmini* comic book, justified the depiction of sati by arguing that different times have different values: "You see, our cultural values today look down upon sati. But cultural values change over time. We have stopped looking at cultural values historically. Sati was considered for ages to be the epitome of a woman's value." When asked whether he was familiar with recent scholarship analyzing the colonial role in debates over sati (see Mani 1998), Sharma stressed the self-sacrificial nature of this act: "Sati was a value throughout India, not just in Rajasthan. Amongst the Hindu masses only, of course. Not the Muslims. But I am not saying that sati should be a value today. You know, a lot of ugly things happened in history. Women of that period were willing to give the ultimate sacrifice for their honor—and this is what the value is, not sati itself."

Producer No. 2 was also familiar with the criticism of the depiction of sati in these comics, and stated that one of her goals in joining *ACK* and writing scripts was to depict strong female characters and to portray gender equity. She recalled several debates that took place in the studio over the depiction of women. Some of these, she said, occurred over surprisingly minor issues, not just over issues like sati. When asked for an example, she recalled the creation of the *Shiva Parvati* issue (no. 29, 1972) just after she joined *ACK* in 1971, during which she required numerous pencil sketches in order to get the characterization of the Hindu goddess Parvati just right: "In this story Parvati does penance in order to get Shiva as a husband. There is one panel—you look at it and see—I made the panel in order to show equality between the two, between Shiva and Parvati. It is not just Parvati wanting Shiva; they want one another equally—she wants him, and he wants her, too."

The *Shiva Parvati* issue does feature a panel in which Shiva and Parvati glance longingly at one another, while Shiva declares himself to be her "willing slave" (26). But this issue is also one that tells the story of a goddess, Parvati, who performs prolonged tapas in order to win a god's attention and love. She is the pativratā par excellence, the wife whose perfect devotion to her lord worshippers strive to imitate through heroic endeavors of their own in order to gain Shiva's blessing (Hansen 1992, 8–9). When asked whether she considered Parvati to be an ideal woman and a role model for girls today, Producer No. 2 replied: "Our women then— epic women—had greater liberties than anything that the West can bring to us now. It was only after the outside invaders came that this changed, that their status was lowered so that they were not equal. Take the British legal and economic system. Our old economic system, the one devised by Chanakya, regarded men and women as equal. But the British and other invaders, they did not think this way."

It is significant that Producer No. 2 has chosen to locate this Indian feminine ideal in the epic period, a past "golden age" of Hindu civilization. She continued:

> Women had it better in the Vedic age and the epic age than they do now. When the marauders came from Mongolia, that is when women's decline happened. That is when purdah was introduced. Then women had to be protected, cur- tained from those men. Previously women were free to choose their own part- ners and could even leave them. Like Satyavati in the *Mahabharat*. She wanted Bheeshma to impregnate her daughters, and she cites examples of women leav- ing their men for other men. It was then that Bheeshma laid down the law that a woman can have only one husband. Before that, polyandry was common— as common as polygamy was for men. This is the case with Draupadi—she knows the legal system, knows about polyandry and polygamy.

This location of the feminine ideal within a past golden age of Hindu civi- lization is built on the idea as it was advanced in the nineteenth century in both Orientalist and nationalist discourses. Like the heroines in Ravi Varma's paintings who embodied the female virtues of modesty, chastity, self-sacrifice, patience, and devotion, and who exercised the modern free- doms that were common to all women in the highly cultured Aryan past, the mythological heroines in *ACK* embody the same virtues and exercise the same freedoms. In Anant Pai's words:

It is certainly not correct to say that the image of women has been negative in *Amar Chitra Katha*. . . . A society that allows a woman to declare her attraction and propose to the man exhibits quite some freedom of thought, doesn't it? Women's right to marry the man of their choice has been portrayed in a number of works. Shakuntala exercises this right and marries Dushyanta by exchanging garlands. (Pai 1987)

As in the nineteenth century, so, too, in *ACK* is the classical heroine Shakuntala upheld as one of the foremost role models for contemporary Indian women.

In the mid-1970s, after several women had joined the growing *ACK* staff—including Kamala Chandrakant, Toni Patel, Meena Ranade, and Mala Singh—debates about the depiction of women increased, resulting in the release of several new comics featuring female protagonists, but of a different nature. These heroines were martial, independent, active, decisive women who fought for their land and people. Unlike the pativratā, who is always depicted in static poses, these martial women are depicted in more active postures: commanding troops, wielding weapons in the midst of battles, and riding horses. For instance, on the cover of the *Rani of Jhansi* issue (no. 51, 1974), the historical Queen Lakshmibai of Jhansi (1835–58) is featured on horseback, with her sword in the air, amid a sea of red-coated British soldiers (figure 14). These martial women do not wear the scanty costumes of the pativratā women, but instead adopt male attire. Kathryn Hansen has contrasted this second type of Indian feminine ideal with the pativrata / tapasvini, and labeled this alternative paradigm of Indian womanhood the *vīrāṅganā,* the woman who manifests the qualities of male heroism (*vīryam*). She describes the vīrāṅganā in the following way:

She is a valiant fighter who distinguishes herself by prowess in warfare, an activity normally reserved for men. She demonstrates her martial skills and courage by direct participation in combat, at the risk of her life; in fact, sometimes she dies in battle or takes her own life on the battlefield to avoid ignominious defeat. She is a leader of women and men, acting as head of state during peace and general in time of war. She adopts male attire, as well as the symbols of male status and authority, especially the sword, and she rides a horse. The vīrāṅganā is dedicated to virtue, wisdom, and the defence of her people. Above all, she is a fighter and a victor in the struggle with the forces of evil. (1992, 22)

The first *ACK* issues to depict this alternative ideal were *Tarabai* (no. 48, 1974), *Rani of Jhansi* (no. 51, 1974), *Chand Bibi* (no. 54, 1974), *Ahilyabai Holkar* (no. 74, 1974), *Rani Durgavati* (no. 104, 1976), and *Sultana Razia* (no. 110, 1976). All of these heroines were historical queens who fought for their land and people as independent agents. "Rani" (Queen) of Jhansi, for instance, ruled the kingdom of Jhansi after her husband's death and

Figure 14. *Rani of Jhansi,* no. 51 [reprint no. 539] (Bombay: India Book House Pvt. Ltd., 1974 [1996]), cover. From *Amar Chitra Katha,* with the permission of the publishers ACK Media, India.

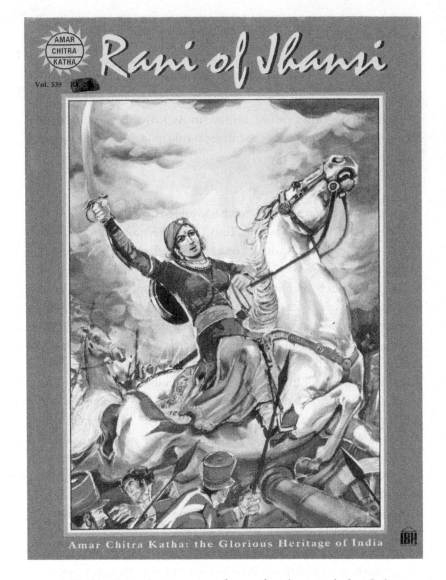

participated in the Indian Mutiny of 1857 after the British decided to annex her territory because her husband had died without a male heir (the son they had adopted was not recognized by the British). As on the cover, inside the *Rani of Jhansi* comic the queen is shown dressed in men's clothing, leading her troops on horseback into battle against the British. Care has been taken, however, to moderate the queen's martial qualities. The introduction to the comic book, for instance, stresses Lakshmibai's "bravery and dauntless courage" while also noting that she was "not aggressive by nature and it was only when the British threatened to annex her small kingdom that she took up arms." The comic book also makes it clear on pages 5 and 6 that the queen did not seek the throne for herself, but ruled on behalf of the king's adopted son, still in his infancy, and for the good of the people. This same emphasis is found in most popular depictions of

Lakshmibai, which show her charging on horseback with her adopted son strapped to her back.

In fact, nearly all of the martial women featured in these comics came into power as regents, ruling the kingdom upon their husband's or father's death and on behalf of a juvenile male heir. Another martial queen featured in the comics is Ahilyabai Holkar, who ruled an area of modern Maharashtra from the time of her husband's death in 1765 until her own death in 1795. Kathryn Hansen has remarked on how the *Ahilyabai Holkar* issue shows her wavering between her desire to become a sati and her eventual decision to dedicate her life to serving others by acting as regent on behalf of her mentally unstable son (1992, 31 and note 69).

Razia Sultana is one exception to this pattern, for she succeeded to the throne of her own accord. Razia is a Muslim, the daughter of Iltutmish, the sultan of Delhi (r. 1229–36), who was chosen over her brothers to follow in her father's footsteps after his death. In the *Sultana Razia* comic (no. 110, 1976), Razia does attain the throne, but the forty *amirs* (governors) object to having a woman as ruler, so Razia abdicates, saying: "My good friends, please stop quarreling. I understand your prejudice against my sex. Therefore let us all swear allegiance to my brother, Ruknuddin" (5). But as Ruknuddin is more devoted to pleasures than to ruling the kingdom, the people rally around Razia, and she is again declared the sultana. She promises her subjects: "My people! I promise before God that I shall prove worthy of your trust. And because I am born a woman, I here and now solemnly pledge that I shall sit on this great throne of our ancestors only if I prove to be as good as any man" (13). The comic book then lists the means by which Razia proved to be as good as a man: she "dressed and acted like a king," "she was the leader of her armies," and she "appeared frequently in public without a veil" (13–15). To this last item an objection is raised that Razia had always veiled in her father's time. Razia responds: "But in my father's time I was not the ruler. Now I face my subjects as their sultana" (15). Razia proves to be a competent and just ruler, but the focus of the second half of the comic book is on the conflict between Razia the woman and Razia the sultana. Razia is unable to marry her true love, the amir Altunia, for fear that the other amirs will become jealous and that the stability of the government will dissipate. Altunia grows jealous of Razia's relationship with another amir and wages battle with her, defeating her forces and capturing her. Upon her defeat Razia's half-brother, Behram, is proclaimed sultan. Razia, however, is concerned only with her relationship with Altunia. She alleviates his jealousy and marries him. The comic ends on a tragically romantic note: following their wedding, Altunia and Razia decide to reclaim the Delhi throne together, but they are killed by Behram's forces.

Discussing the popular Bollywood film *Razia Sultan* (directed by Kamal Amrohi), which was released in 1983, just a few years after the *Sultana*

Razia comic book, Uma Chakravarti and Kumkum Roy note how in this medium as well Razia's life story has been transformed into a tragic love story:

> While the historical Razia has yet to find her place, the mythical Razia, her polar opposite in every sense, has found an audience of many lakhs of people. The real Razia fought tooth and nail to keep herself in power, the mythical Razia proclaims in a Laila-like fashion that the "emperor's garb" is a "shroud" which she would relinquish without the slightest hesitation, because it was an impediment to the fulfillment of her love. Not a single historian protested against the gross distortion of history, and the government of India, which is apparently committed to raising the status of women, considered its duty towards women complete when it gave the film a tax exemption. (1988, WS7)

Although the comic book producers incorporated this alternative feminine ideal after much debate in an effort to celebrate these historical queens' independence and martial deeds, and to provide an alternative female role model to the pativratā, the vīrāṅganā ideal nonetheless demonstrates the limited range of that debate. In several important ways, the vīrāṅganā ideal overlaps with the pativratā (or tapasvinī) ideal: the emphases on regency, motherhood, romantic love, and, above all, the heroines' ultimate sacrifice. All of these alternative heroines ultimately die on the battlefield. *Rani Durgavati* (no. 104, 1976), for example, concludes with a final battle between Queen Durgavati (1524–64), the regent of Gondwana, and Asaf Khan, the Muslim leader of Akbar's imperial army. Rani Durgavati's badly outnumbered forces lose heart and flee after her son is killed on the battlefield, but she fights on, despite the impossible odds and her own wounds. Finally, her charioteer advises her to cease fighting and seek safe harbor. Durgavati rejects his suggestion and instead takes out her dagger and takes her own life, proclaiming, "I would rather die in honour than live in disgrace" (31) (figure 15). Significantly, on this final page Durgavati expresses sentiments that are similar to Padmini's before she committed sati in order to save herself from being physically defiled at the hands of the invaders.

This overlap between the two feminine ideals, the pativratā and the vīrāṅganā, is a modern phenomenon. Cynthia Talbot has discussed in some detail one medieval martial queen, Rudrama-devi (r. 1262–89), the fourth independent ruler in the Kakatiya dynasty in Andhra, who was chosen by her father as his successor (1995b). Like the historical martial queens who are depicted in the comic books, Rudrama wore masculine clothing and acted like a male warrior, even to the extent of dying in battle. Talbot argues that this is because Hindu gender ideology of the time mandated that rulers be males. However, it was also flexible enough to accommodate women like Rudrama-devi whose overt behavior was sufficiently masculine. Thus while Rudrama was understood to be a male socially, she was also understood to be a female biologically. One inscription alternates

THE RANI HAD TO THINK FAST. THE ENEMY WAS CLOSING IN UPON HER.

RANI, PLEASE LET ME TAKE YOU TO A SAFE PLACE.

THE RANI SCORNED HIS SUGGESTION.

AND PERCHANCE FALL INTO THE HANDS OF THE ENEMY. NO! I AM OVER-COME IN BATTLE. GOD FORBID THAT I ALSO BE OVERCOME IN NAME AND HONOUR.

SHE PULLED OUT HER DAGGER.

I WOULD RATHER DIE IN HONOUR THAN LIVE IN DISGRACE.

AND LIKE THE TRUE RAJPUTNI THAT SHE WAS, THE PROUD RANI STABBED HERSELF.

Figure 15. *Rani Durgavati,* no. 104 [reprint no. 606] (Bombay: India Book House Pvt. Ltd., 1976 [2000]), 31. From *Amar Chitra Katha,* with the permission of the publishers ACK Media, India.

between the feminine and masculine versions of her name (Rudrama-devi and Rudra-deva), praising feminine virtues (her generosity and beauty) and then masculine virtues (her ruling and fighting skills). In the privileging of maternal and wifely obligations and romantic scenarios, these comics seem to demonstrate a marked and more recent discomfort with the medieval Indian gender ideology that recognized a difference between sex as a biological given and gender as an enacted social role.

Like the first feminine ideal, the pativratā, the construction of this alternative feminine ideal, the vīrāṅganā, also has its origins in the nineteenth-century debate about the place of women in Indian society. While many Indian nationalists turned toward Vedic and epic heroines as spiritual and cultural models for the modern Indian woman, others turned toward historical female warriors as examples of women who, guided by the *Kshatriya* (warrior caste) values of courage and bravery, were able to resist the might of alien rule. However, such resistance was almost always characterized in a "helpmate" way, so that women's actions were shown to be valuable precisely because they enabled men to resist to the very end. In nationalist stories and images of female warriors, the martial woman quickly became an emblem of the nation itself, Mother India personified, and emotional appeals were made to men to liberate her from her foreign oppressors. Bal Gangadhar Tilak and other nationalists of the Extremist nationalist party, for instance, upheld the Rani of Jhansi as an example of Mother India engaged in righteous struggle against the British (Lebra-Chapman 1986, 143–46). As with the pativratā, then, here too there is slippage between the secular and the sacred, as historical women are likened with martial goddesses such as Durga and Kali and with the nation of India personified as a goddess. Aware of this slippage and the political ramifications of such potent allegories during the colonial period, the British banned literature and images of these martial heroines, historical and mythological alike.[14] Nonetheless, such allegorical associations continued to be made throughout the colonial period and beyond in the various print media. Prime Minister Indira Gandhi (d. 1984), for instance, was often likened to the goddess Durga during her term in office. Uma Chakravarti argues that the normative model of womanhood from the late nineteenth century forward was the pativratā, but the martial woman was also incorporated into the equation as a response to the colonial criticism of the status of women in contemporary India: "Reaction to the attacks by colonial writers ensured that Indian women were almost built up as superwomen: a combination of the spiritual Maitreyi, the learned Gargi, the suffering Sita, the faithful Savitri, and the heroic Lakshmibai. . . . In this model of womanhood there was no difference between the perceptions of progressives and of conservatives" (1990, 79).[15]

Such superwomen—pativratā and vīrāṅganā, mythological and historical—are the heroines featured in *ACK*. Heroines like Shakuntala and the Rani of Jhansi may at first glance seem to be opposites: Shakuntala is a devoted wife and mother, while the Rani of Jhansi is a warrior fighting the British; Shakuntala is shown on her cover in a static pose, dressed in a glamorous outfit and ornaments, while the Rani of Jhansi is shown on her cover in an active pose, dressed in male attire and on horseback; Shakuntala is a pativratā who embodies female heroism, while the Rani of Jhansi is a vīrāṅganā who embodies male heroism. Yet all of these heroines are united in the way they epitomize voluntary sacrifice and suffering. The "superpowers" of Indian comic book heroines, therefore, are nothing physical or external like Wonder Woman's magic lasso and her bulletproof bracelets; they are the internal female virtues of chastity, faithfulness to husband, children, and country, and willingness to make the ultimate sacrifice.

Discussing the portrayal of women in this comic book series, Frances Pritchett writes:

> There are as yet no women on the "Makers of Modern India" list—no Sarojini Naidu (surely the obvious first choice), no Kasturba Gandhi, no Kamala Nehru, no Durgabai Deshmukh, no Anasuyabehn Sarabhai, no Vijayalakshmi Pandit. (And, it should be noted, no Indira Gandhi.) Moreover, even outside the "Makers of Modern India" category, there are no educated, urban, twentieth-century women in the *Amar Chitra Katha* series at all. (1995, 95)

Conclusion: Modern Indian Heroines

The *ACK* series includes a wide range of male protagonists—politicians, revolutionaries, social activists, scientists, industrialists, and religious leaders—from the late nineteenth and twentieth centuries, including *Chandra Shekhar Azad* (no. 142, 1977), *Vivekananda* (no. 146, 1977), *Bagha Jatin* (no. 156, 1978), *Babasaheb Ambedkar* (no. 188, 1979), *Jayaprakash Narayan* (no. 206, 1980), *Lokamanya Tilak* (no. 219, 1980), *Bhagat Singh* (no. 234, 1981), *Rash Behari Bose* (no. 262, 1982), *Lal Bahadur Shastri* (no. 271, 1982), *Senapati Bapat* (no. 303, 1984), *Veer Savarkar* (no. 309, 1984), *Jagdish Chandra Bose* (no. 325, 1985), *Deshbandhu Chittaranjan Das* (no. 344, 1985), *Khudiram Bose* (no. 364, 1986), and *Ghanshyam Das Birla* (no. 382, 1987). However, female protagonists remain limited to ancient mythological and medieval historical heroines. When asked whether Padmini was a role model for girls today, Yagya Sharma, author of *Padmini* and other issues, replied, "No. The *Padmini* issue is not teaching girls today to perform sati. But at the time I wrote it, I didn't think about this stuff, you know? With hindsight I do. . . . Scholarly ladies would be better role models for today's girls. But the lives of scholarly ladies are devoid of the dramatic events that comics need. So it is hard to depict good role models for girls."

In 2005, nearly forty years after *Amar Chitra Katha* was founded, the first modern Indian heroine was featured in a comic book: *Kalpana Chawla* (no. 736, 2005). This is a biographical issue about the Indian-born NASA astronaut. The introduction states: "Kalpana met her end on the morning of February 1, 2003, after the *Columbia* space shuttle exploded during re-entry over Texas. She always reached out to the stars, she went there and beyond. Hers is a story of unusual courage, ambition, and achievement that will inspire young people for all time to come." Scripted as a brave woman who flew through the stars and then met a tragic demise, Kalpana Chawla is the only "scholarly lady" from modern India yet to be featured as a heroine in this series.

The absence of modern Indian heroines—politicians, revolutionaries, social activists, scientists, industrialists, and religious leaders—in the *ACK* series is not due to the fact that such women do not exist, nor are their lives are any less dramatic than their male counterparts. Instead, the absence is due to the many ways in which ideal Indian womanhood has been located within the past Hindu golden age. Like Varma and Phalke before him, Anant Pai looked to the Indian epics and other mythological literature for inspiration as he worked to indigenize a new medium, the comic book, by presenting within its pages Indian stories, characters, and virtues. Shakuntala was to him the obvious first choice in crafting an Indian comic book heroine: she was the pativratā par excellence—the foremother of all Indians who epitomizes the female heroic virtue of voluntary long-suffering devotion to one's husband. To this normative ideal a second, alternative heroine was later added: the martial vīrāṅganā who epitomizes the male heroic virtue of voluntary self-sacrifice out of devotion to one's country. With this formula in place, there is no room for heroines who do not fit either of these molds. Although astronaut Kalpana Chawla stretches the mold as a contemporary vīrāṅganā who entered the "man's world" of space exploration, she was scripted to fit rather than break this male heroic model precisely because her ultimate self-sacrifice demonstrated her devotion to the NASA mission and to both India and the United States.

Sequencing the Tales of Goddess Durga

3

When Anant Pai had an epiphany in the mid-1970s and realized that many readers looked to the *Amar Chitra Katha* comic books as a legitimate source of sacred Hindu stories, he began to feel responsible for textual authority. As a devout Hindu and yet a man educated in science, Pai initially questioned the veracity of the miracles related in Sanskrit narratives of the Hindu gods. Thus although he had based the script of the first comic book, *Krishna* (no. 11, 1969), on the *Bhāgavata Purāṇa* scripture, he updated it in accordance with modern scientific reasoning by eliminating all miracles, including the famous miracle of Krishna lifting the Govardhan Mountain on his finger. But when repeatedly asked why he had eliminated this and other miracles that so many Hindus feel are a crucial part of Hindu mythology, Pai rethought his own religious convictions and decided to revise his comic book template to incorporate miracles. Around 1980 a new, revised *Krishna* was released, prominently showing Krishna lifting the mountain.

Since his change of heart, Pai and his team have marketed this comic book series based on its accuracy and authenticity. They insist that in their recastings of sacred Hindu scriptures no symbolic meanings have been altered, no new interpolations have been inserted, and no facts have been left unchecked. Parents, educators, students, and other consumers can therefore rest assured that when they purchase these comic books, they get the real thing, only better—the "original" Indian story, now in a fun, short, and colorful format.

One of the first issues created following Pai's epiphany—even before the revised *Krishna* issue was finished and released—was *Tales of Durga* (no. 176, 1978) (figure 16). Pai based the script for this issue on the *Devī Māhātmya,* a circa sixth-century classical Sanskrit text, and emphasized that this recasting of that sacred scripture must be done "accurately, without changes." But what does it mean to tell Durga's story accurately in the comic book medium? As one of the earliest comic books to be created under this new directive, *Tales of Durga* represents an important evolution in the interpretation of scripture in this popular medium. Through a careful reading of the *Devī Māhātmya,* content analysis of the *Tales of Durga*

The *Tales of Durga* issue is based on the *Devi Mahatmya.* In the story Durga shoots her arrows at the demon [Raktabeeja], and from every drop of blood that the demon sheds a new demon arises. This has a symbolic meaning: it means that you can't cure violence with violence. But if I changed the story because it is not scientific, then these symbolic meanings are also altered. All of the mythological stories have symbolic meanings that are changed if you change the story. So we must tell these stories accurately, without changes.

Anant Pai, personal interview

comic, a consideration of the unique characteristics of the comic book medium, and interviews with the comic book creators, I hope to provide insight into one modern interpretation of the *Devī Māhātmya* and evolving Hindu attitudes toward the martial goddess Durga and her place within the Hindu pantheon of gods.

The Making of Tales of Durga

In the decade following the release of *Krishna,* many more mythological comic books featuring Hindu gods and goddesses were created: *Rama* (no. 15, 1970), *Hanuman* (no. 19, 1971), *Shiva Parvati* (no. 29, 1972), *Surya* (no. 58, 1974), *Indra and Shachi* (no. 71, 1974), *Ganga* (no. 88, 1975), *Ganesha* (no. 89, 1975), *Sati and Shiva* (no. 111, 1976), *Krishna and Rukmini* (no. 112, 1976), *Garuda* (no. 130, 1977), *Krishna and Jarasandha* (no. 147, 1977), *Tales of Vishnu* (no. 160, 1978), *Tales of Shiva* (no. 164, 1978), *Krishna and Narakasura* (no. 167, 1978), *Indra and Vritra* (no. 170, 1978), and *Krishna and the False Vasudeva* (no. 172, 1978). Most of these titles were Vaishnava (concerning the god Vishnu or his incarnations); however, a number of Shaiva (about the god Shiva) and Shakta (about the forms of the Great Goddess) titles were also printed. All of the goddesses featured were of the idealized pativratā type (including Parvati and Sati); they were chaste, wifely, and maternal. No fierce, martial, independent goddesses resembling the alternative vīrāṅganā type of Indian feminine ideal had yet been featured, despite the fact that Durga, Kali, and other martial forms of the Goddess are incredibly popular among Hindu devotees in parts of eastern, northern, and southern India. Throughout the 1970s, Durga—the martial goddess known for her battlefield victories over demons—was slated on the production charts as one of the Hindu deities whose story remained to be told. In 1978, Anant Pai decided it was finally time to assign the *Tales of Durga* title.

Pai chose the author and artist very carefully. The artwork was assigned to Souren Roy, a Hindu freelance artist living in Kolkata, capital of the eastern Indian state of West Bengal. Because Bengal is one of the regions where the worship of Durga is concentrated, Pai was certain that Roy was the best artist for the job and would depict Durga accurately:

> We give the stories set in Bengal to Souren Roy because he will know what the fashion is like there, what the buildings are like, etc. And Mohandas Menon knows these things for Kerala. These are things that not every artist will know. And we have used a Sikh artist for some of our Sikh issues, Devender, because in the past we had errors with the bracelet, with earrings, etc., so it is better that a Sikh artist do these issues or, if that is not possible, that a Sikh like Mr. Rajinder Singh Raj check the story for accuracy before it is printed.

Pai chose Producer No. 1, a Hindu but not a devotee of Durga, to write the *Tales of Durga* script because of his strong research skills:

Figure 16. *Tales of Durga*, no. 176 [reprint no. 514] (Bombay: India Book House Pvt. Ltd., 1978 [2000]), cover. From *Amar Chitra Katha*, with the permission of the publishers ACK Media, India.

[Producer No. 1] was a good author. He was a teacher before, so he knew how children read, what they like. And he knew the textbooks, knew history very well. He was also good with mythology. He did a lot of research on his own before writing a script. So some issues he picked out himself. But many I assigned to him, like *Tales of Durga,* because I knew he would do the research, read the original texts, and write a good script.

Pai gave the author and artist both explicit instructions to retain important miracles as they worked up the script and pencil sketches and also to remain as faithful as possible to the "original" text. These instructions reflected Pai's new emphasis on accuracy and authenticity in the production of the mythological *Amar Chitra Katha* comic books that followed in the wake of his epiphany.[1] Producer No. 2 discussed this new emphasis on authenticity and her role in achieving it by reading English translations of classical Hindu scripture that were produced during the colonial period and are housed in the libraries of the Royal Asiatic Society and Bharatiya Vidya Bhavan in Bombay. She also stressed the significance of the introductions that she had placed inside the front cover of each comic book:

> My aim was that one day the readers of *ACK* would want to read the more elaborate originals and would like to know where the *ACK* was drawn from. The late Mr. Purushottam Nedungadi wrote most of the introductions for *ACK*. By now *ACK* had gained the acceptance and approval of schools and parents. Children loved them; the family enjoyed them. I was achieving all I had set out to achieve. *ACK*s were not brushed aside as mere comics but had achieved a standing and were even being used as authentic reference material by many.

Producer No. 3, an author and associate editor who joined the company in the late 1970s, similarly maintained that preserving the authenticity of the "original" source was a top priority with all of the mythological issues. When asked whether she had any flexibility to update a script and make it more relevant for modern times, she replied:

> Not at all. If it's from a mythological title, not at all. Because it is supposed to be based on a certain source. So you have to be true to that. And that, I think, has been the staying power of *Amar Chitra Katha*. You don't make it relevant to modern times. And I would say, even the language is a little archaic in the mythological titles. Not only the language style, but also the content is true to the original. You don't play around with mythology. But if it's lighter, like a story or a folktale, you have a lot of play. You can change it, you can add to it, you can put in flourishes—whatever you like, that's fine.

But putting into practice this policy of recasting mythology "accurately, without changes" in the comic book medium while making *Tales of Durga* raised several questions about scriptural interpretation. First, for the scriptwriter, which version of the "original" text was he or she to be true to? Hinduism has a relatively open canon with a vast array of authoritative scriptures about the Hindu pantheon, as has been demonstrated by research on the many *Rāmāyaṇa*s, or stories of god Rama, in Sanskrit and vernacular Indian languages (see Richman 1991, 2001). For Durga, like Rama, many texts relate her mythology, each with its own distinct emphases, including the *Devī Māhātmya* and the later *Devī Bhāgavata Purāṇa*. When asked about the possibility of multiple "original" mythological texts, Anant Pai's response was simple: "If there are three or four texts, then I choose one, and list the source in the comic book." For the *Tales of Durga* issue, he explained, the *Devī Māhātmya* was chosen because it is the oldest—and hence in his opinion the most authoritative—source on Durga. The introduction to *Tales of Durga* therefore notes that the three short stories that are told in this comic book are "based on the Durga-Saptashati of the Markandeya Purana." *Devī Māhātmya* means "Glorification of the Goddess" and is the title commonly given to the 81st to 93rd chapters of the

Sanskrit *Mārkaṇḍeya Purāṇa* scripture; these same chapters are also known as the *Durgā Saptaśatī* or "Seven Hundred Verses to Durga."

The *Devī Māhātmya* is a philosophical treatise on the nature of the Great Goddess (Devī) as the Supreme God and ultimate reality of the universe. Thomas Coburn, who has translated and analyzed this scripture, describes it as the earliest text "in which the object of worship is conceptualized as Goddess, with a capital *G*" (1991, 16). Whereas previous Purāṇic stories had equated male gods like Krishna, Rama, and Shiva with the ultimate reality, the *Devī Māhātmya* was the first text to make the case for the Great Goddess as the ultimate reality. It begins with a frame story in which a king and a merchant ask a Hindu renouncer, Sage Medhas, about the nature of their woes, for the king has lost his kingdom and the merchant has been banished by his own family. Sage Medhas replies that it is the Goddess who is responsible both for deluding them and for the eternal knowledge that can bring them liberation. He then narrates three stories of this Goddess to guide them down the path to moksha.

In the first story, the god Vishnu lies sleeping on his serpent in the cosmic ocean during the interval between the cyclical creation and destruction of the universe. As the god Brahma prepares to create the next cycle of the universe, two demons (*asuras*)—Madhu and Kaitabha—suddenly arise from the dirt in Vishnu's ear and attack Brahma. To wake Vishnu so that he can kill the demons, Brahma sings a hymn to Goddess Mahamaya ("She Who Is the Great Illusion"), who here takes the form of Yoganidra, the yogic sleep of Vishnu. After praising the Goddess and her cosmic forms, Brahma asks her to withdraw from Vishnu so that he may awaken. The Goddess consents, Vishnu wakes and decapitates Madhu and Kaitabha, and Brahma creates the universe. As Coburn has demonstrated, this is a familiar story that has been cleverly refashioned in this scripture: "[T]he story has previously been 'owned' by Vishnu, for all previous accounts portray him as the agent of the Asuras' demise. Now, in our text, Vishnu's very capacity to act as agent is shown to be derivative, contingent upon the withdrawal from him of the Goddess" (1984, 221). Here it is instead claimed that it is the Goddess, not Vishnu or Brahma, who is ultimately responsible for the death of the demons and the creation of the universe.

The second story in the *Devī Māhātmya* is the most popular one, in which Durga battles and defeats the buffalo demon Mahisha. This story, according to Coburn, has few earlier precedents, and functions to "demonstrate not only that the Goddess has an earthly career, but that of earthly creatures, she is the supreme ruler" (1984, 229). Whereas the first story demonstrated the transcendent power of the Goddess, this second story demonstrates her immanent power.

The third story is a lengthy one in which the Goddess takes on many forms to battle many demons, including Raktabeeja, Chanda and Munda, and Shumbha and Nishumbha. This story teaches that the many goddesses are ultimately one Great Goddess. In Coburn's words: "There need be no paradox or contradiction between transcendence and immanence, nor between either of these and internality, because all of these are manifestations of one power. The forms of power are many, but the fact of power is one" (1984, 305). The *Devī Māhātmya* then concludes by returning to its frame story, wherein the king and the merchant are persuaded to worship the Goddess by the sage's stories. After three years of prayer, the Goddess appears before the men to grant them each a boon. The merchant chooses liberation, while the king chooses eternal kingship. By worshipping the Goddess as the king and merchant have, readers can hope for their own boon.

But after an "original" text like the *Devī Māhātmya* is decided upon as the source for the *Tales of Durga* comic book, a second question arises: How do the creators accurately transform this weighty poetic scripture into a book of thirty-two pages? Because comic books are a form of sequential art that tells stories through a procession of panels, each of which contains a mixture of text and image, the processes of creating and reading comics are more complex than is often realized. Discussing this with regard to English-language comics in particular, Lawrence Abbott writes:

> The order in which one perceives the various textual and pictorial elements of a single panel—not to mention a series of panels—depends on eye movement. Eye movement in a panel is determined by both the left-to-right, top-to-bottom conventions of reading and by the freer patterns associated with the contemplation of pictures. The good comic artist knows how to work the two seemingly unrelated eye operations to his advantage. (1986, 159)

Like Abbott, Ann Marie Seward Barry has recognized the complexity of comics in their sequential nature and their intimate blending of two systems of expression: a verbal language, which is "essentially a linear system," and visual imagery, which is "closely associated with direct perception and experience" (1997, 107). Together, Barry argues, the combination of word and image in sequential comic panels forms a system that encourages us as readers to focus our attention on details, such as the narrative text and visual landscapes and backgrounds, as well as on more universal patterns, such as the expressions and postures of the characters, "into which we project our own experience" (1997, 109). As we progress from panel to panel, following the linear narrative text and reading the dialogue, our gaze also lingers on the characters' frozen postures, gestures, and expressions, and in the process we absorb their emotional states and, ideally, identify with them. "Meaning," Barry concludes, "is thus derived from experiential sequence" (1997, 113).

In his own way, comics artist Scott McCloud posits a similar argument when he explains—through sequential panels that depict a man in glasses speaking directly to the reader via dialogue balloons—that reader-identification is a specialty of comics and cartooning: "You give me life by reading this book and by 'filling up' this very iconic (cartoony) form. Who I am is irrelevant. I'm just a little piece of you. But if who I am matters less, maybe what I say will matter more. That's the theory, anyway" (1993, 37).

Like continuity editing in classic Hollywood cinema, which encourages strong character identification and maximizes narrative clarity through an "invisible" editing style (utilizing establishing shots, eyeline match, the 180° rule, etc.; see O'Brien 2005 and Bordwell 2006), classic American comic books have their own editing system that clarifies the story and encourages character identification. Formally, the *Amar Chitra Katha* series was modeled on American comics of the 1950s and 1960s (*Tarzan, Phantom,* and *Mandrake,* as well as *Classics Illustrated*), thus this editing system also dictates how Indian stories are told in this medium. The first step is to single out a hero or heroine to organize the narrative around. In *Tales of Durga,* the obvious choice is the Goddess. But the comic book creators found the *Devī Māhātmya* to be a particularly challenging text to transform into this visual medium, for the Goddess is not a character in the frame story where she is only mentioned by Sage Medhas, nor is she physically present in the first story where she takes the form of Yoganidra, Vishnu's yogic sleep, the transcendent but intangible form of the Goddess. Not until the second story, in which Durga slays the buffalo demon, does the Goddess appear as a physical character. How, then, to even begin the comic book?

According to classic comic book continuity editing, the hero must be presented to the reader in the first, or "splash," page. American comic artist Will Eisner explains the importance of the splash page:

> The first page of the story functions as an introduction. What, or how much, it contains depends on the number of pages that follow. It is a launching pad for the narrative, and for most stories it establishes a frame of reference. Properly employed it seizes the reader's attention and prepares his attitude for the events to follow. It sets a "climate." (1985, 62)

In the *Amar Chitra Katha* series the style of the splash page varies depending on a number of factors, including which artist designed the page and how much room the artist had to work with, but these pages are always specially designed to grab the reader's attention by introducing the hero with strong visual appeal. If room allows, the splash page is a full-page panel. But if space is tight, the splash page may be subdivided into a half- or two-thirds-page panel on top, featuring the hero and the title of the issue, and two square panels on the bottom of the page with more narrative text that begins to move the story forward. In either case, the splash page visually presents the hero and provides some information about the hero's personality and situation, so that we begin the identification process and eagerly proceed to the next page to learn more about our hero and to partake in his or her adventures.

Rama (no. 15, 1970), for instance, opens with a full-page splash panel that immediately draws the reader's eye to Rama, the handsome blue-skinned youth standing in the center of the image with the bow and arrow. After looking him over, the eye moves to the right, taking in the title "Rama" in the top corner and one of Rama's brothers poised slightly behind him, before moving to the left to take in the other two brothers lined up behind him and the city of Ayodhya in the background, then finally dropping to read the narrative text which informs us that King Dasharatha ruled Ayodhya and fathered four sons. Thus this splash page not only introduces Rama as a young prince of Ayodhya but also sets up the epic themes of battle (through the inclusion of the bow and arrow) and the potential for conflict over a throne (through the mention of Dasharatha fathering four sons and the visual inclusion of Rama's brothers) that are so central to the story of this Indian hero.

Shakuntala (no. 12, 1970) also opens with a full-page splash panel, which features a lush forest hermitage (plate 5): Green trees, climbing creepers, and flowering bushes frame the image, and a simple thatched hut sits in the upper right-hand corner, with a small fire pit for ritual oblations in front of it and two deer peacefully grazing at its front stoop. Opposite the hut, standing against a tree in the lower left-hand corner of the page, is the beautiful nymph Menaka. She holds a newborn baby cradled in her arms and gazes across the fire pit at the hut, an outsider looking in upon this forest idyll. In the middle of the page the title of this comic book, "Shakuntala," is printed in large bold letters, and the narrative text in the small box beneath it reads, "Menaka, a heavenly nymph, left her new-born baby near Sage Kanva's hermitage." Thus this splash page introduces the heroine of this comic book, Shakuntala, as an abandoned baby, invoking the reader's sympathy and simultaneously setting up the situation in which the first half of her story will take place: the forest hermitage of Sage Kanva, where Shakuntala grows up to become a beautiful maiden. It also suggests for the discerning reader the themes of marriage, motherhood, and abandonment that are so central to the story of this Indian pativratā heroine.

Like the mythological issues, the historical comics also begin with splash pages that introduce the hero. *Subhas Chandra Bose* (no. 77, 1975) opens with a full-page splash panel that contains a large and detailed image of the ancestral home of the Indian nationalist leader "Netaji" (Leader) Subhas Chandra Bose (1897–1945?). The title of the issue—the hero's name—spans the top of the page, above the home. To the bottom left is a circular inset panel featuring baby Subhas upon his mother's lap, with his father standing at their side. This inset invites us as readers into the ancestral home that fills the rest of the page, allowing us to join this biographical narrative at the very beginning. To the right of this round panel the text in the narrative box reads: "Subhas Chandra Bose was born in Cuttack, Orissa, on January 23, 1897. His mother was Prabhavati and his father, the famous lawyer, Janaki Nath Bose." When discussing this splash page and the visual instructions he had received, artist Souren Roy stated with a mischievous smile:

> Well, you don't have to follow the visual instructions carefully. You can make additions, changes. And they appreciate it when we do so, because often the visual artist knows better how something should be put into image. I did a lot of research for *Subhas Chandra Bose*. I visited Janakinath Bhavan, where Netaji was born, and made some sketches. It is where his life began, so it is where the story must begin also. And I looked at photos and many books. The artist must do a lot of work. Back then, you know, Janakinath Bhavan was not in good condition. It was neglected, so I had to imagine what it was like in Netaji's time. Now that it is a museum, it is protected. I wanted to show what it was like, a nice home, so that everyone would know Netaji's birthplace.

For this artist, then, the splash page was so important that he decided to exercise his creative freedom and conduct his own research to produce a full-page splash panel that would both educate and entice the reader.

The *Tales of Durga* comic book begins with a splash page that is quite different from the usual formula: In a two-thirds-page panel at the top of the page, the buffalo demon Mahisha (a Sanskrit term meaning "buffalo") stands on one leg in austere prayer (figure 17). Here the eye wanders from Mahisha as he stands performing tapas, to the right, taking in the approaching chariot that flies through the air in the background, as well as the title of this first story, "Durga—The Slayer of Mahisha," which is printed in the upper right-hand corner. As the eye drops to read the narrative text at the bottom of this panel, we learn that Mahisha has performed these difficult austerities as a form of prayer, hoping to propitiate and win a boon from Lord Brahma, who now approaches him in the chariot. Next the eye moves to the bottom left panel, in which Brahma has landed his chariot and appeared before Mahisha, holding his right hand in the air in a beneficent gesture. Mahisha bows before Brahma, asking in a dialogue balloon to be made immortal. Brahma replies that because he was born a mortal he cannot escape death. As the eye crosses to the bottom right panel, it focuses on the close-up image of Mahisha and his thought balloon in which he ponders what other boon to ask for.

The entire focus of this splash page is therefore upon the demon Mahisha, for the first panel introduces him as an austere figure who commands the attention of Lord Brahma; the next introduces Mahisha's desire for immortality; and in the third Mahisha tries to think of a way to use his boon to achieve immortality. This page uses only moment-to-moment panel transitions, which require little work or input from the reader to render the

Figure 17. *Tales of Durga*, no. 176 [reprint no. 514] (Bombay: India Book House Pvt. Ltd., 1978 [2000]), 1. From *Amar Chitra Katha*, with the permission of the publishers ACK Media, India.

sequence meaningful, as the activity and duration between each panel is minimal. Such transitions are standard in comic book continuity editing, helping readers to focus on a single subject: the hero.[2] Here, however, the focus is Mahisha, and the only clue on this page that signals that Mahisha is not the hero is the story title in the upper right-hand corner.

If the first rule of classic comic book continuity editing is that the hero should be the focus of the splash page, the second rule is that all elements within the comic book should be subservient to the plot. Dialogue balloons, narrative text, images, panel transitions, page layout—these elements must work together to clarify the story. This rule, too, is broken in *Tales of Durga*. At the top of the second page Mahisha asks that he may only be killed at the hands of a woman, which he figures is as good as immortality. The boon is granted, and the following panels continue to focus on

Mahisha as he commands his troops, wages war against the gods, achieves victory, and ascends their throne at the bottom of the fourth page. As the battle rages between Mahisha and the gods, action-to-action panel transitions highlighting the exchange of blows on the battlefield are interspersed with subject-to-subject panel transitions that shift the perspective of the scene, alternating between the gods as they lose ground and Mahisha as he emerges victorious. In these first thirteen panels there are no standard visual clues (aside, perhaps, from his dark skin color) that Mahisha is the villain. Only through the contrasting montage on pages 4 and 5 is the first such visual suggestion made: on page 4 Mahisha sits on the throne, a victorious king surrounded by his loyal demon horde; on page 5 in an opposing panel an enthroned idol of Mahisha is worshipped by citizens under duress who secretly call out to their own gods for salvation. Here as one Brahmin bows before the idol of the buffalo demon, two thought balloons emanate from him. The first contains his silent prayer, "O God of Gods! When will you save us from this plight?" The second contains an image of Shiva, showing us whom he really prays to. But if Mahisha is not the hero, then who is?

Durga finally appears in the twentieth panel at the bottom of page 6 (plate 4). In this panel the goddess has just been conjured up by the gods. She is resplendent, illuminated by the rays of light (*tejas*) that the gods used to create her and her radiant golden crown and jewelry. She shines, in contrast to the dark-skinned Mahisha.[3] The miraculous nature of this occurrence is highlighted in both the text and the image. The narrative text takes on a reverent tone when discussing the miracle of the creation of the Goddess: "And lo! The next moment, out of that light a female form with a thousand arms came into being! It was Devi Durga" (6). The image is equally reverent, depicting a majestic and serene many-armed Durga shrouded in a radiant halo and encircled by the other gods. It recalls the description of the Goddess in verses 2.36–38 in the *Devī Māhātmya*, who is described just after her creation as:

> Filling the triple world with her radiance,
> Causing the earth to bow down at the tread of her feet, scratching the sky
>   with her diadem,
> Making all the nether regions tremble at the sound of her bowstring,
> Standing (there) filling all the directions with her thousand arms. (Coburn
>   1991, 42)

In this panel, Anant Pai's recent decision to embrace the miraculous in mythological narratives is made abundantly evident.

But Durga's appearance, majestic and miraculous though it is, is brief. In the four panels on the next page her presence is only suggested, not shown. Instead, the subject shifts so that we first see the gods in prayer, while their joint speech balloon tells us that they pray to Durga hoping that she will be able to defeat Mahisha. In the next three panels the gods are shown offering up their various weapons, asking Durga to accept them in preparation for her martial mission. Thus at the end of page 7, half-way through this story, the heroine of this issue has appeared in only one panel.

Durga reappears at the top of page 8, riding her lion and ready for battle, emitting a "blood-curdling roar." But in the next panels the focus shifts away from her. With scene-to-scene panel transitions we see the seas tremble and the mountains shake at that fierce roar, and in the bottom panel Mahisha takes notice of the disturbance. At the top of page 9, in the twenty-ninth panel, Durga makes her third appearance, this time before Mahisha (figure 18). But who is the hero and who is the villain in this panel? Durga's presence is larger, for she is in the foreground and occupies half of the panel, with her lion and her array of arms and weapons. Yet her back is to the reader, making it difficult to identify with her by hiding her expression—we do not know if she looks fierce and confident or if she is intimidated by Mahisha. Mahisha, on the other hand, faces the reader, and it is to him that the eye is drawn as he proclaims, "Ho! A mere female!" Mahisha stands in a challenging posture, with his muscles taut, his sword ready, and the hint of a smirk on his face.

On the bottom half of page 9, the perspective finally shifts with a moment-to-moment transition to indicate that Durga is the real hero. In the bottom left-hand panel Durga advances, asserting that she is "no mere female," while Mahisha steps backward, thrown off balance. Here it is Mahisha's back that is presented to the reader and Durga that we look up to in all of her martial glory. In the next panel Mahisha steps further back and turns to his men for help, and from this point forward Durga has him on the run as he shape-shifts into buffalo, lion, and elephant forms to battle the Goddess. On the following six pages, in panel after action-packed panel, their battle wages on, until the final showdown on page 15: Here our heroine leaps upon the charging buffalo's back, stabs him with her trident, and decapitates him with her sword, all while retaining a serene half-smile. In the final half-page panel at the bottom of this page Mahisha lies dead beneath Durga's feet, and the gods reappear to offer their grateful salutations to the Goddess, praising her as the "upholder of virtue" and the "destroyer of evil" (figure 19).

In its complex narrative sequencing and prolonged focus on the villain from the splash page forward, *Tales of Durga* violates the rules of continuity editing and stands apart from other issues in the *Amar Chitra Katha* series. Whereas it is the archfiend Mahisha whom we see on the splash page of *Tales of Durga*, and Mahisha who is featured in the first six out of seven panels and who wins the first battle sequence, in the *Rama* issue Rama remains the object of focus—the clear hero—throughout the comic book.

Figure 18. *Tales of Durga,* no. 176 [reprint no. 514] (Bombay: India Book House Pvt. Ltd., 1978 [2000]), 9. From *Amar Chitra Katha,* with the permission of the publishers ACK Media, India.

It is Rama who is featured on the splash page and in the first six out of seven panels. After a panel showcasing Rama's archery skills immediately following the splash page—in which Rama stands with his admiring brothers, his hand still in the air, having just released an arrow to pierce the bull's-eye of a target in the distance—the villains are introduced in the next panel with a subject-to-subject transition. Here, in a large panel at the bottom of the second page, Sage Vishwamitra is shown being interrupted in his ritual offerings by a pack of demons who pollute the sacred fire. Rama is not depicted, but the narrative text at the bottom and Vishwamitra's thought balloon inform us that, with his bow and arrow, "Rama alone can help" (2). In the next panel, at the top of the third page, the visual focus returns to Rama as he battles the giant demon Tataka. In the sequence of four action panels on this page that makes up the battle scene, each of the panels can be

Text in image: THE NEXT MOMENT, MAHISHA FELL DEAD, AT THE FOOT OF DURGA. THE DEVAS WERE OVERJOYED.

O DURGA, UPHOLDER OF VIRTUE, DESTROYER OF EVIL, WE HUMBLY SALUTE YOU! O DEVI, CONTINUE TO PROTECT US!

Figure 19. *Tales of Durga*, no. 176 [reprint no. 514] (Bombay: India Book House Pvt. Ltd., 1978 [2000]), 15. From *Amar Chitra Katha*, with the permission of the publishers ACK Media, India.

understood without the accompanying text, for the visual action depicted here is very clear. In the top panel Tataka approaches, sword drawn, and is pointed out to Rama by Sage Vishwamitra. In response, Rama grabs an arrow. In the second panel Rama raises his bow and arrow, taking aim at Tataka, who shields her face in fear. Here the angle of the shot has moved in a counterclockwise direction, so that the view of the scene is no longer from a point between Rama and Tataka, but almost directly behind the demon. In this way our attention is focused on Rama as he faces Tataka. In the next panel, Tataka lies supine at Rama's feet, with an arrow shaft standing vertically up out of her chest. The perspective is such that the viewer looks up at Rama, his bow still in hand, for he is the clear victor. Finally, in the last panel Rama and his brother fend off the other demons, while Sage Vishwamitra successfully performs his prayers in the background (3).

This last panel on the third page of the *Rama* issue is juxtaposed with the bottom panel on the second page, suggesting a resolution to this narrative segment: Vishwamitra's prayers to the gods had been interrupted by the demons, but Rama now has that problem well in hand. These panels have been purposefully grouped together on these two pages in a complete narrative segment, so that a new episode in Rama's story can begin on the fourth page. Will Eisner has commented on the significance of such sequential groupings:

Pages are a constant in comic book narration. They have to be dealt with immediately after the story is solidified. Because the groupings of action and other events do not necessarily break up evenly, some pages must contain more individual scenes than others. Keep in mind that when the reader turns the page a pause occurs. This permits a change of time, a shift of scene, an opportunity to control the reader's focus. Here one deals with retention as well as attention. The page as well as the panel must therefore be addressed as a unit of containment although it too is merely a part of the whole comprised by the story itself. (1985, 63)

The Rama-Tataka battle presents a great contrast with the Durga-Mahisha battle. The villain Mahisha is the dominant figure, with an emphasis on his size and fearless charges in battle as he rages across the pages in his buffalo, lion, human, and elephant forms, while the heroine Durga is frequently eliminated from the panel altogether or minimized so that only her back, arms, or weapons are included. Furthermore, the Durga-Mahisha battle lacks the visual cohesion of the Rama-Tataka battle and relies on the text for explanation (figure 20): Is Durga holding her ground at the top of page 10 or losing it to the demons? Are the soldiers in the middle panel fighting at Durga's side or fleeing? Is Mahisha featured in the last panel on this page because he is winning or because he is losing? Without textual explanations, all of these images are unclear. For those Indian readers who already know the story because they have previously learned Durga's mythology, this does not present a problem. But for those readers who are less familiar with Durga, this is potentially quite confusing. Finally, the Durga-Mahisha battle goes on and on, spanning twenty-three panels and extending from the ninth to the fifteenth page, without any attempt to control the reader's focus through the purposeful grouping of panels into a "unit of containment." In these pages our heroine is nearly sequenced out of her story.

In the *Devī Māhātmya*, on the other hand, this long battle sequence serves to glorify the Goddess by showcasing her ability to fight and defeat a wide array of fierce opponents. It is a powerful, often gruesome account of Durga's awesome martial abilities, as in this description of her battle with the demon army in verses 2.54–58:

> Then the Goddess with her trident, club, and showers of spears,
> With sword and the like slew the great Asuras by the hundreds,
> And she felled others who were deluded by the sound of her bell.
> And having bound some Asuras on the ground with her noose, she dragged
>   them along.
> Others were cut in two by sharp blows from her sword.
> Still others, crushed by the fall of her club, lay on the ground,
> And some, much smitten by her mace, vomited blood.
> Some fell to the ground, their chests rent by her spear.
> Others were destroyed on the field of battle, cut by the flood of arrows.
>   (Coburn 1991, 43–44)

Figure 20. *Tales of Durga,* no. 176 [reprint no. 514] (Bombay: India Book House Pvt. Ltd., 1978 [2000]), 10. From *Amar Chitra Katha,* with the permission of the publishers ACK Media, India.

The passage goes on, describing decapitated heads and limbs strewn across the battlefield, and torrents of blood flowing from the deceased soldiers. In the classical text, Durga remains the focal point as she defeats Mahisha in his many forms: snaring him as a buffalo, beheading him as a lion, ripping him to shreds as a human, and cutting off his trunk as an elephant. Durga, the immanent form of the Great Goddess, takes on a royal role at a time when all other kings and gods have been overpowered by the demon-king. Thus as the regal challenger who is invested with the sovereign weapons and blessings of all other deities, it is her sacred duty to defeat Mahisha so that order may be restored, and this is a duty she both excels at and seemingly relishes. Finally, after the Goddess has had enough play, she quaffs a "superior beverage," laughs with intoxication, and slays Mahisha (Coburn 1991, 46–47).

In *Tales of Durga,* two other short stories are told following "Durga—the Slayer of Mahisha." "Chamundi" concerns the battle between the goddess Kali and the demons Shumbha, Chanda, and Munda. It begins with a splash page featuring the demon Shumbha wreaking havoc in the gods' abode. The gods flee to Mt. Himavat, where they again pray to Durga for their salvation. Goddess Parvati walks by at this point, and suddenly the beautiful goddess Ambika springs forth from her. When the demons learn of Ambika's beauty and report it to Shumbha, he decides that he must have her at any cost. However, when the demons approach Ambika, she frowns and Kali springs forth from her forehead. Kali is a fierce goddess with dark skin, a bloodstained tongue, and a garland of skulls. She rushes into battle with the demon army, quickly slays Chanda and Munda, and is therefore given the epithet "Chamundi" in the final panel.

The third story, "How Durga Slew Shumbha," continues where the second left off, featuring even more incarnations of our heroine. To defeat the demon Shumbha, hundreds of "Shaktis—the inner force of various gods—issued forth assuming female forms" (24). These shaktis—including Brahmani, Vaishnavi, Maheshwari, and Chandika—battle Shumbha's army alongside Kali, eventually defeating even Raktabeeja, the demon endowed with the ability to create a new replica of himself out of each drop of his blood that spills upon the ground. Ultimately, when all of the demons except Shumbha are defeated, Shumbha complains to Durga, telling her that she should not take any pleasure in her victory, since she achieved it only with the help of many others. In reply, Durga explains: "I am alone. The goddesses you see are but different forms of myself" (30). On the final page, all of the shaktis merge into Durga before Shumbha's eyes, proof of her statement that the hundreds of shaktis and Kali are really incarnations of Durga, who is the Great Goddess, at once immanent and transcendent, many and One. Durga and Shumbha then engage in one-on-one battle, and Durga is victorious. In the final panel, the gods appear once again to thank their savior.

Keeping in mind the directive to recast scripture "accurately, without changes," the elimination of the frame story and first story of the *Devī Māhātmya* and the rearrangement of the classical scripture's third story to constitute the comic's final two stories is striking. Would it have been possible to create a more authentic rendering of the *Devī Māhātmya,* one that at least included the first story? Are there visual references that the authors and artists at the studio could have drawn upon to write the script and illustrate it? Certainly, the story of the Great Goddess has been referred to for centuries in visual media like sculptures and illuminated manuscripts, testifying to the significance of the Goddess in the Hindu pantheon and to the strength of Shakta devotion. Yet the vast majority of these depictions are of the Goddess as Durga Mahiṣāsuramardinī, the slayer of the buffalo demon. Indeed, the popularity of such images of Durga from the seventh century forward has led art historian Vidya Dehejia to write:

> The worship of a mother goddess as the source of life and fertility has prehistoric roots, but the transformation of that deity into a Great Goddess of cosmic powers was achieved with the composition of the *Devī Māhātmya* (Glory of the goddess), a text of the fifth to sixth century, when worship of the female principle took on dramatic new dimensions. Images of Devi killing the buffalo demon Mahishasura, her most renowned feat, appeared across the country in caves and temples, in metal and stone, in clay and paint. . . . Everywhere, it seems, devotees gave her a local habitation and a name. (1999, 215–16)[4]

The third episode of the *Devī Māhātmya,* however, was not popular with premodern artists and was only occasionally envisioned in sculpted form (see Dehejia 1999, 216–17), and sculpted images of the Goddess as Yoganidra from the first episode are practically unknown.[5] Even in the tradition of manuscript illumination from the sixteenth to nineteenth centuries in South Asia, martial images of Durga slaying Mahisha are prevalent, and images of the slaying of Chanda and Munda are known yet less frequent, while painted images of the first episode of the *Devī Māhātmya* are rare— so rare, in fact, that when discussing the illustrated folios of a sixteenth-century *Devī Māhātmya* manuscript from Nepal, Mary Slusser expresses excitement over the existence of just such an image: "One of the most remarkable miniatures in this manuscript has nothing to do with Devi's martial deeds but pertains to the first story of the *Devī Māhātmya*" (in Dehejia 1999, 228–29).

In modern visual arts as well, images of the first episode of the *Devī Māhātmya* are practically unknown. As nationalist sentiments rose during the colonial period, the Great Goddess was increasingly used as an allegory for the motherland: in her maternal pativratā form she represented the long-suffering country that would persevere in spite of oppression, while in her martial vīrāṅganā form she represented the country's ability to fight and defeat its "demonic" oppressor. This allegorical use of the Goddess can be seen in Raja Ravi Varma's painting *Durga* (1898), where she is draped in a red sari and golden ornaments and holds in her hands emblems of war and peace and state power (Neumayer and Schelberger 2003, 60–61), or Abanindranath Tagore's famous painting *Bharat-mata* (Mother India, 1905), or in the lesser-known painting *Nirjatite Ashirvad* (1906) by Avinash Chandra Chattopdhyay, in which Durga rewards a freedom fighter with heavenly blessings (Guha-Thakurta 1992, 196–97, 226–312). Throughout the twentieth century, images of Durga and Kali were also widely available in the form of poster art, including an abundance of nationalist prints of the Goddess as Mother India that circulated at the height of the nationalist movement in the 1930s and 1940s, religious prints of the ten-headed cosmic Kali and the ever-popular Durga as Mahiṣāsuramardinī.[6]

Given the scarcity of images of the first episode in the *Devī Māhātmya*, there was very little available in the way of handy visual references for the comic book creators as they wrote the script for *Tales of Durga* and composed the pencil sketches. When asked whether he felt it was important that he be familiar with the entire *Devī Māhātmya* to create this issue, artist Souren Roy replied:

> Yes. There are descriptions of the events, and the asuras, in the text. But as you know there are images of Durga everywhere in Kolkata. So I was already quite familiar with Durga. We Hindus grow up with Durga, we know the stories, we know how she looks.

Like the artist Ram Waeerkar, who mentioned that while making the first comic book, *Krishna,* he didn't need any visual references for the issue because as a Hindu he had been "studying" Krishna since he was a young boy, here Roy similarly maintains that modern storytelling patterns and devotional images are as authoritative as classical texts, if not more so. For modern Hindus like Roy who worship Durga, the most important story of the Goddess is when she slays the buffalo demon, because it is ritually recalled every year during the Durga Puja (or "Nine Nights") festival through oral narrations told by parents and grandparents, scripture readings by priests, reenactments of the slaying in plays or ritual sacrifices, and the all-important creation of festival statues of Durga slaying Mahisha. Indeed, while some devotees do pay to have the *Devī Māhātmya* recited in its entirety during this festival, audience members come and go during such recitations, leaving during "boring" parts and gathering for the defeat of Mahisha, and little attention is otherwise paid to the entire narrative of the classical text.[7]

Likewise, when asked about the textual research conducted when writing the *Tales of Durga* script, Producer No. 1 stated that translations of both the *Mārkaṇḍeya Purāṇa,* containing the *Devī Māhātmya,* and the later *Devī Bhāgavata Purāṇa* are equally authentic sources:

> *Markandeya Purana* is available in English translation. You could refer to any standard translation—there may be two such translations. For Durga, *Devi [Bhagavata] Purana* is another source. You may refer to it also. I do not recall whether I compared the two and decided on the *Markandeya,* or whether *Markandeya* was just easily accessible.

Together, the comments of Souren Roy and Producer No. 1 indicate that despite the editorial directive to recast the "original" *Devī Māhātmya* scripture "accurately, without changes," they considered a wide variety of sources—ritual and festival practices, oral traditions, and popular visual traditions, as well as multiple canonical texts in English translation—in creating the *Tales of Durga* comic book.

Reflecting upon the many attempts that various artists have made over the past hundred years to render *Hamlet* in comic book format, Marion Perret has commented that it seems highly improbable that "Shakespeare's complicated, introspective Prince Hamlet could become the hero in a medium privileging visual, physical action." However, Perret continues, "even the most philosophical soliloquy can become visually active when the artist, recognizing that its action lies primarily in the slowly developing speech and the responses of the reader, draws for the mind as well as the eye" (2001, 123). While most artists fail, in her opinion, to express the philosophical nature of *Hamlet*, Perret finds success in the new *Classics Illustrated* issue of *Hamlet* (no. 5, 1990), illustrated by Tom Mandrake. Through a full-page panel featuring Hamlet walking across the great hall and surrounded by a trail of sixteen small speech balloons, each containing a brief segment of the famous "To be or not to be" soliloquy, Mandrake invites his readers to take in this speech as a whole by presenting it on a single page, yet encourages them to pause between each balloon to glance back at the hero and his surroundings while considering the words and reflecting upon them:

> In this medium, as the eye moves, the mind moves, nimbly reassessing and reinterpreting. Mandrake's graphics keep us measuring verbal text against visual context, pondering Hamlet's analysis of why men don't act and how this truth applies to him—for this prince, especially in his soliloquies, thinking *is* acting and leads toward further action. Hamlet's mind is a stage on which he rehearses. (Perret 2001, 140)

As a philosophical work the *Devī Māhātmya*, like the play *Hamlet,* is not easy to visualize as action. Yet despite the lack of visual references, the creators of the *Tales of Durga* comic could have produced a more "authentic" rendering of the philosophical treatise of the *Devī Māhātmya* in the *Classics Illustrated* style, had that been their foremost goal.[8] The brief first story of the *Devī Māhātmya* could have been incorporated in just two pages: On the top half of page 1 Vishnu would lie asleep upon his snake, beneath the title of the story. The narrative text at the bottom of this panel would explain, paraphrasing verses 1.49–53 of the *Devī Māhātmya,* that the Goddess was the yogic sleep of Vishnu and had made her abode in his eyes. Here the Goddess could be rendered in a large fadeout across the sky, to visually introduce her transcendence to the reader. In the bottom left panel, while Vishnu continued to sleep, the demons Madhu and Kaitabha would arise from his ear. In the bottom right panel, Vishnu would remain in his oblivious slumber in the background while Madhu and Kaitabha attacked Brahma in the foreground. At the top of the second page in a large half panel, the narrative text would explain that in order to awaken Vishnu, Brahma praised the Goddess. This panel would feature Brahma kneeling before Vishnu's eyes, praising the Goddess therein through several short speech balloons, each containing segments of his prayer, drawn directly from verses 1.54–67. In the bottom left panel on this second page, Vishnu would awaken, and in the bottom right panel he would slay the demons. The final narrative text would proclaim that this victory was due to the majesty of the Goddess. In such a rendering, readers would be invited to join Brahma in praising the Goddess by reading his prayers and to pause between the verses and also between the panels to consider the Goddess's relationship with Vishnu and Brahma and her nature as the ultimate reality.

But the creators of *Tales of Durga* did not arrive at the same solution as Mandrake in his vision of *Hamlet*. Instead of including the original philosophical speeches and devotional hymns, this comic book rendering of the *Devī Māhātmya* opted for action shots and lengthy battle sequences. One might conclude that despite the producers' emphasis on the accuracy and authenticity of the comic book version of this mythological tale, *Tales of Durga* fails to capture even the basic storyline of the classical text. However, unlike Marion Perret's take on *Hamlet*, the point here is not that the only good comic book rendering of Durga's story is one in which its philosophical nature is expressed and that all other renderings are failures. Instead, what is most important about *Tales of Durga*, particularly in light of its proclaimed accuracy and authenticity, are its innovations.

Three innovations are particularly significant in this comic book recasting of the *Devī Māhātmya*, which together point to an active rethinking of this martial Hindu goddess. First, as we have seen, *Tales of Durga* eliminates the frame story and first story of the *Devī Mahatmya* and rearranges its latter two stories into three. For the scriptwriter and illustrator, this decision made sense because they located the comic's authenticity not only in its fidelity to classical scripture but also in its continuity with the larger Goddess tradition as it is expressed in oral, visual, ritual, and festive practices, all of which share in common the event of Durga slaying the buffalo demon. They also believed that focusing on Durga slaying the buffalo demon was most suitable for the comic book medium, which emphasizes heroic action. However, this innovation results in a focus that overlooks the *Devī Māhātmya*'s central claim that it is the Goddess, not Vishnu or any other god, who is the Supreme God and the transcendent reality responsible for the creation of the universe and its preservation in the face of evil. In effect, by eliminating the first story of the classical scripture, *Tales of Durga* places the Goddess within the Hindu pantheon alongside Vishnu, Shiva, and other deities as equals, each of whom is a holy superhero worthy of a comic book title. The ramifications of this are interesting: it could be interpreted as an inclusive move, meant to incorporate various Hindu sects together as equals under the larger umbrella of "Hinduism"; it could also suggest discomfort with the central philosophical argument of the

Devī Māhātmya as a Shakta scripture in favor of competing philosophical claims, such as the Vaishnava claim that Vishnu is the Supreme God and ultimate transcendent reality, which is given voice in this series in *The Gita* (no. 127, 1977) and other issues.

A second innovation in *Tales of Durga* is the incorporation of the notion that Durga is created by the gods because of the demon Mahisha's boon that he can be killed only at the hands of a woman. In the *Devī Māhātmya*, the beginning of the second story is much simpler. Mahisha conquers the gods and takes over their abode and their throne. All of the exiled gods then approach Vishnu and Shiva, who grow angry when they learn of Mahisha's doings. Thus "with furrowed brows and twisted faces," a great fiery splendor emerges from the collected gods, and out of that splendor the Goddess rises: "That peerless splendor, born from the bodies of all the gods, unified and pervading the triple world with its luster, became a woman" (verses 2.1–12 in Coburn 1991, 39–40). Significantly, there is no boon to explain why the Goddess was incarnated as a woman; in the *Devī Māhātmya*, the Goddess emerges in the form of a woman simply because ultimate reality is feminine.[9] But in the comic book, Mahisha earns a boon from Brahma for his austerities, and with that boon requests, "If I must die, Lord, let it be at the hands of a woman." "So be it," replies Brahma, and immediately after he leaves, Mahisha chuckles to himself, believing he has outwitted Brahma, stating, "How can a woman, a helpless creature, kill me? You have as good as granted me the boon of immortality!" (2). This is an interpolation that dates to the later *Devī Bhāgavata Purāṇa* scripture and has remained popular ever since.[10] Its incorporation in the comic book further demonstrates the range of sources considered authoritative by the scriptwriter. However, by beginning the story with this focus on Mahisha's boon, and pairing it with the prolonged visual focus on Mahisha, Durga's role as the heroine becomes ambiguous. This reflects the difficulty the creators encountered in molding the Durga of the *Devī Māhātmya* into *Amar Chitra Katha*'s heroic template. Prior to *Tales of Durga*, the mythological martial heroes featured were all male (like Rama and Krishna). Mythological heroines, on the other hand, were all chaste, long-suffering goddesses who were devoted to their husbands (like Sati, Savitri, and Sita). Although the creators had produced a few issues featuring martial heroines of the alternative vīrāṅganā type of Indian feminine ideal, all were historical queens (like Rani Durgavati and the Rani of Jhansi). *Tales of Durga* was the first attempt to expand this heroic type to the mythological genre. As an independent goddess with martial qualities, Durga just didn't fit the established formula for either male or female mythological heroes. But Mahisha, although a villain, was more suited to the established heroic template. The ambiguity concerning Durga's role as heroine also has important ramifications: it may suggest discomfort with the immanent power of the Goddess and her martial role as the "supreme ruler" of earthly creatures.

Finally, the third innovation to the classical narrative of the Goddess as told in *Tales of Durga* is the sanitized presentation of the goddess Kali. Whereas Durga is always described in the *Devī Māhātmya* and other Sanskrit texts as having a serene countenance even in the midst of battle, Kali is described as a gruesome, even horrifying presence, with an emaciated figure, a widely gaping mouth and lolling tongue, and sunken, reddened eyes (see verses 7.5–7 in Coburn 1991, 61). When battling the demon Raktabeeja, Kali (also called Camunda and Chamundi) heartily drinks all of his spilled blood in verses 8.58–61, and thereby miraculously prevents further Raktabeeja clones from arising:

> Camunda took it [the blood] all into her mouth, from every direction,
> And also into her mouth entered the great demons who were born from his
> blood.
> Camunda chewed them up, and drank his blood.
> With spear, thunderbolt, arrows, swords, and lances the Goddess
> Wounded Raktabija, whose blood was being drunk by Camunda.
> Mortally wounded by that constellation of weapons, the great demon
> Raktabija
> Fell to the earth bloodless, O king!
> And then, O king, the gods entered into boundless joy. (Coburn 1991, 67)

But in *Tales of Durga*, Kali is not fearsome. Her gruesome characteristics are minimized so that, despite the lolling tongue and garland of skulls around her neck, she is not emaciated nor does her expression seem particularly fearsome without the sunken eyes and gaping mouth that prominently features her fangs. Here Kali has a curvaceous figure, full cheeks, a calm demeanor, and a pleasant expression behind her tongue. Just as Durga is not the dominating warrior of the *Devī Māhātmya* who plays with Mahisha as a cat would a mouse, so this is not the horrific, bloodthirsty Kali of the *Devī Māhātmya*. Even the matter of the blood drinking is circumscribed in the comic book. When Durga asks Kali to prevent the blood of Raktabeeja's clones from reaching the ground, Kali replies, "Leave it to me. Not a drop of their blood shall stain the earth again" (28). In the next panel, Durga and the various shaktis vigorously hurl their various weapons at the demons. The narrative text informs us only that during this attack "Kali prevented the birth of any more asuras," but not how she accomplishes this, and neither does the image show us just how Kali managed to prevent further asuras (figure 21). Instead, Kali occupies the left foreground of the panel, apparently overseeing the battle from the air. Neither textually nor visually are we told how Kali prevented more Raktabeejas from arising; instead, just as readers of the first *Krishna* comic book had to infer that Krishna had miraculously lifted the Govardhan Mountain on one finger, here the reader must infer that

Kali miraculously drank the blood of every wounded demon before that blood could fall to the earth.

Anant Pai first spoke of this scene when discussing his change of heart about miracles, commenting on his interpretation of the idea that a new demon arises out of every drop of blood that Raktabeeja sheds: "This has a symbolic meaning: it means that you can't cure violence with violence. But if I change the story because it is not scientific, then these symbolic meanings are also altered." In light of Pai's new policy that all mythological stories must be told "accurately, without changes," including the depiction of miracles, the omission of the miracle of Kali drinking Raktabeeja's blood stands out. When asked about this, Pai recited another of his guiding policies, which here seems to have trumped the policy of authenticity and accuracy: "'One must tell the truth, one must tell what is pleasant; but don't tell what is unpleasant just because it is true.' In Sanskrit this is 'satyam bruyāt priyam bruyāt mā bruyāt satyam apriyam.'"[11] Yes, Pai insisted, Kali had a thirst for blood in the *Devī Māhātmya,* but this need not be depicted just because it is true or authentic, especially if it might alienate modern readers' sensibilities.

John Stratton Hawley has noted that Anant Pai downplays not only violence but also the emotion associated with it—fear—in the comic books featuring goddesses in particular:

> Pai rejected a proposal to do an issue on the snake goddess Manasa because it might have stimulated too much fear in children, and for the same reason he several times fended off an *Amar Chitra Katha* entry on Santoshi Ma. The culminating episode in the story, in which this goddess goes on a rampage of destruction because someone had tampered with food offered to and blessed by her (*prasād*), was dismissed by Pai as being not only fearsome but unworthy and superstitious, a "degradation of Hinduism." (1995, 118)

When I asked Anant Pai if the decision not to depict Kali drinking blood was made to protect children from gratuitous violence and the fear associated with it, Pai clarified: "It is not just too violent for children. It is also too violent for adults. You see, Hindus do not do blood worship, sacrifice. They do not want to see blood drinking." For Pai, an upper-middle-class, upper-caste, vegetarian Hindu in western India, a more sanitized version of the Goddess and her story was needed than the one found in the *Devī Māhātmya.* Thus even in Pai's statement explaining the need to retell scripture accurately, the reasoning he gives is not that he believes in the literal veracity of these texts; rather, he interprets them symbolically, so that for him Kali's miracle actually has nothing to do with blood drinking, which he regards as a "degradation of Hinduism," and therefore this fearsome activity need not be shown.

The scriptwriter, Producer No. 1, who is also an upper-caste, middle-class Hindu in western India, similarly expressed discomfort with the

As Chandika and the other Shaktis attacked the Raktabeejas...

...Kali prevented the birth of any more Asuras.

Figure 21. *Tales of Durga,* no. 176 [reprint no. 514] (Bombay: India Book House Pvt. Ltd., 1978 [2000]), 28. From *Amar Chitra Katha,* with the permission of the publishers ACK Media, India.

portrayal of the Goddess in the *Devī Māhātmya* and with those devotees of the Goddess in Bengal and elsewhere who engage in blood sacrifice. He confessed:

> To be honest, at that point of time I was uncomfortable with this theme. I'm not a worshipper of Mother Goddess, who to me appeared bloodthirsty. For story value I chose this theme. Much later, about ten years after I wrote the title, I understood the principle of the Mother Goddess—as an embodiment of Nature at once benevolent and devouring. This is a philosophical concept. I do not think I had this in mind when I wrote this script. In fact, I do not rate *Tales of Durga* as one of my good scripts at all.

This discomfort with the Great Goddess and the martial elements of the *Devī Māhātmya* scripture is not unique to the creators of the *Tales of Durga* comic book, but extends to its readers as well. Whereas hundreds of readers wrote to Anant Pai in response to the *Krishna* issue, stating that they loved the comic but couldn't understand why he had left out the miracle of Krishna lifting the mountain, according to Pai not a single reader has complained about the elimination of the miracle of Kali drinking the demons' blood. It would appear that while the readers of these comics do want to see Krishna lifting the Govardhan Mountain, no one wants to see Kali's bloodlust. In their study of Kali, Rachel Fell McDermott and Jeffrey Kripal have also pointed out that many modern middle-class Hindus—not to mention non-Hindus in India—are uncomfortable with the extreme martial nature of the Goddess: "[E]very culture has its own category of the exotic; for those in the Hindu mainstream, this includes Kali's various provenances—Tantra, tribal culture, historical links to social revolution, and a bloody temple cult—all of them both alluring and dangerous" (2003, 9). Today this discomfort is expressed in imagery extending beyond the medium of comic books, as Kajri Jain has noted in her study of modern bazaar art and god posters, in which she found that Kali is now rarely depicted in her gruesome form:

> [U]gly or otherwise depressing depictions are seen as inauspicious, and this forms the basis for a picture's acceptance or rejection by a customer.... Indeed, there is evidence to suggest that earlier depictions of divine power that are not unambiguously benign, such as those of the inauspicious Shani (Saturn), Krishna's cosmic form (*viraat roop*) revealed to Arjun on the battlefield in the Mahabharata, or Kali in her more terrifying aspect, have gradually disappeared from calendar prints, or have given way to interpretations with a quite different affective charge: the Krishna you see nowadays is much more the sweet, seductive, androgynous child, and similarly the sensuous treatment of Kali's tongue can sometimes verge on soft-focus eroticism. (2000, 162)

Conclusion: A Story for All Thinking Indians

In creating these mythological comic books, Anant Pai and his team at the *Amar Chitra Katha* studio have learned over the years that much of their audience regards these comics as far more than entertainment; in Pai's words, the comics are "something sacred" to their Hindu readers. In that case, just as scholars have studied the many *Rāmāyaṇa*s, the many stories of god Rama from the earliest Sanskrit version to its myriad modern mediated recastings, in the effort to understand the ongoing interpretation of the classical epic, so too must we examine the many *Devī Māhātmya*s, or stories of the Great Goddess. With *Tales of Durga,* the creators set out to popularize the classical Sanskrit *Devī Māhātmya* scripture through the comic book medium, insisting that they had recast it "accurately, without changes," so that their modern middle-class, English-educated audience in urban India and abroad could become familiar with classical Hindu mythology, even if they never learned Sanskrit or took part in temple rituals or annual festivals in India. Yet despite the creators' claims that in retelling classical mythology in the comic book format "you don't make it relevant to modern times," *Tales of Durga* demonstrates that in making the *Devī Māhātmya* appealing to themselves and their audience, the creators reinterpreted the classical scripture in accord with modern middle-class, upper-caste Hindu beliefs and practices: beliefs and practices that minimize the transcendence of the Goddess as well as her immanent and often gruesome yet regal martial qualities. What is significant, therefore, about the discourse of authenticity surrounding *Tales of Durga* is that it is not just a marketing ploy to attract consumers, but is also indicative of an active effort to legitimate this interpretation of Durga and the *Devī Māhātmya* scripture, and to redefine this particular interpretation as the authentic one.

Hinduism is notoriously difficult to define as a unified and systematic religion due to its multiplicity of sacred texts, historical teachers, philosophies, and regional and sectarian traditions. However, beginning in the late nineteenth century, leading Hindus set out to define Hinduism and project it as India's national religion. Today in postcolonial India this process is ongoing, and comic books are one important public medium in which the questions "What is Hinduism?" and "Who speaks for Hinduism?" are being considered. The comic book producers insist that their comic book renderings of classical Sanskrit scripture like the *Devī Māhātmya* are not just for Hindus but for all Indians. Producer No. 2 explained that such comics should appeal to "all thinking Indians," no matter what religion they adhere to:

> In scripting the *ACKs* and editing or rewriting them, I made conscious attempts to keep out narrow religious bigotry and bring out the essence of the great perceptions captured in the vast body of our Sanskrit-language literature in a manner and a metaphor that would appeal to all thinking Indians, no matter what their religious persuasion. Our great literary heritage belongs to all our countrymen and should appeal to all of them.

Her sentiments echo Anant Pai's repeated declarations that the mythological comic books based on classical Sanskrit texts are not for Hindus alone: "When a group in Goa charged me of Hindu propaganda, I countered it by saying that epics like the *Ramayana* and the *Mahabharata* were the heritage of all Indians" (2000, 39). The dominant Hindu nationalist trend has been to put forth a definition of Hinduism as the national religion of India that is based on high-caste Brahminical traditions and draws directly upon Sanskrit scripture, yet reflects modern, urban, middle-class Indian values, wherein "mantras, chanted scripture, and vegetarian eating are highly recommended," but one "rarely finds reference to village deities, blood sacrifice, possessions, or exorcisms" (Falk 2005, 288). For these reasons, *Tales of Durga* presents a holy Indian superheroine who cannot be considered a "degradation of Hinduism" by Anant Pai and his middle-class Hindu readers but who is in fact far less "super" in terms of both her transcendent and immanent significance than the Great Goddess of the Sanskrit *Devī Māhātmya*.

4 The Warrior-King Shivaji in History and Mythology

Shivaji was a great liberal. He had many people in his court and at his side in battle—many religions, many castes. He is a hero for that reason. He fought for all of India, for India's independence. He fought against Aurangzeb to make his own kingdom.

Anant Pai, personal interview

After publishing nearly a dozen successful mythological comic books in the *Amar Chitra Katha* series, including *Krishna* (no. 11, 1969), *Shakuntala* (no. 12, 1970), *Rama* (no. 15, 1971), *Hanuman* (no. 19, 1971), and *Mahabharata* (no. 20, 1971), Anant Pai felt that it was time to branch out. In an effort to promote national unity and integration, he decided to introduce historical subjects into the series, featuring stories of kings and queens from throughout India to teach "people in one region of the country the culture, history and ways of life of people in another" (Gangadhar 1988, 140). The first historical figure chosen was Shivaji Bhonsle (1627–80), a Hindu Maratha king who was featured in the *Shivaji* issue (no. 23) in 1971. Shivaji is famous throughout India, but especially in the western Indian state of Maharashtra among Marathi-speaking Hindus, for founding his own independent Maratha kingdom in 1674 after battling the Mughal Empire—the Muslim empire that began in northern India in 1526 and rapidly expanded throughout the subcontinent during the seventeenth century, especially during the reign of the emperor Aurangzeb (r. 1658–1707).

As Anant Pai's statement indicates, he chose Shivaji to be the subject of his first historical comic book because he viewed him not merely as a regional historical figure but also as a national Indian hero. The *Shivaji* comic casts Shivaji as one of independent India's founding fathers and the Mughal emperor Aurangzeb and his Muslim cohorts as the villains, enemies of the nation-state. Pai's comments recall the comments made a century earlier by another Hindu Brahmin in Maharashtra, the Indian nationalist leader Justice M. G. Ranade (1842–1901). In his book *Rise of the Maratha Power*, which challenged the colonial portrayal of Shivaji and his regime, Ranade wrote: "There are many who think that there can be no particular moral significance in the story of the rise and fall of a freebooting Power, which thrived by plunder and adventure, and succeeded only because it was the most cunning and adventurous among all those who helped to dismember the Great Moghul [Mughal] Empire after the death of Aurangzeb. This is a very common feeling with the readers, who derive their knowledge of these events solely from the works of English historians" (1900, 1). Ranade argued that the formation of a Maratha kingdom under the leadership of Shivaji in the late seventeenth century was the beginning of the modern process of nation making. He characterized it as an upheaval of the whole population, "strongly bound together by the common affinities of language, race, religion, and literature and seeking further solidarity by a common independent political existence" (6–7). He argued that this was the first experiment of its kind in India, and described it as the work "of the people, of the masses, and not of the classes. At its head were Saints and Prophets, Poets and Philosophers, who sprang chiefly from the lower orders of society—tailors, carpenters, potters, gardeners, shopkeepers, barbers, and even *mahars* [an "untouchable" or Dalit caste]—more often than Brahmans" (10).

Both Justice Ranade and Anant Pai seek to portray Shivaji as a unifying nationalist leader who inspired Indian people from multiple class, caste, and religious backgrounds to unite as a single political entity in the quest for independence. From the late nineteenth century forward, the figure of Shivaji has acted as a locus for the articulation of multiple and often contested identities—religious, regional, and caste-based—in modern India. This chapter investigates the wide range of late nineteenth- and early twentieth-century visual and textual antecedents of the *Shivaji* comic book and then considers which prior visual and textual narratives the comic book producers have drawn upon and which they have excluded to construct their narrative of Shivaji as a "great liberal." In addition to considering how debates over issues of religion, region, and caste play out in the production and consumption of this comic book, this chapter also discusses the ramifications of applying the now-established mythological heroic template to this first historical comic book hero.

On the cover of the *Shivaji* comic book (figure 22), Shivaji is depicted astride his horse, leading his Maratha soldiers through the hills of Maharashtra. They have presumably just left the fort that sits atop the hill in the background and are now on their way to engage in another battle, for the soldiers have their weapons raised, and Shivaji wields his sword above his head, as if all were united in chanting their famous Hindu religious chant-cum-war cry, "Har Har Mahadeo!" (In the name of Lord Shiva!). A sense of urgency is conveyed by the angle of the horse's legs and the flow of its tail in the wind, and the combination of dark red, saffron, and purple in the color palette further heightens the sense of melodrama, suggesting that Shivaji and his troops are in the midst of a whirlwind campaign, leaving one fort at sunset and traveling through the night to the next, without time to rest or even celebrate their victories. The artist who created this cover image, Pratap Mulick, stated that "all of the criss-crossing lines in the *Shivaji* cover are meant to create a sense of action," because he believed that "Shivaji on horseback, in that pose, should be a very active figure."

The People's King

These active, narrative elements of the comic book cover work to remind the reader of the whole of Shivaji's heroic story. But as the reader looks at Shivaji in the center of the image, a deliberate suspension of the narrative action occurs, achieved through what Svetlana Alpers has called a "fixity of pose and an avoidance of outward expression" (1976, 15). Shivaji's face does not betray any emotion that would forward the narrative action or help the comic book fan to read the image. Indeed, despite the narrative elements that frame Shivaji, no specific event is actually told—Shivaji could be leaving any fort and traveling on to any battle. In this way, the cover presents not a pictorial narrative but an abstraction of Shivaji's narrative: Shivaji is here presented as an icon, an immortal hero. He is the martial Maratha warrior who is forever ready to ride off into the sunset to battle his enemies.[1] In this cover image, the pictorial modes of narrative and icon are combined, neither mode completely separate from the other, establishing a dynamic between realism and idealism, between Shivaji's past actions and his timeless heroism, between history and mythology.

In the West, scholars have generally spoken in oppositional terms about narrative and iconic representation. Drawing upon studies of narratology in the field of literary criticism, which differentiated between "narration" as a discussion of events that moves the plot forward and "description" as a static representation of people, things, and situations that halts the plot flow (Lukács 1970), scholars arrived at a definition of pictorial narrative that similarly set up a binary opposition between narrative (or active) and iconic (or static) representation (see Brilliant 1984, 17). What is more, a further binary came into play between history and mythology when narrative images were equated with historical events and iconic images with mythological personas. This latter binary has been particularly prevalent in the academic study of Indian art.[2] Fortunately, several scholars have begun the work of deconstructing these binaries. Scholars of Indian art, in particular, are now attempting to dislodge the strict division between narrative and iconic representation, arguing that such a division is not necessarily applicable in the Indian context. For instance, in her discussion of Orissan illustrations of the *Rāmāyaṇa* epic, Joanna Williams writes that although we may be tempted to distinguish the narrative picture from the iconic (in India) or from the descriptive (in the West), there are many mixed examples of both, particularly when only one moment is depicted (1996, 110). The power of the *Shivaji* cover image—and of the comic book as a whole—lies in that mixture of narrative and icon, history and mythology. Like the introduction to the *Ganga* issue about the Hindu river goddess (no. 88, 1975), which claims that "mythology is not all fact, we know, but yet, in its vast poetic exaggerations, one can always trace an outline of truth," the cover of *Shivaji* proclaims the complementarity of the narrative and the iconic modes and of historical and mythological "truths."

Figure 22. Cover of *Shivaji,* no. 23 [reprint no. 564] (Bombay: India Book House Pvt. Ltd., 1971 [2000]). From *Amar Chitra Katha,* with the permission of the publishers ACK Media, India.

The *Shivaji* comic book begins with Shivaji's birth and then describes his schooling in such subjects as reading and writing, archery, and horsemanship. His mother, Jijabai, tells him stories from the great Hindu epics, including the *Bhagavad Gītā,* teaching young Shivaji about Lord Krishna's lesson that "even death in the cause of one's duty should be dear to a hero's heart." In response, Shivaji wonders aloud what his duty is, whether it is "to fight for a foreign king by the side of my father? Or to fight for my people, against the king?" His mother responds, "Your duty lies in fighting for your people" (3–4). Shivaji takes his mother's lesson to heart and begins to gather a band of boys around him who agree to fight for their freedom. After they capture their first fort, Shivaji receives blessings and congratulations from his mother, but his father, Shahji, who was allied with the regional Muslim ruler, Sultan Ali Adil Shah II (r. 1656–72) of Bijapur, is arrested.

Figure 23. *Shivaji,* no. 23 [reprint no. 564] (Bombay: India Book House Pvt. Ltd., 1971 [2000]), 12. From *Amar Chitra Katha,* with the permission of the publishers ACK Media, India.

The Sultan sends troops to battle Shivaji, but Shivaji and his friends are quickly able to defeat them. It is at this point in 1659 that the Sultan sends his general, Afzal Khan, together with a large army, to face Shivaji.

After one of Shivaji's spies warns him of Afzal Khan's plans to assassinate him during their meeting, Shivaji begins to prepare carefully: he stops at a Hindu temple to pray to Goddess Bhavani, he puts on armor under his clothing, and he affixes his easily hidden tiger claw weapon to his right hand. Then he bravely walks down the hill from the Pratapgarh Fort to the appointed meeting spot, accompanied by only two guards. The next panel focuses on Afzal Khan and highlights his treachery. Afzal Khan is depicted as a humongous man, dressed in heavy robes and finery, with a duplicitous smile on his face. As Afzal Khan stands awaiting Shivaji with open arms he

Figure 24. *Shivaji,* no. 23 [reprint no. 564] (Bombay: India Book House Pvt. Ltd., 1971 [2000]), 13. From *Amar Chitra Katha,* with the permission of the publishers ACK Media, India.

says, "Come, my son," while simultaneously thinking to himself, "Your end is near!" (11). In greeting in the following panel, Shivaji embraces the giant Afzal Khan, who holds a raised dagger in his right hand behind Shivaji's back. But our wiry hero Shivaji is alert, waiting only for some indication of Afzal Khan's intent. In the next full-page panel (figure 23), Afzal Khan cries out, "Ya Allah!" ("Oh, God!") as Shivaji wrenches the dagger from his hand and stabs him with it, piercing his stomach (12).

The encounter between Shivaji and Afzal Khan is presented not only as an epic struggle between two men, one a hero and the other a villain, but also as a communal one. When Afzal Khan first sets out with his army against Shivaji, he is shown commanding his troops to pull down Shivaji's favorite temple to the Hindu goddess Bhavani, the very goddess that

Shivaji is shown praying to before his meeting with Afzal Khan. Thus Afzal Khan is here depicted as an invading, plundering Muslim iconoclast—his religious affiliation is made indisputable by his death cry, "Ya Allah!"—while Shivaji is depicted as a devout, persecuted Hindu forced to defend his faith and his land. After Afzal Khan is decapitated and Shivaji emerges victorious, "wave after wave of Maratha soldiers" descend from the surrounding hills, raising their war cry (13) (figure 24). This two-page center spread featuring the slaying of Afzal Khan and the victorious emergence of Shivaji's troops pairs the Khan's death cry to his Muslim god on the left, "Ya Allah!" with the troops' war cry to their Hindu god on the right, "Har Har Mahadeo!" But when read sequentially, as the comic book format demands, it becomes clear that these cries are not equally paired. Khan, big and intimidating though he is on the left, falls in the first panel on the right, his cry drowned out by the Maratha war cry. It is the latter cry to the Hindu god, Shiva, rather than the former cry to the Muslim god, Allah, that continues to resonate with the reader at the end of these two pages.

In addition to the central episode of the slaying of Afzal Khan, the *Shivaji* comic book features several other famous episodes in the life of this warrior king: Shivaji's escape from Panhalgarh, which highlights the martyrdom of his loyal captain, Baji Prabhu Deshpande; Shivaji sneaking into the Lal Mahal in Pune and chasing away the villainous Muslim Shayista Khan, depriving him of three fingers in the process; and Shivaji's attack on the port city of Surat. The climax comes when Shivaji and his son, Sambhaji, are invited to Emperor Aurangzeb's palace in the Mughal capital city, Agra. Shivaji cannot refuse the invitation, but fears that it is a trap that places him and his son in grave danger. In the royal court, Shivaji and his son refuse to bow before the emperor; Sambhaji daringly states, "I only bow before God and my mother, sir!" (27). Held prisoner for weeks by the trappings of royal etiquette and surrounded on all sides by Aurangzeb's men, Shivaji devises a clever plan of escape. He feigns illness for several days and each day orders that large baskets of sweets be given to the poor. After the baskets have become so routine that the guards let them pass without inspecting them, Shivaji and his son each climb into a sweetmeat basket and make their escape from the palace. Disguised as a wandering Hindu renouncer accompanied by a young disciple, Shivaji eventually makes his way home to his own palace, where his troops wait for him and his mother greets him with a tear in her eye. Ever the underdog, Shivaji has succeeded in outwitting even the most powerful of men, Aurangzeb.

The *Shivaji* comic ends victoriously on the next page, with Shivaji's coronation ceremony in 1674 (plate 7). In this final full-page panel, Shivaji is seated on a grand throne, with his mother on one side and his son on the other. His supporters surround him, proclaiming him to be "a people's king." The final lines in the narrative box at the bottom of the panel read:

"As a king he ruled only for five years; but the Maratha power which he had built flourished for many years after him" (32). In this full-page final panel featuring Shivaji's coronation ceremony, no mention is made of the great lengths to which Shivaji had to go to prove his Kshatriya (warrior caste) lineage in order to silence those who questioned the legitimacy of his rule. Instead, there is a deliberate erasure here of the fact that Shivaji did not just assume the throne after outwitting and defeating all of his enemies, that he still had to convince many Hindu Brahmins that he was worthy of such a position. There is also an active attempt to forget the remainder of Shivaji's life after his coronation in 1674, including his death in 1680. The final six years of his life are by no means as heroic as the earlier years: Shivaji was unable to convince his half-brother, Shahji's heir in the south, to join his cause; his own son, Sambhaji, defected to the Mughals, thereby leaving him without a worthy heir of his own; and ultimately Shivaji died from an illness in 1680. In this final panel, Shivaji's death is not visually depicted and is only vaguely hinted at in the narrative text, when it mentions that Shivaji ruled as a king for only five years. Shown seated before a court full of loyal and cheering subjects, who declare that "as long as freedom is cherished, his name will shine and inspire millions" (32), both text and image are united here in preserving the memory of Shivaji's ultimate victory. How did this regional medieval king come to be remembered as a national Indian hero? To answer this question, to understand how Shivaji came to epitomize the Indian freedom fighter, we must investigate the archetype of the martial Indian warrior that was constructed within the context of colonial modernity.

Finding the "Real" Shivaji

The Indian artist Raja Ravi Varma (1848–1906) is known to have created several paintings of Shivaji, including a portrait, an equestrian image, and a painting of the king's coronation ceremony. Varma's narrative paintings of mythological and historical subjects received praise from both colonial Orientalists and Indian nationalists, and through lithographic technology they became incredibly popular with a large Indian middle-class audience as well during his lifetime. Varma's paintings of Shivaji, though equally acclaimed by both Orientalists and nationalists, were put to very different uses by these groups. Colonial historian H. G. Rawlinson, for instance, used a portrait of Shivaji painted by Varma as the frontispiece to his history textbook, *Shivaji the Maratha: His Life and Times* (1915). Rawlinson discusses the portrait only in his preface, where he writes: "I have to acknowledge my indebtedness to Rao Bahadur B. A. Gupte, Curator of the Victoria Memorial Exhibition, Calcutta, for permission to reproduce the picture of Shivaji, by Raja Ravi Varma, said to be copied from a contemporary Dutch print."[3] For Rawlinson and other colonial historians, paintings of Shivaji by Varma and other artists had value only as illustrations for the textual narratives they were producing.

Throughout the nineteenth century, European historians had worked to construct a history of India, and in so doing they wanted to separate the "real" Shivaji from the legendary one, the historical from the mythological. The glorification of Shivaji had begun in his own lifetime, when his court poet, Kavindra Paramananda, began composing a biographical Sanskrit epic of Shivaji's life, *Śivabhārata,* and others composed Marathi ballads (*povāḍas*) and prose histories (*bakhars*) of Shivaji's battles. In the *Śivabhārata,* Shivaji is described as the Hindu god Vishnu incarnate, present to protect the gods, Brahmins, and cows from Afzal Khan and other Muslims, who are in turn said to be demons incarnate. James Laine, who translated this text into English with S. S. Bahulkar, describes it as "both an historical chronicle, and a laudatory *mahākāvya* (epic poem) in which the poet must describe his hero in a mythic manner conforming to the canons of taste of that genre" (2001, 8). Greatly disturbed by such perceived genre mixing, colonial historians mined sources like the *Śivabhārata* for kernels of historical "truth." But as they worked to separate the real Shivaji from the legendary one, these historians excised what they considered to be fiction—all references to deities and demons—and left behind the other half of the epic story—the Hindu versus Muslim rhetoric—in their belief that the *Śivabhārata* epic and other precolonial narratives of Shivaji were based on a factual history of communalism.

James Grant Duff (1789–1858) published *A History of the Mahrattas,* the first British history of the Maratha people of western India, in 1826. In this work, Grant Duff attempted to set the record straight in his telling of the encounter between Shivaji and Afzal Khan. He reports that Afzal Khan arrived for the meeting dressed in a thin muslin garment, armed only with his sword and attended by a single armed follower; Shivaji, on the other hand, "put on a steel chain cap and chain armour under his turban and cotton gown, concealed a crooked dagger, or *beechwa,* in his right sleeve, and on the fingers of his left hand he fixed a *wagnuck,* a treacherous weapon well known among Mahrattas." Shivaji then approached Afzal Khan, stopping frequently along the way so as not to alarm him, "a supposition more likely to be admitted from his [Shivaji's] diminutive size," and as Shivaji and Afzal Khan were introduced, "in the midst of the customary embrace, the treacherous Mahratta struck the wagnuck into the bowels of Afzool Khan," and then "instantly followed up the blow with his dagger . . . the whole was the work of a moment, and Sivajee was wresting the weapon from the hand of his victim before their attendants could run towards them" (Grant Duff 1826, 1:171–73). Unlike the comic book's recounting of this incident, which focuses on Afzal Khan's treachery and Shivaji's heroism, Grant Duff viewed Shivaji as the treacherous villain. After concluding his narrative of

Shivaji, Grant Duff gave a summary of Shivaji's character, wherein he again returned to this episode of the slaying of Afzal Khan. In this passage we can see how Grant Duff has excised all references to Shivaji's divinity, yet has retained the dramatic antagonism between Shivaji and Afzal Khan: "Sivajee's admirers among his own nation speak of him as an incarnation of the Deity, setting an example of wisdom, fortitude, and piety. Mahrattas, in general, consider that necessity authorises a murder, and that political assassination is often wise and proper . . . few of them acknowledge that Afzool Khan was murdered. The vulgar opinion is, that the Khan was the aggressor; and the event is spoken of rather as a commendable exploit than a detestable and treacherous assassination" (1:297)

In 1883, James Douglas (1826–1904) published his *Bombay and Western India,* wherein he similarly characterized Shivaji's victory over Afzal Khan as premeditated murder. Douglas writes, "Sivaji, the founder of the Maratha power, met Afzul Khan, the Bijapur general, at an arranged conference, pretending to embrace him, and having previously armed his own hands with steel claws—the *wagnak*—tore him open" (1893, 1:341). Once again, in a colonial history of Shivaji, Shivaji is designated as the treacherous villain. In final confirmation of Shivaji's despicable character, Douglas concluded his history of Shivaji by commenting on the lack of regard for Shivaji in his day: "No man now cares for Sivaji. Over all those wide domains, which once owned him lord and master, acquired by so much blood and treasure, and which he handed down with care to the Rajas of Kolapur, the Bhonsles of Satara, and their Peshwahs in Poona, not one man now contributes a rupee to keep or repair the tomb of the founder of the Maratha Empire" (2:179–80). This comment did not go unnoticed.

As the British investigated and recorded the Indian past, they assimilated Indian history to the history of Great Britain, resulting in a narrative that, according to Ranajit Guha, was henceforth used as a measure of difference between the colonizer and the colonized. In this context, nationalist Indian historiography arose as a form of resistance in a "simultaneous relationship of affinity with and opposition to colonialist historiography" (Guha 1989, 212). Several scholars have written of the sudden production of nationalist histories by Indians in nineteenth-century Bengal. Discussing the work of Bankimchandra Chatterjee, Sudipta Kaviraj has argued that he and others writing in Bengal at this time discovered the constructedness of historical "truth": that in telling the history of India, the British were constructing an image of a people whose whole history destined them for British conquest—or, as Bankimchandra put it, that the lion is always shown being defeated because it was man who painted the picture. Bankimchandra realized that history was not just the chronological arrangement of events but also the narrative arrangement of stories through which those events attain meaning. He and other Bengali historians, therefore, set out to paint a new self-portrait, highlighting the deeds of their ancestors in order to show the ability of the lion to defeat the man (Kaviraj 1998, 107–9).

In western India as well, Indians in the late nineteenth century also began to compose their own national histories, the vast majority of which centered upon Shivaji (O'Hanlon 1985, 164). Justice Ranade heard James Douglas's lament about the state of neglect that Shivaji's *samadhi* (tomb) was in, and initiated a movement to restore it and, with it, the proper memory of Shivaji. In May 1885, Ranade convened a gathering of Pune aristocrats to petition for restoration funds. In response, Lord Reay, governor of Bombay, set aside four rupees to clear the plinth of weeds and to erect a railing to keep out cattle (Cashman 1975, 101). After this victory Ranade continued his work, publishing *Rise of the Maratha Power* in 1900 to challenge the colonial portrayal of Shivaji and his regime. But it was "Lokamanya" (Beloved of the People) Bal Gangadhar Tilak (1856–1920) who presented the greatest challenge to the colonial portrayal of Shivaji and who recognized the role that images of Shivaji could have in that challenge.

In 1895, Tilak took up the Shivaji memorial cause. An aspiring nationalist leader, Tilak hoped that Shivaji might be the figure behind which all the castes and classes of western India—and all Hindus across the nation—could unite in the quest for self-rule. A member of the Extremist Party of the Indian National Congress (as opposed to the Moderate Party that Ranade was a member of), Tilak had previously used the annual Ganapati Hindu religious festival as a setting for nationalist agitation, for while the British often suppressed political meetings at this time, they were more hesitant about interfering with religious meetings and festivals.[4] Tilak convened a meeting in Pune to raise further funds for the reparation of Shivaji's samadhi, including the erection of a *chatra* ("parasol," a sign of royalty and divinity), and for an endowment for an annual commemorative festival. As editor of the Marathi-language newspaper *Kesari*, Tilak was able to publicize the memorial movement through the newspaper. Richard Cashman has discussed in detail his campaign to collect donations, noting that Tilak enlisted the support of wealthy and common folk alike by acknowledging every donation, large and small, in *Kesari*. By December 1895, 15,000 rupees had been donated by nearly 60,000 contributors (Cashman 1975, 106–7). The campaign was so successful, in fact, that the first Shivaji festival was held at the Raigarh hill-fort the next year, April 15–17, 1896.

At the Shivaji festival, the major events of Shivaji's life—especially his victory over Afzal Khan, his escape from Agra, and his coronation ceremony—were reenacted through a variety of media, allowing those present to participate in the performance of the new nationalist historiography: a narrative of struggle, sacrifice, and eventual victory. Devotional songs and plays like Anna Martand Joshi's *Victory to Shiva Chhatrapati* celebrated the slaying of Afzal Khan in order to demonstrate Shivaji's ability to rid the land of "foreigners" (Deshpande 2002). Another relatively new and very successful medium that was used to disseminate the new narrative to the larger public was that of poster art. Whereas Rawlinson and other colonial historians valued paintings of Shivaji by Varma and other artists only as illustrations for their textual narratives, Bal Gangadhar Tilak realized that images of Shivaji had a far greater potential.

When Tilak saw Ravi Varma's painting *Shivaji Maharaj*, he reportedly remarked that, unlike prevailing images of Shivaji, "this painting takes the view of eighteenth-century politics. . . . Looking at [it] one immediately thinks of the whole . . . of the great warrior. So he must be congratulated" (Mitter 1994, 204n82). In this image, which was later reprinted as a popular lithograph (figure 25), Shivaji sits astride his horse, leading his Maratha soldiers through the hills of Maharashtra. They appear to have just left the fort that sits atop the hill in the background and are now on their way to engage in another battle, for the soldiers behind Shivaji hold their weapons aloft, as if—again—united in the cry "Har Har Mahadeo!" By referring to eighteenth-century politics in his discussion of this painting, Tilak per-haps suggests that Varma was not influenced by the colonial perception of Shivaji, but instead saw him as a great leader, a divinized hero, in the manner of the *Śivabhārata* epic and other precolonial narratives. Tilak's comment that one immediately thinks of the whole Shivaji narrative when one looks at this frozen moment suggests that he believed that narrative, figural images combining realism and idealism could remind the viewer of the glorious past, valorize previous struggles, and even suggest the possibility of future victory.

Indeed, recognizing the power that such heroic images could have in disseminating his nationalist message beyond elite audiences, Tilak ar-ranged for a portrait of Shivaji to be unveiled at the Shivaji festival in 1896, and a procession of the portraits of Shivaji and Saint Ramdas—believed by many to be Shivaji's guru—was held on the first day (Cashman 1975, 109). Furthermore, at the time of the festival the Ravi Varma Lithographic Press—which had been founded just two years previously—put out litho-graphs of Shivaji, Tilak, and Ranade. Even after Varma sold his press, along with the right of reproduction of eighty-nine of his paintings, to the Ger-man technician Fritz Schleicher in 1901 due to ongoing financial difficul-ties, the press continued to issue posters of Shivaji and Tilak in recognition of their overwhelming popularity in Maharashtra (Venniyoor 1981, 38–40). Through the darśanic display of these popular lithographs and others pro-duced by the Poona Chitrashala Press, the procession of paintings, the singing of devotional ballads, scripture recitations, and prayer offerings, the 1896 Shivaji festival took on the character of a Hindu religious festival,

Figure 25. *Shivaji Maharaj,* lithograph print by Raja Ravi Varma. Courtesy of Ganesh V. Shivaswamy, Bangalore.

with the historical figure of Shivaji cast as a mythological hero much akin to the god Rama: fighting invading "demons" in order to protect Hindu *dharma* (religion) and to guarantee the people's freedom. At the close of the first Shivaji festival, plans were discussed for the building of an equestrian Shivaji statue at the Raigarh fort, along with a Hindu temple complex.

In the years that followed, the popular lithographs of Shivaji by Varma and other artists, along with the plays and devotional ballads, helped Tilak bring his message to the local masses in the Bombay presidency and to a larger pan-Indian audience as well. Tilak organized Shivaji festivals throughout the Deccan and exclaimed in newspaper editorials that Shivaji was a national hero, one that all Indians—or at least all Hindus—should embrace in their national struggle against the British. Works such as the poems "Pratinidhi" (1897) and "Shivaji Utsav" (1904) by the prominent Bengali nationalist Rabindranath Tagore give some indication that the plea that Shivaji be recognized as a national hero had at least a limited sway outside of western India.[5] In fact, fearing that the Shivaji movement was gaining too much momentum too quickly, the British Raj charged Tilak with sedition in 1898, prosecuting him and other regional newspaper editors for "giving a political turn" to the Shivaji celebration by publishing articles that encouraged the use of the festival as an occasion to "attempt to excite disaffection to the present rulers" (Extracts from the Home Dept. 1898).

The sedition charge against Tilak revolved in part around his interpretation of the slaying of Afzal Khan. Tilak and other nationalists believed that the Orientalist historians' characterization of Shivaji as a murderous villain was unacceptable. In June 1897, at a gathering held to commemorate Shivaji's birth, Professor Bhanu of Fergusson College in Pune argued in a public lecture that in killing Afzal Khan, Shivaji was not a murderer because he was above the usual canons of morality, for he was fighting for the larger cause of Maratha freedom. Commenting on this speech in *Kesari*, Tilak similarly defended Shivaji's act by agreeing that great men are above common principles of morality:

> Did Shivaji commit a sin in killing Afzal Khan? The answer to this question can be found in *Mahabharata* itself. Shrimat Krishna preached in the *Gita* that we have a right even to kill our own *guru* and our kinsmen. No blame attaches to any person if he is doing his deeds without being actuated by a desire to reap the fruit of his deeds. (Cashman 1975, 113–14)

Just one week after Professor Bhanu's speech and the printing of Tilak's editorial, a young man named Damodar Chaphekar shot W. C. Rand, a British military officer with a reputation for severity during the bubonic plague epidemic that struck the Deccan in 1896. Chaphekar stated that he and his associates were moved by the Shivaji festival and Tilak's narrative of Shivaji's life to take such measures in their quest to overthrow the colonial regime (Cashman 1975, 112–16; Vora 1999). After this incident, on the evidence of the above and other *Kesari* editorials, Tilak was given a six-year penal transportation sentence.

British fears of the momentum of Tilak's movement aside, however, Tilak encountered significant resistance to his efforts to take his history of Shivaji to the masses. One of the strongest points of contention was the Kshatriya caste status assigned to Shivaji in Tilak's narrative. Shivaji's status as a Kshatriya was disputed during his lifetime, when his supporters sought to confer the title "Chhatrapati" upon him at his coronation ceremony in 1674. This title, which literally means "Lord of the Umbrella," denotes one who is entitled to have a chatra, an umbrella or parasol, a sign of royalty and/or divinity. In practical terms, the title would signify that Shivaji was now an independent monarch, no longer a vassal. But in order to be invested with this title, Shivaji first had to be declared a Kshatriya, the caste of kings and warriors. Some Brahmins objected, and so Shivaji employed Gaga Bhatt, a Marathi Brahmin living in Banaras, to investigate the Bhonsle family lineage. He declared that they were directly descended from the Sisodia Rajput kings (undisputed Kshatriyas), and that Shivaji was of the Solar lineage, descended from the god-king Rama. His genealogy thus established, the coronation ceremony proceeded, and Shivaji was from then on known as the Chhatrapati.[6] Both Tilak and Ranade described Shivaji as a Kshatriya king who, together with his Brahmin spiritual advisor Saint Ramdas, had established an independent Maharashtrian nation. Although Tilak and Ranade believed that Shivaji and Ramdas together symbolized the potential for Brahmins and non-Brahmins to unite in the face of colonial oppression, many others felt that this vision of unity was exclusive of many segments of the Indian population who were neither upper caste nor Hindu: *Shudras* (peasant caste), Dalits, tribals, and Muslims.

A second, related point of contention was the role Saint Ramdas (1608–81) was given in these nationalist histories. Ranade described Ramdas as Shivaji's spiritual advisor and wrote that it was Ramdas who encouraged Shivaji to unite all Maharashtrians and to propagate the dharma of Maharashtra (Ranade 1900, 143). Tilak similarly believed Ramdas to be Shivaji's spiritual advisor, and therefore took care to include references to him in public commemorations of Shivaji through the parading of a portrait of Ramdas alongside Shivaji's portrait and the recitation of Ramdas's writings before the masses at the Shivaji festival. But by attributing Shivaji's success to his Brahmin advisor, the narratives of Ranade and Tilak—both Brahmins themselves—alienated many non-Brahmins.[7]

Jotirao Phule (1827–90), then a leading non-Brahmin activist in Maharashtra, disagreed with the depiction of Shivaji as a protector of cows and Brahmins. In his *Chhatrapati Shivaji Raje Bhosleyanche Povada* (Ballad of the Raja Chhatrapati Shivaji Bhonsle, 1869), he depicted Shivaji as a non-Brahmin ruler of the low Shudra caste, not the higher Kshatriya caste, who protected the common man. In this ballad and his 1873 book *Gulamagiri* (Slavery), Phule argued that the elites of his day were the descendants of Aryan invaders who had enslaved the natives of India through their caste system and religion. He also maintained that the masses—laborers, tribals, Shudras, and Dalits—were the original inhabitants of India. Pairing Shivaji's past righteous wrath against Muslim "invaders" with the lower castes' current righteous wrath against Brahmin/Aryan "invaders," Phule skillfully crafted a counternarrative of Shivaji for those disenfranchised by the elite nationalist movement.

In 1877, Phule founded the Marathi-language newspaper *Din Bandhu* to act as a counterforce to the Brahmin-run *Kesari* and *Mahratta* newspapers. As Tilak's Shivaji movement was gaining momentum in the 1890s,

Din Bandhu launched a campaign against the Brahminic interpretation of Shivaji. Under the direction of its non-Brahmin editor, Narayanrao Meghaji Lokhande, editorials ran arguing that the memorial was in danger of being transformed into a temple and Shivaji into another incarnated Hindu god. Fearing that a heroically sculpted statue of Shivaji could too easily be transformed into a figure of mythological proportions, these non-Brahmin protestors wrote that instead of a heroic sculptural complex complete with a *linga* (an aniconic form of the Hindu god Shiva) and priest, the memorial should be created along the lines of the secular memorials designed for George Washington, the Duke of Wellington, and Napoleon (O'Hanlon 1985, 295–96).

What is particularly fascinating about this comment is that the Washington Monument in Washington, D.C. (completed in 1884), the Wellington Testimonial in Dublin (completed in 1861), and the Place Vendôme Column in Paris (completed in 1810; reerected in 1873) are all monolithic stone obelisks. By advocating a nonfigurative, abstract memorial, these non-Brahmins hoped to resist the elite effort to recast Shivaji as an iconic deity incarnate in the burgeoning myth of the nation-state. For many Hindus, a sculpted image of Shivaji on horseback could easily call to mind images of Kalki, the final incarnation of the god Vishnu, who according to Puranic lore will appear on horseback, armed with a sword and prepared to eradicate evil and protect the Hindu dharma. Given this mythology, and the fact that images of a significant number of other historical martial figures—often depicted on horseback with swords or spears—are ritually worshipped in some regions of India (see Harlan 2003), one can see how a monolithic, abstract memorial might more easily allow for multiple memories of Shivaji, memories that are not specifically connected to Hindu mythology or ritual practices. Nonetheless, the elite Hindu community dismissed the appeals for a nonfigurative memorial.

The upper-caste Hindu community also dismissed Phule's narrative of Shivaji as a low-caste king. The Daksina Prize Fund Committee, for instance, rejected Phule's ballad, awarding its prize to another work: *The Advice Given to Maharaj Shivaji by Dadoji Kondadev* (1877) by Ekanath Annaji Joshi, which emphasized the role of Brahmin spiritual advisors and likened Shivaji's rule to "Ramraj," the golden era of the god-king Rama. Phule, on the other hand, had completely dismissed Ramdas and other Brahmins, and instead of Ramraj likened Shivaji's rule to "Baliraj," referring to the mythological demon-king Bali who—according to the subaltern interpretation of the myth—was an ideal king unjustly sent to hell by a Brahmin.[8] Yet Phule's narrative was carried on into the twentieth century by Shahu Chhatrapati (1874–1922), the maharaja of Kolhapur. As a Maratha prince and descendant of Shivaji, Shahu Maharaj's support was sought by nationalist leaders for their ongoing annual Shivaji festivals. However, in

1900 when he learned that his priest had been performing for him only the Hindu Vedic rituals that Shudras were fit to receive, not the rites performed for Kshatriyas, he became an advocate of the non-Brahmin cause.

In 1917, Shahu Maharaj and some associates organized the Shri Shivaji Maratha Memorial Society in Pune. One of the goals of this non-Brahmin society was to build a statue of Shivaji (Omvedt 1976, 124–36). For this new generation of activists, an abstract sculpture would no longer do. They wanted to sponsor their own figural statue of the equestrian Shivaji as a way of clearly reclaiming the hero as their own. In 1921 they were successful, for when the Prince of Wales visited Maharashtra, Shahu Maharaj persuaded him to inaugurate a monument to Shivaji as well as a memorial to the Maratha soldiers lost in World War I by explaining that it was Shivaji who "instilled into [the Marathas] the soldierly qualities which were manifested in the great World War" (Laine 2003, 79). From 1922 forward, non-Brahmin activists continued to make public their counternarratives of Shivaji—which dismissed Ramdas and Brahminical Hinduism—by reenacting their memories of Shivaji through statues, festivals, plays, songs, posters, and other media.

Thus a single narrative image—such as the equestrian Shivaji—has the potential for tremendous multivalence, although the account of Shivaji as a Kshatriya defender of Marathi Brahmins and the larger Hindu nation continues to be reinforced as the hegemonic narrative in postcolonial India. After independence, as the movement for a state composed of the Marathi-speaking population grew in western India in the 1950s, the Samyukta Maharashtra Samiti (SMS) promoted an image of Maharashtra as the nation's protector and argued that as the descendants of the first real Indian nationalist, Shivaji, the Marathas deserved their own territory.[9] On January 16, 1956, after Prime Minister Jawaharlal Nehru declared Bombay a Union Territory, a large protest erupted. In this six-day "Battle for Bombay," over eighty demonstrators were killed by police fire, becoming instant martyrs for the Maharashtrian cause. After the battle was over, Nehru, who had previously denounced Shivaji as a "predatory adventurer," made an effort to appease the Marathi people and incorporate Shivaji into the national memorial landscape by unveiling a new statue of Shivaji at the Pratapgarh fort in 1957 (T. Hansen 2001, 41–45). Notably, this statue was figural, featuring Shivaji astride his horse, wielding his sword. For many who visit this statue today, after the formation of the state of Maharasthra in 1960, the memory of Shivaji is now inextricably linked with this regional protest movement. For them, the statue calls to mind the narrative of struggle, sacrifice, and ultimate victory of those who fought for Maharashtra in the seventeenth *and* twentieth centuries.

In 1966, political cartoonist Bal Thackeray founded the Shiv Sena political party in Bombay. Shiv Sena means "Shivaji's Army," and the men who join this "army" are likened to Shivaji's soldiers, willing to bravely sacrifice even their lives defending the Marathi community and the larger Hindu nation (*Shiv Sena Speaks* 1967). Initially, the Shiv Sena appealed to lower- and middle-class families who felt some resentment toward the South Indian and Gujarati upper class in Bombay; in the 1970s, communists were targeted, and projecting Muslims as the latest enemy helped the Shiv Sena to redefine itself as a Hindu nationalist organization in the 1980s as Hindu nationalism was on the rise throughout India. Based on its Hindu nationalist platform, the Shiv Sena became the majority party in Maharashtra in 1995. Despite this flexibility of the "other," the characterization of the "self" in the Shiv Sena's rhetoric has remained constant: the "self" is a manly, Marathi-speaking Maharashtrian who is the martial guardian of the Hindu nation. By sponsoring figural statues, posters, pamphlets, neighborhood parades, and festivals throughout the state, members of the Shiv Sena continually define Shivaji as the first true Indian hero, a Kshatriya protector of cows and Brahmins, and a sanctified figure beyond reproach.

However, non-Brahmin activists throughout Maharashtra continue to resist this now-dominant characterization of Shivaji and to interpret this icon in their own way. In the past few years, members of the non-Brahmin groups Sambhaji Brigade and Maratha Seva Sangh have begun to advocate a new religion that has not yet received much academic attention, Shiv Dharma, which rejects Brahminical Hinduism and regards Shivaji's mother, Jijabai, as its reigning deity (Salunkhe 2002). Drawing heavily on Phule's interpretation of Shivaji, these non-Brahmins have begun to propagate their religion and make public their claim on Shivaji through a variety of visual media: they have produced posters of Shivaji (using both equestrian and portrait-style imagery) and distributed them at religious festivals; sponsored plaques with their organization's name inscribed upon them at Raigarh, Sindhudurg, and other forts associated with Shivaji; and donated figural statues of Shivaji to various locales, including the bust of Shivaji that now stands in the Chhabutar at Raigarh Fort.

The cover of the *Shivaji* comic book (figure 22) demonstrates Ravi Varma's continued influence. It is remarkably similar to Varma's *Shivaji Maharaj* print of the equestrian Shivaji (figure 25) in its composition and its combination of iconic and narrative modes. All of the comic book artists at the *Amar Chitra Katha* studio were familiar with Varma's subjects and style, and several admitted looking at his many lithographs for inspiration. Ram Waeerkar, for instance, discussed the importance of having a large visual reference library at the studio for the comic artists that included the works of Ravi Varma and other artists, both Indian and western:

Showing and Telling Shivaji's Story in *Amar Chitra Katha*

We use all the references, whatever reference is there we look at, from all the artists. Ravi Varma, S. M. Pandit, all artists. At first there were not enough. We [at *ACK*] had to start a library, build up the references. And I have my own references at home. Many references are necessary because there are many frames [panels] for each character, 150 frames per comic, and they must be done quickly. So I look at all the references for that character. Then I make the drawings very fast. I am the fastest artist. . . . But not just Indian references, not just Ravi Varma. Also there is Fortunino Matania, and American comic artists. All of these I look at, too.

Pratap Mulick, the artist who created the *Shivaji* comic book cover and illustrated the issue, has worked for years for *ACK* and has also freelanced for the Delhi-based *Raj* and *Manosh* comic book series. A native Maharashtrian, Mulick takes pride in the *Shivaji* cover and has also created a number of Shivaji oil paintings, including a recent series of eleven 11′ × 8′ paintings of Shivaji's life commissioned by a Pune-based company. When asked about his influences, Mulick listed a series of American comics artists, including John Prentice (of *Rip Kirby* comic strip fame) and Hal Foster (*Prince Valiant*). When asked about Indian influences specifically, including Varma, his reply was terse: "Of course, Ravi Varma, other Indians. All Indian painters know other Indians' work. I have many books, many posters around to look at." Sitting in his home studio one morning and browsing through his personal reference library of Indian and western lithographs, posters, books, and comic books, I was amazed by the stacks of aged lithographs that he had carefully preserved, including many from the Ravi Varma and Poona Chitrashala presses. As Christopher Pinney has commented, due to this tradition of preservation, similar images have "pictured the nation of India" for more than a century now, shaping the national canon of gods and heroes and the ways they are remembered: "The creation of popular visual symbols is facilitated by the archives of early images maintained by most commercial artists. These ensure the circulation of these images and prevent their sedimentation. Forming part of a relatively closed repertoire, they migrate endlessly, cutting back and forth across new times and contexts (1997b, 835)."[10]

Just as the images of Shivaji created by Varma and other artists continue to inspire artists today, so do the stories of Shivaji told by Tilak and other Indians more than a century ago continue to inspire authors today. The presentation of the encounter between Shivaji and Afzal Khan, in particular, in the *ACK* comic book narrative is indebted to Tilak's nationalist narrative of events in a number of ways. For instance, despite the long-standing editorial policy of minimizing violence (according to which Pai decided not to show goddess Kali drinking blood), the slaying of Afzal Khan is prominently featured—his decapitation by one of Shivaji's soldiers is shown in the first panel on page 13 (figure 24). Furthermore, the decapitation of Khan is morally justified in the comic book. As had

Tilak, so have the creators of the comic used the *Bhagavad Gītā* to defend Shivaji's actions. In the early discussion featured between Shivaji and his mother, our young hero is taught the *Gītā's* lesson that fighting is at times an inescapable duty and that "even death in the cause of one's duty should be dear to a hero's heart" (3).

In other ways as well, the comic book's depiction of the encounter between Shivaji and Afzal Khan draws more upon Tilak's nationalist narrative of Shivaji than any other history. In the comic, Shivaji is presented as a small, wiry character, while Afzal Khan is enormous (figure 23). This is true of all the colonial-era narratives discussed above—for instance, James Grant Duff had written of Shivaji's "diminutive size" (1826, 1:172), while James Douglas noted his weight of "only 112 pounds," which he characterized as "good riding weight" (1893, 1:337–38). But unlike the Orientalist historians' accounts, the differing size of the two characters in the comic is meant to suggest a David versus Goliath scenario, where the righteous man, no matter how small, is ultimately able to overcome the oppressive giant. As in Tilak's account, there is no doubt that it is Shivaji who is the hero and Afzal Khan who is the villain. Thus Afzal Khan's treachery is doubly articulated in the comic book: visually through his enormous size and the knife he attempts to stab into Shivaji's back, and textually through his double-speak, his habit of saying one thing while thinking another. Similarly, Shivaji's innocence and bravery are doubly articulated: visually through his small size, his courageous approach, and his hesitancy to fight without provocation, and textually through the verbal explanation that Shivaji wore armor and carried a weapon only because he had been informed that Afzal Khan would try to kill him (10).

But the comic book narrative of Shivaji also departs from Tilak's account in a significant way. When the *Amar Chitra Katha* issue on Shivaji was first planned in 1970, the Shiv Sena was rising as a prominent political force in Bombay and surrounding areas. In an effort to take advantage of this resurgent interest in Shivaji, the studio decided to release the *Shivaji* comic book in 1971. Yet the producers wanted their comic book to appeal to a large audience of Brahmins and non-Brahmins alike, and therefore they decided to overlook the controversial issue of Shivaji's relationship with Saint Ramdas. Anant Pai stated that from the very beginning he has sought to promote national integration by creating comics that featured mythological and historical figures—including Shivaji—that everyone could enjoy, no matter their caste, class, regional, or religious identity. Furthermore, he explained, ever since he was taken to court by the Valmiki Sabha, a Dalit group, for depicting Valmiki, author of the earliest Sanskrit version of the *Rāmāyaṇa* epic, whom they revere as god, as a dark-skinned dacoit in the *Valmiki* issue (no. 46, 1973), he has taken the extra step of having comics on "sensitive subjects" approved by various organizations, such as the Shiromani Gurdwara Prabhandhak Committee in Amritsar for the Sikh comic books:

> You see, in 1976 I was presented with a lawsuit by the Valmiki Sabha in the Punjab for defaming their community in the *Valmiki ACK.* They objected to the presentation of Valmiki as a dacoit. The lawsuit was filed under Section 295, which forbids the disparaging of a religious community—I can't remember the technical language, but that is what it does. Anyway, it was a big commotion when I went to the Punjab to defend myself in court—they even burned effigies of me in the Punjab, and there was a lot of press coverage, some negative and some positive. But the chief minister of the Punjab, a Sikh, he eventually dismissed the case. Before then, I was careful. But since then, I get the approval of religious communities whenever I print an issue about a religious figure. That way I don't offend anyone.[11]

Like Shivaji, Valmiki is a sanctified historical figure who is differently interpreted by Brahmins and non-Brahmins. Unwittingly, Anant Pai—a Brahmin—excluded the non-Brahminic understanding of Valmiki when he decided to base the comic book's script on popular traditions, including the tradition that Valmiki was a robber before he became an enlightened Hindu renouncer and composed the *Rāmāyaṇa,* a tradition that is offensive to many non-Brahmins. Anant Pai stresses that his comic books are for upper and lower castes alike and that, although he was very careful when making *Shivaji,* he learned his lesson from the *Valmiki* issue and now maintains that same level of care with all of his comic titles.

However, Shivaji's relationship with Ramdas has been raised in several other issues in this comic book series. *Chhatrasal* (no. 41, 1973) tells the story of Chhatrasal's fight against the Mughal emperor Aurangzeb and features a discussion between Chhatrasal and Shivaji about Ramdas. When Chhatrasal approaches Shivaji for advice in fighting the Mughals, Shivaji tells him that although the Mughal army is large, it cannot withstand surprise attacks. At this point, Chhatrasal asks Shivaji about a framed picture that is shown hanging on the wall. In the next panel—a close-up of the framed picture of a guru—Shivaji tells Chhatrasal, "He is my patron saint and guru, Swami Ramdas. I draw my strength and inspiration from him" (17). Chhatrasal takes Shivaji's words to heart, and shortly after their meeting he finds his own guru, Pran Nath, and thereafter attains victory in his martial quest.

The cover of the *Samarth Ramdas* issue (no. 222, 1980) about Saint Ramdas paints an even clearer picture of Ramdas as Shivaji's spiritual advisor. In this image, Shivaji kneels in prostration before Saint Ramdas. In the background Shivaji's troops wait patiently while Ramdas blesses their leader; and in the foreground a small *murti* (statue) of the Hindu monkey-god Hanuman oversees the meeting between Shivaji and Ramdas, lending his blessing to Shivaji's mission as well. Posters of Shivaji kneeling before the Brahmin Saint Ramdas have been sold in Maharashtra for a century and reflect the now-dominant understanding of Shivaji as a Hindu leader, rightly guided by his Brahmin advisor, that has been promoted since Tilak's time. But throughout the latter half of the twentieth century, Dalits and other non-Brahmins have countered such imagery with posters of their own, depicting Shivaji kneeling before the non-Brahmin Saint Tukaram. *Amar Chitra Katha* has released a *Tukaram* issue (no. 68, 1974), but Shivaji is not featured on the cover, and within the issue, although the popular legend of Shivaji's meeting with Tukaram is briefly recounted (30), Shivaji is nowhere depicted kneeling before Tukaram or otherwise presented as his disciple. Thus although the *Shivaji* issue can be read and embraced by Brahmins and non-Brahmins alike, the series as a whole does not allow for multiple interpretations of Shivaji, but instead reflects the more dominant Brahminical interpretation of Shivaji that is most familiar to Anant Pai and the majority of creators of this comic book series.

Producer No. 1 mentioned that when the *Shivaji* issue was written, there was a general consensus in the comic book studio that the "gray episodes" of Shivaji's life should be left out in order to better portray him as a hero. But after its publication, he stated, some journalists and others questioned whether it was appropriate to mythologize a historical figure in this manner. He continued: "There was much criticism about this, and also about how the Muslims were portrayed in it. But still the comic book is a bestseller; it has not been cancelled, it has instead been reprinted, and you can find it for sale everywhere, not just in Maharashtra, but all over India."

In a brief article published in the *Illustrated Weekly* in 1993, Nancy Adajania criticized the *Shivaji* comic book, writing that the main culprits responsible for stripping historical figures such as Shivaji of their humanity and homogenizing them into superhuman symbols of nationalist history are "comic strips of the *Amar Chitra Katha* variety, and textbooks serving State-licensed curricula for the humanities," whose "ability to parrot a limited number of points allows students to ingest a neat scheme of things. Unconfused by the facts, students thus pass on, having liberated themselves from the burden of studying any real history at all" (1993, 34). Adajania argued that the popular images of Shivaji stabbing the "treacherous" Afzal Khan and battling "alien" Mughal aggressors are false. Echoing the nineteenth-century narratives put forward by colonial historians like James Grant Duff and James Douglas, she reminded readers that the "true" Shivaji had levied exorbitant taxes and pillaged territories in Rajputana, the Gangetic plains, Bengal, and the Deccan. He was not a national hero, she suggested, but a regional despot.

Adajania's article was published in April 1993, just four months after Hindu nationalists destroyed the Babri Masjid mosque in Ayodhya, claiming that the Mughal emperor Babar had it built on the hallowed site of god Rama's birthplace. Following the destruction of the mosque, Hindu-

Muslim riots erupted in Bombay (December 1992 to January 1993), killing approximately 1,000 people.[12] In the wake of this violence, Adajania's article was likely an attempt to forestall the further communalization of figures like Rama and Shivaji. Nonetheless, this small article created a rather large furor. Both houses of the Maharashtra state legislature resounded with angry protests, as Mangesh Kulkarni has chronicled, and members of the Shiv Sena, the (right-wing) Bharatiya Janata Party, and the ruling (left-wing) Congress Party throughout the nation jointly demanded that stern action be taken against the *Illustrated Weekly* and Adajania for offending the sensibilities of the Marathi people (Kulkarni 1997, 126). Despite the public apology offered by Anil Dharker, editor of the *Illustrated Weekly*, in that publication (April 24–30, 1993) and in the *Times of India* (April 14, 1993), the issue of the magazine in which Adajania's article appeared was banned, and cases were registered against the author, editor, publisher, and printer under Section 153(A) of the Indian Penal Code, which prescribes "promoting enmity between different groups on grounds of religion." Although these cases were eventually dismissed by the Bombay High Court, the two-week-long protest of this article by liberal and conservative officials alike testifies to the way in which the historical figure Shivaji has continued to be memorialized as a sacred figure, one whose "proper" memory state officials are now vested in maintaining.

More recently, the controversy surrounding scholar James W. Laine's book *Shivaji: Hindu King in Islamic India* (2003) demonstrates that the memory of Shivaji continues to be policed by multiple parties. In November 2003, just a few months after the book's release, the Shiv Sena began to protest both the book and its author, accusing Laine of maligning their beloved leader and his mother. In January 2004, the Sambhaji Brigade attacked the Bhandarkar Oriental Research Institute (BORI) in Pune, lashing out at the institution where Laine conducted his research as well as the librarians, scholars, and staff members who worked there. Members of this non-Brahmin group embrace Shivaji as a low-caste king who fought for the upliftment of the low-caste Marathi community, and his mother, Jijabai, as the reigning deity of their new religion, Shiv Dharma. These activists targeted BORI because they blamed the Brahmin scholars there for misguiding Laine in his interpretation of Shivaji. Despite the apology that Laine tendered to the Indian public via the major newspapers, criminal proceedings were launched against him later that month, and his book was banned by the government of Maharashtra, then ruled by an alliance of the Congress Party and the Nationalist Congress Party (Vajpeyi 2004).

In the days following the BORI attack, Indian prime minister Atal Behari Vajpayee announced his plans to unveil an equestrian statue of Shivaji at the Bombay airport, recently renamed the Chhatrapati Shivaji International Airport, and added that he supported the actions Maharashtrian officials had taken against James Laine ("Shivaji Is My Ideal" 2004; "PM to Unveil Shivaji Statue" 2004). Equestrian statues of Shivaji with his sword aloft—similar in theme to the *Shivaji* comic book cover—now abound throughout Maharashtra, testimony of the esteem with which Maharashtrians of multiple political, religious, caste, and ideological persuasions regard this seventeenth-century king. After the Bharatiya Janata Party came into national power in the 1990s, Hindu nationalist politicians commissioned new Shivaji statues and organized public activities in Shivaji's honor on a national scale. When Union home minister L. K. Advani unveiled a Shivaji statue in Agra in 2001, he stated that he was proud to present a statue of the "warrior legend who sowed the seeds of Indian independence," and further noted that it was due to the presence of this statue that "for a patriot this place now could be another pilgrimage" (D. Sharma 2001). In this speech Advani not only claimed Shivaji as a national hero but also suggested that the statue had transformed Agra into a hallowed site. Rather than remembering Agra—home of such architectural testaments to Mughal strength as the Taj Mahal and the Agra Fort—as a Mughal city, it could now be remembered as a site of Hindu victory: namely, the site where the underdog Shivaji outwitted the Mughal emperor Aurangzeb. There are no statues of any of the Mughal emperors in Agra.

For Producer No. 1, the continued popularity of the *Shivaji* comic book confirms that the creators made the right decision in incorporating historical figures into the *Amar Chitra Katha* series and in eliminating some of the "gray episodes" of Shivaji's life in order to portray him more heroically. While other *ACK* comics have faced declining sales and are no longer reprinted, *Shivaji* has been reprinted numerous times since its initial press run in 1971, and the issue is still widely available throughout India today, complete with a superior "deluxe edition" laminated cover. However, the popularity of this issue must be understood in light of the culture wars that have dominated South Asian culture and politics in recent decades. As the communal interpretation of Indian history has become deeply rooted in modern social memory, politicians in Maharashtra and, increasingly, throughout the nation have drawn upon the hegemonic Shivaji narrative—and especially Shivaji's battle with Afzal Khan—to motivate and unify Hindu voters.[13] And the producers of popular media, including comic books, have responded to and benefited from this interest in Shivaji. In Bombay in particular, the demand for images of Shivaji slaying Afzal Khan increased dramatically in the 1990s in the wake of the controversy over Adajania's article in the *Illustrated Weekly* in 1993–94 and the devastating communal violence of the Bombay riots of December 1992 and January 1993. These events fueled sales of the *Shivaji* comic book throughout the 1990s, as well as posters, calendars, and other items featuring Shivaji as a Hindu king who was victorious over his Muslim enemies.[14]

Conclusion: Sanctifying Shivaji

The fact that *Shivaji* was the first historical issue produced in the *Amar Chitra Katha* series demonstrates that this seventeenth-century Maratha king is one of the foundational figures of Indian history, at least in the eyes of the creators and consumers of these comic books. In addition to the *Shivaji* issue, ACK has also released a *Tales of Shivaji* issue (no. 268, 1982) that relates several legendary incidents that occurred at his hill-forts; a *Tanaji* issue (no. 40, 1973) that tells the story of Shivaji's Maratha companion Tanaji Malusre in more detail; and a *Sambhaji* issue (no. 250, 1981) featuring Shivaji's son. Furthermore, numerous historical figures from all regions of India are compared with Shivaji in the introductions to other titles in this comic book series: In *Chhatrasal* (no. 41, 1973), Chhatrasal from Bundelkhand "met and was inspired by Shivaji, and like him was a freedom-loving warrior"; in *Lachit Barphukan* (no. 169, 1978), which is set in Assam, "Lachit Barphukan—like Shivaji—fought relentlessly to check the expansion of the Mughal Empire"; and in *Guru Gobind Singh* (no. 32, 1972), set in the Punjab, "Guru Gobind Singh and his Sikhs in the north" worked alongside "Shivaji and his Marathas in the Deccan" to hasten the end of the Mughal empire. By comparing the similar martial qualities of various rulers throughout India with Shivaji's and emphasizing their similar efforts to fight the Mughals, a larger image is created of Indians—Hindus along with Sikhs—united in the struggle against "invading" Muslims, or as the introduction to the *Shivaji* issue puts it, united to "throw off the yoke of alien rule." Shivaji is thus remembered not just as one of the many national heroes who fought for India's independence but as the foremost among those heroes.

The ending of the *Shivaji* comic book (plate 7) is particularly poignant for understanding why the seventeenth-century warrior-king was chosen to be the first historical Indian hero in the *ACK* series and what he means to its creators and readers. Here Shivaji sits on his throne beneath a golden umbrella, alongside his mother, Jijabai, and son, Sambhaji, where the courtiers bow before him and proclaim him to be "a people's king" (32). Like other images of Shivaji's coronation, including the large figural statue of Shivaji seated on his throne that now stands at the Raigarh fort memorial site, this comic book image of Shivaji's coronation could conceivably be interpreted in various ways. For some, Shivaji's coronation could signify the victory of Indian independence and the founding of a secular nation-state by a "great liberal," as Anant Pai's quote at the outset of this chapter suggests; for others, it could signify the victory of Hindu solidarity in the face of a perceived Muslim onslaught; and for still others it could signify the victory of a low-caste hero over elite Brahminical culture.[15] Yet despite the potential multivalence of this final image, the comic book narrative as a whole encourages readers to remember Shivaji as a victorious Hindu king. As we have seen, both visually and textually the comic book producers had many narrative options to choose from. Ultimately, they chose to side with the dominant Brahminical, Hindu nationalist interpretation of Shivaji by eliding references to his caste struggles, depicting him as a devout Hindu, and by portraying his struggle with Afzal Khan and other Indian Muslims as a communal one. Furthermore, when read across the large corpus of comic books in the series, this final image of Shivaji's coronation encourages readers to remember Shivaji not as a mortal human, but instead to immortalize him as a forever-victorious Hindu god-king.

In discussing the historical fiction novels of the nineteenth-century Indian writer Bankimchandra Chatterjee (1838–94), Sudipta Kaviraj raises the issue of narrative closure, writing about the novel *Rājsinha*: "By narrativity, the simple act of telling and not telling, the narrator can gerrymander events—not by directly falsifying them, but by the most unanswerable of his narrative weapons, his right of closure. In history, Rajsinha's victory against Mughal power must have been the merest of reprieves. But in the narrative, Rajsinha's victory stands out indelibly. This difference is simply because history does not have an end, but the narrative has" (1998, 153).

Shivaji lived until 1680, when he succumbed to an illness, leaving behind no loyal heir. But in the comic book, Shivaji's ultimate victory—the founding of a Maratha kingdom, independent of Mughal rule—"stands out indelibly" due to this strategy of narrative closure. Bankimchandra and other authors of historical fiction in the late nineteenth century often felt that their patriotic duty was to convey the general truth about a period of history, supplementing the historical record with their imagination when necessary, in order to arrive at a "true history," one which related the memory of the glorious deeds of past heroes in a way that was relevant in the present (Kaviraj 1998; also Chatterjee 1993:76–94). Like these authors, the creators of the *Shivaji* comic book have also gerrymandered events by actively forgetting the final six years of Shivaji's life in order to arrive at their "true history."

Other historical comic books in the *ACK* series featuring martial historical figures end with a heroic death scene, typically on the battlefield, as in *Prithviraj Chauhan* (no. 25, 1971), *Tanaji* (no. 40, 1973), and *Rani Durgavati* (no. 104, 1976) (figure 15). But in its concluding image, *Shivaji* has more in common with the comic book about the mythological god-king Rama than with any historical comic. *Rama* (no. 15, 1970) also ends with a coronation ceremony, after Rama has defeated the demon-king Ravana and returned victoriously to Ayodhya (figure 1). The final panel shows Rama seated on his throne with his wife and brother at his side, and the narrative text states that Rama was "crowned king in Ayodhya and he ruled for many years" (32). When the *Valmiki's Ramayana* bumper issue (no. 10001) was released in 1992—at the time that Hindu nationalist agitation over Ayodhya was at its height—it also ended with a coronation image: a full-page panel that is remarkably similar to the *Shivaji* panel (plate 8). Such parallels serve to subtly suggest that Shivaji is a latter-day Rama and to liken Shivaji's reign to "Ramraj," rather than the "Baliraj" that it was hailed as by the non-Brahmin activist Phule. They also indicate that, in preparing the visual templates and storyboards for these comics, mythology and history were considered to be complementary rather than oppositional—that together, they tell the "whole truth" of India and its immortal heroes. The next chapter considers the other side of this coin: the combination of history and mythology not only results in the warrior-king Shivaji being sanctified as a godlike hero in this comic book series; it also results in those he struggled against being demonized as villains.

Vol. 504

Rama

Amar Chitra Katha: the Glorious Heritage of India

Plate 1. *Rama,* no. 15 [reprint no. 504] (Bombay: India Book
House Pvt. Ltd., 1970 [1998]), cover. From *Amar Chitra Katha,*
with the permission of the publishers ACK Media, India.

Plate 2. *The Gita*, no. 127 [reprint no. 505] (Bombay: India Book House Pvt. Ltd., 1977 [1999]), 27. From *Amar Chitra Katha*, with the permission of the publishers ACK Media, India.

Plate 3. *Bhagawat: The Krishna Avatar*, not numbered (Bombay: India Book House Pvt. Ltd., 2000), 72. From *Amar Chitra Katha*, with the permission of the publishers ACK Media, India.

Plate 4. *Tales of Durga*, no. 176 [reprint no. 514] (Bombay: India Book House Pvt. Ltd., 1978 [2000]), 6. From *Amar Chitra Katha*, with the permission of the publishers ACK Media, India.

Plate 5. *Shakuntala,* no. 12 [reprint no. 530] (Bombay: India Book House Pvt. Ltd., 1970 [2001]),
1. From *Amar Chitra Katha,* with the permission of the publishers ACK Media, India.

SHAH JAHAN BUILT THE EXQUISITE MONUMENT, THE TAJ MAHAL, FOR MUMTAZ. TWENTY THOUSAND MEN WORKED ON IT FOR SEVENTEEN YEARS. THE TAJ MAHAL IS A DREAM IN WHITE MARBLE, THE WORLD'S GREATEST MONUMENT TO TRUE LOVE.

SHAH JAHAN DIED IN 1666 AT THE AGE OF SEVENTY-FOUR. HE WAS BURIED BESIDE HIS BELOVED MUMTAZ MAHAL.

31

Plate 6. *Shah Jahan,* no. 204 [reprint no. 642] (Bombay: India Book House Pvt. Ltd., 1979 [1999]), 31. From *Amar Chitra Katha,* with the permission of the publishers ACK Media, India.

Plate 7. *Shivaji*, no. 23 [reprint no. 564] (Bombay: India Book
House Pvt. Ltd., 1971 [2000]), 32. From *Amar Chitra Katha*, with
the permission of the publishers ACK Media, India.

RAMA WAS CROWNED KING OF AYODHYA.

RAMA RULED HIS KINGDOM WISELY AND STRICTLY FOLLOWED THE PATH OF DHARMA. PEOPLE FOLLOWED HIS EXAMPLE AND CARRIED OUT THEIR RESPECTIVE DUTIES. UNDER RAMA'S RULE, THERE WAS UNIVERSAL HAPPINESS.

95

Plate 8. *Valmiki's Ramayana*, no. 10001 (Bombay: India Book House Pvt. Ltd., 1992), 95. From *Amar Chitra Katha*, with the permission of the publishers ACK Media, India.

Plate 9. *Sati and Shiva*, no. 111 [reprint no. 550] (Bombay: India Book House Pvt. Ltd., 1976 [2000]), 3. From *Amar Chitra Katha*, with the permission of the publishers ACK Media, India.

Plate 10. *G. D. Birla*, no. 382 [reprint no. 733] (Bombay: India Book House Pvt. Ltd., 1987 [2001]), 29. From *Amar Chitra Katha*, with the permission of the publishers ACK Media, India.

Muslims as Secular Heroes and Zealous Villains

5

Following the release of *Shivaji* (no. 23, 1971), the issue about the seventeenth-century Hindu king from western India, Anant Pai added a range of other historical comic books to the ever-growing *Amar Chitra Katha* corpus in the 1970s. These issues were written in the same formula pitting medieval martial Hindu "heroes" from various regions of India against Muslim "villains." Especially favored for the role of the villain in these issues are the Mughal emperors, Muslims who controlled a vast swath of the Indian subcontinent from 1526 until 1707, when the empire began to decline as British colonial influence increased. *Rana Pratap* (no. 24, 1971), for example, features a sixteenth-century Hindu king from Rajasthan in northwestern India who battles the Mughal emperor Akbar (r. 1556–1605). In this comic book, Rana Pratap (r. 1572–97) vows before the Hindu goddess Kali that he will sacrifice his life for his kingdom and that he and his men will refrain from luxuries like sleeping on beds and wearing nice clothes until they have attained freedom (4–5). When Akbar's commander, a Hindu Rajput named Man Singh, meets with Rana Pratap in a peace-making effort, Rana Pratap cannot disguise his feelings about Akbar: "He may be a king for you, but to us he is an invader, an enemy" (11). Throughout the comic book, the underdog Rana Pratap—shown repeatedly posed heroically on his horse Chetak—fearlessly battles the Mughal forces that both outnumber him and outstrip him in weaponry (figure 26). It is for such sentiments and his brave death that Rana Pratap is remembered today, immortalized in the introduction to the comic as a hero whose "freedom was his honour, which he cherished even more than his own life."

The *Rana Sanga* issue (no. 106, 1976) pits the Hindu Rajput king Rana Sanga (r. 1509–27) against Babur (r. 1526–30), founder of the Mughal Empire. In one particular panel toward the end of the comic, after making vows to the Hindu goddess Chandi and on the Muslim Quran, respectively, Rana Sanga and Babur gather their troops and face off against one another. Here there is no doubt that the war being waged by these forces is religious: The forces at the bottom left-hand corner are marked with the Hindu color, saffron, while the forces at the upper right-hand corner are marked with the Muslim color, green (29). Reminiscent of the saffron and green stripes

Rana Pratap and Akbar fought one another, but both are heroes. Rana Pratap is a hero in *his* issue, and Akbar is a hero in *his* issue. Rana Pratap was right. He was fighting for his country, for the land of his fathers. But Akbar's father's father also claimed India as his homeland. And Akbar was a good king. He was very accommodating. He removed the tax on Hindu pilgrims, and he spread the word that all religions are equal.

Anant Pai, personal interview

SOON AFTER MAN SINGH LEFT, RANA PRATAP ATTACKED A CAMP OF MUGHAL FORCES AND KILLED MANY OF THEM.

Figure 26. *Rana Pratap,* no. 24 [reprint no. 563] (Bombay: India Book House Pvt. Ltd., 1971 [1994]), 14. From *Amar Chitra Katha,* with the permission of the publishers ACK Media, India.

of the tricolor Indian flag, which are separated by a plain white field, here the image works in the opposite way: it does not suggest unity in diversity but an unbreachable divide. Similarly, in the *Amar Singh Rathor* issue (no. 171, 1978), which features the Mughal emperor Shah Jahan as the villain, the battle between the Hindu Rajputs and the emperor's forces is cast as a religious battle when the Rajputs cry out the names of Hindu deities Shiva and Bhavani on the battlefield ("Har Har Mahadev!" and "Jai Bhavani!"), while the Mughal soldiers charge in the name of Allah and the prophet Muhammad ("Allah-Ho-Akbar!" and "Ya Rasool!") (24).

Prior to *Shivaji,* the *ACK* comics had featured mythological Hindu gods like Krishna and Rama as heroes who battled demons like Putana, Tataka, and Ravana. In making these first historical issues in the 1970s, this same formula was utilized, resulting in some historical figures—Hindus— being cast as heroes and other historical figures—Muslims—being cast as villains. Just as Rama battles and defeats Tataka and the other pesky demons who have invaded Vishwamitra's holy realm, so does Rana Pratap battle and defeat the pesky Mughal soldiers who have "invaded" north-western India. In both *Rama* and *Rana Pratap,* our heroes calmly hold their weapon of choice ready in exercised poses, while their foes scramble about, waving their arms and weapons in frantic, destructive gestures. For a number of Indians—Hindu and Muslim—this decision to feature historical subjects in this previously mythological comic book series has been worrisome. Indian journalists Sanjay Joshi and Rajni Bakshi, for instance, wrote in the early 1980s after the release of these historical issues that the *Amar Chitra Katha* series is "history with a strong 'great man' bent and a decided Hindu chauvinist bias. Most stories are full of 'patriotic' (Hindu) kings defending the 'motherland' against 'foreign' (Muslim) rulers. In all battles soldiers are shown shouting, 'Allah O Akbar' or 'Har Har Mahadev,' as if religion were all that the battles were fought about. The 'two nation thesis' is drummed into impressionable minds from this young age" (Joshi and Bakshi 1983).[1]

Anant Pai is aware of such criticisms of these comic books. In an article published in India's *Gentleman* magazine in February 2000, he proclaimed the secular nature of this series, explaining that the wide array of available titles is meant to appeal to all Indians, regardless of their religious identities: "To mythology, we added history, folktales, regional heroes, heroines. Feedback from readers and from educationists and savants at seminars helped a lot. When a group in Goa charged me of Hindu propaganda, I countered it by saying that epics like the *Ramayana* and the *Mahabharata* were the heritage of all Indians. I was quick to add titles like *Babur, Humayun,* a title on Jesus Christ, and tried to make the series more secular" (Pai 2000, 39).

In 1977, ten years after the comic book series was founded, the first issue to feature a Muslim figure as its hero—*Babur* (no. 134)—was published in an attempt to appease critics who alleged that the series had a Hindu bias. Babur, the founder of the Mughal Empire in India (r. 1526–30), is clearly conceived of as a hero, for the introduction to the comic book tells us that "Babur was not just a good soldier or an able general; he was also a wise and just ruler, with qualities of generosity and good humour." Issues on the rest of the Great Mughals followed, though not in strict chronological order: *Humayun* (no. 140, 1977), *Noor Jahan* (no. 148, 1977), *Akbar* (no. 200, 1979), *Shah Jahan* (no. 204, 1979), *Jahangir* (no. 221, 1980), and *Dara Shukoh and Aurangzeb* (no. 232, 1981). This chapter examines several of these issues about the Mughal emperors in order to take a closer look at the representation of Muslims as heroes and as villains in the *ACK* series. In addition to considering how the binary portrayal of Muslims as heroic rulers who embrace pluralism and as villainous puritans who attack Hindus is indebted to colonial historiography, this chapter also discusses the contested meaning of the term *secular* in these comic books in particular and in postcolonial India more generally.

Shah Jahan and *Akbar* are the two bestselling issues in the *Amar Chitra Katha* series featuring Muslim heroes. Unlike the other comics on the Great Mughals, these two have been reprinted numerous times and are still widely available today. In fact, I have encountered the *Shah Jahan* issue being hawked to foreign and domestic tourists alike outside the Taj Mahal, the famous mausoleum that was built by Emperor Shah Jahan (r. 1627–58). "See the love story," said one hawker on my first visit to the Taj in 1999, pointing at the cover of the comic book and winking. As the hawker's statement suggests, much of the appeal of this comic book is its romantic characterization of Shah Jahan. On the cover, Shah Jahan is featured as an old man, lying under a blanket with his head propped up so that he can look out the window at the Taj Mahal, which sits in the distance on the bank of the Yamuna River (figure 27). In this image, which recalls impressionist painting in its visible brushstrokes and play of light, the sun is just setting beyond the Taj, causing the reflection of the Taj Mahal to dance on the surface of the golden-hued water. Shah Jahan's glance at the Taj is a longing, almost wistful one, a look of yearning that is ripe with romantic sentiment. From the outset, then, it is apparent that Shah Jahan is not a hero in the same martial way that Shivaji and Rana Pratap are, both of whom are shown on their covers dressed in battle gear and in imposing equestrian stances, Shivaji with his sword aloft and Rana Pratap with his spear raised.

The story within the *Shah Jahan* issue begins in 1592 with the birth of Prince Khurram, who would later be known as Shah Jahan, "King of the World." The court astrologer tells Khurram's grandfather, Emperor Akbar, that his grandson will earn both fame and fortune in his lifetime. Reading on, we learn that the prince was schooled in mental and physical arts and that he excelled at everything he attempted, pleasing his grandfather greatly: he is a brave hunter, an able swordsman, and a good scholar. At the age of twenty he is married to Arjumand Banu, who would later be known as Mumtaz Mahal, "Beloved of the Palace." From this point forward, the focus of the remaining twenty pages of the comic book is on the romantic sentiments of love-in-union and love-in-separation that the couple experiences over the years.

Shah Jahan and Mumtaz Mahal must endure many lengthy separations from one another during various military campaigns. The comic book highlights these separations and the ensuing happy reunions: Shah Jahan defeats Rana Amar Singh in Mewar and then rushes home to his wife and newborn daughter; Shah Jahan engages the Deccani rulers in battle and then quickly returns to celebrate his victory; he holds a council of war in Burhanpur and then returns for his wife's political advice. Although Shah Jahan's creative strategies in battle and his compassion in dealing with his enemies are mentioned, the overarching theme of this

Figure 27. *Shah Jahan,* no. 204 [reprint no. 642] (Bombay: India Book House Pvt. Ltd., 1979 [1999]), cover. From *Amar Chitra Katha,* with the permission of the publishers ACK Media, India.

issue is the great love that exists between Shah Jahan and his wife, who is portrayed as his soul mate and his most loyal political advisor. When Shah Jahan is eventually estranged from his father, Emperor Jahangir, the narrative again shifts to focus on the romantic couple: Shah Jahan's wife and children bravely decide to accompany him as he flees the imperial forces. Mumtaz Mahal justifies this decision to her husband, saying, "As long as we are together, nothing matters" (24). Like true romantics, Shah Jahan and Mumtaz Mahal would risk everything to forego any further periods of separation from one another.

Not long after Shah Jahan is finally crowned emperor, however, the romance takes a tragic turn as Mumtaz Mahal gives birth to her fourteenth child. On the penultimate page of the comic book, Mumtaz Mahal lies dying, and she asks Shah Jahan to build her a tomb "such as the world has never before seen" (30). Shah Jahan promises to do so. The comic book then ends with a full-page panel of Shah Jahan looking out the window at the Taj Mahal, the exquisite mausoleum that he built for his beloved wife (plate 6). In this panel he is a lonely, decrepit man with gray hair and white mourning attire. Here Shah Jahan lies dying, taking his last glimpse of the Taj Mahal. Described in the narrative text as "the world's greatest monument to true love" (31), the Taj Mahal is here made the supreme symbol of the bond of love between man and woman.

By framing Shah Jahan's story with this scene—which is featured as both the cover image and the final panel—Shah Jahan is cast in the role of a great lover in this comic book. His martial prowess, his extensive architectural programs, and his generous patronage of the arts are all overshadowed by the story of his undying love for his wife, Mumtaz Mahal. Today, in Hindi films like *Taj Mahal: A Monument of Love* (dir. Robin Khosla, 2003) and *Taj Mahal: An Eternal Love Story* (dir. Akbar Khan, 2005), this romantic narrative lives on. How did a tomb ever come to have such a romantic connotation? Under what circumstances was this one-dimensional romantic image of the Taj—and of its creator—constructed? Certainly the Taj Mahal could have other meanings, in addition to being a monument to true love: it could also signify Shah Jahan's might and wealth as an emperor; it could be a symbolic image of the Islamic concept of paradise (Leoshko 1989) or a visual representation of the Throne of God on Judgment Day (Begley 1979). Significantly, however, as Pratapaditya Pal and other scholars have cogently argued, the trope of the romance of the Taj Mahal is "essentially a creation of Western enthusiasm" (Pal et al. 1989, 194). To understand this portrayal of Shah Jahan as a romantic hero on the cover and within this comic book, we must examine the significance of this emperor and his monument in the context of colonial modernity.

During the seventeenth century, western travelers to India wrote about their dealings with the Mughal rulers, sparking the curiosity of their readers back home. Two such travelers to India during Shah Jahan's lifetime were Jean-Baptiste Tavernier and Francois Bernier, both from France. Tavernier, a jeweler, visited Agra in 1641 and wrote about the "most splendid" tomb then being constructed by Shah Jahan (1925, 1:90–91). Bernier, a physician, stayed in India for over a decade. In his memoir, *Travels in the Mogul Empire AD 1656–1668*, he wrote about the Taj Mahal, which had been completed by the time of his arrival, stating that Shah Jahan had erected it in memory of his wife, "that extraordinary and celebrated beauty, of whom her husband was so enamoured that it is said he was constant to her during life, and at her death was so affected as nearly to follow her to the grave" (Pal et al. 1989, 194). Aside from Shah Jahan's undying love for his wife, however, what most intrigued Bernier was the "war of succession" that Shah Jahan's four sons waged for the imperial throne during his lifetime. Bernier wrote about this struggle in his *Histoire de la Dernière Revolution des etats du Grand Mogul,* published in 1670. This book was translated into English the next year and served as the inspiration for John Dryden's popular play *Aurang-Zebe* (1675), which was repeatedly reprinted and staged even into the nineteenth century. The beginning of the play, which is taken directly from Bernier's *History,* sets the stage for this war of succession as it was then recounted:

> I found also at my arrival that this king of the world, Shah Jahan, of above seventy years of age, had four sons and two daughters; that some years since he had made these four sons vice-kings or governors of four of his most considerable provinces or kingdoms; that it was almost a year that he was fallen into a great sickness, whence it was believed he would never recover: which had occasioned a great division among these four brothers (all laying claim to the empire), and had kindled among them a war which lasted five years. (Link 1971, xv)

These two aspects of Shah Jahan's life—his undying love for his wife, as embodied in the mausoleum he built for her, and the war of succession waged by Aurangzeb and his three other living sons during his lifetime— became the focus of his legend throughout the colonial period, inspiring both texts and images, and eventually reducing the emperor to a romantic and tragic figure. Whereas the Mughals themselves were initially the primary focus of authors and artists, the Taj Mahal gradually received more attention as the British consolidated their power in India from the end of the eighteenth century and throughout the nineteenth century. This is because India became more accessible to western travelers—who began to think of the Taj as one of India's greatest attractions—as the British Raj was ascendant (Pal et al. 1989, 199) and because the surveys and repairs of the Taj that were undertaken by the British from the early nineteenth century also commanded greater attention for the monument (Leoshko 1989, 53 and 86).

This way of thinking about the Taj as a monument to love (not as a symbol of imperial Mughal grandeur or as a religious edifice) and about Shah Jahan as a romantic and tragic figure (not as a powerful ruler or devout Muslim) continued to develop as the British were establishing themselves as the new seat of power in the region. An essay by Sir William Wilson Hunter, "The Ruin of Aurangzeb; or, The History of a Reaction," first published in 1887, illustrates this point. Hunter describes Shah Jahan as an ill and aged figure as a prelude to his discussion of the war of succession: "[T]he Emperor, now sixty-seven years of age, lay stricken with a terrible disease. The poor old palace-builder well knew the two essential conditions for retaining the Mughal throne—namely, to be perfectly pitiless to his kindred and to be in perfect health himself" (1903, 83). Hunter then gives a rather favorable account of Aurangzeb's role in the war of succession, arguing that Aurangzeb did not initially aspire to the throne but was instead "forced by his eldest brother's intrigues to assume the defensive" (83–84). However, Hunter's favorable description of Aurangzeb ends there. He next states that after the war of succession, "[h]aving thus disposed of his three brothers, Aurangzeb got rid of their sons by slow poisoning with laudanum, and shut up his aged father in his palace till he died. Then was let loose on India that tremendously destructive force, a puritan Muhammadan monarch. In 1658 . . . Aurangzeb, at the age of forty, seated himself on the throne of the Mughals. The narrative of his long reign of half a century is the history of a great reaction against the religious compromises of his predecessors, and against their policy of conciliation towards the native races" (85). According to Hunter, a "bitter war of religion" between the native Hindus and the ruling Muslims was the result of Aurangzeb's reign, and it was this war of religion that caused the downfall of the Mughal Empire. Hunter sees this downfall as an object lesson for the British, and concludes his essay with the following warning: "It was by the alienation of the native races that the Mughal Empire perished; it is by the incorporation of those races into a loyal and a united people that the British rule will endure" (96).

Earlier writings about Mughal dynastic figures, including Dryden's play *Aurang-Zebe*, focused on the war of succession and thus portrayed Shah Jahan as the aged king whose advanced years and illness provided the occasion for the war. Hunter's essay and others like it by nineteenth-century colonial figures went further, seeking to differentiate between the current and the previous regimes, and thereby to demonstrate the lasting vitality of the current colonial regime. In such works Shah Jahan was remembered as the "poor old palace builder" who had been locked up in the Agra Fort by his own son, Aurangzeb, and characterized as an impotent old man whose greatest achievement was his monument to love, the Taj Mahal.

The cover and last panel of the *Shah Jahan* comic book are part of this colonial legacy, for they call to mind not only the tragic loss of Shah Jahan's wife but also his ultimate dethronement by his son. The text of the comic book nowhere mentions that Aurangzeb had imprisoned his father in the Agra Fort—an interesting oversight that was perhaps intentionally committed so as to gloss over the unpleasantness of the war of succession. However, the reader who is familiar with this part of Shah Jahan's legend will immediately discern that Shah Jahan is here shown in the Jasmine Tower of the Agra Fort, where he spent the final years of his life under lock and key, a prisoner of Aurangzeb. The loss that Shah Jahan mourns here, then, is not just that of his beloved wife but of his own former might and vitality as emperor as well. Here too the exalted and powerful Shah Jahan—the "King of the World" who created the Taj Mahal in Agra and also the new capital city Shahjahanabad in Delhi as an expression of his political might and majesty—is reduced to a pathetic old man.

Souren Roy is the freelance artist who illustrated the *Shah Jahan* comic book, and P. G. Sircar created the cover image. According to Roy, the covers are usually done in-house in the Bombay studio:

> They take the cover from one of the panels inside. It works like this: They look at the whole issue, at all of the panels that I have created. Then they pick one panel and design the cover based on it. It should feature the hero of the comic book, and it should show him in a way that reveals something about him and about the story. For example, if the story is about a historical king who won an important battle, then the cover should show that king, should depict something about that battle, and should depict the king's bravery in battle.

Although Shah Jahan did experience several military victories, the cover does not show him riding bravely into battle like Shivaji or Rana Pratap. Instead, the panel that was chosen for the *Shah Jahan* cover as the image that most reveals something about Shah Jahan and his story is the final image of the comic book, in which the old man lies in his prison bed staring at the Taj Mahal. It is the romantic sentiment, rather than the heroic, therefore, that should be stirred up in the reader when he or she first looks at this comic book.

When asked about the visual references used while working on *Shah Jahan*, Roy replied that he had visited the Taj Mahal and the Agra Fort and taken several photographs.

> You need very good art training in perspective. Otherwise you don't know what snapshots to take, what angles to look from. And for the Mughals there are lots of portraits, lots of miniature books, lots of paintings from that time and later. Some drawings I collected in the miniature style—they are mainly profiles. The artist must have references. He must collect as many as possible in order to be accurate, correct. So I looked at the profiles, and then from the profile image I would imagine the full face of Shah Jahan, Akbar, others. You know, live models are difficult to get. And anyway, how can you get a live model of Aurangzeb? The references are also important for style of dress and other details. And I look at photos of the landscape, the buildings—like the Agra Fort. Sometimes Mr. Pai sends us Xeroxes, sometimes I go myself and take snapshots. With lots of authentic references, you get confidence in what you are doing, in doing it the right way.

The paintings of Shah Jahan that were done by the artists of the Bengal School of Art in the early twentieth century were among the many "paintings from that time and later" that Souren Roy examined while seeking visual references for *Shah Jahan*. As a Bengali who was trained at the Government School of Art in Calcutta, the same school with which many of the Bengal School artists had been affiliated, Roy was familiar with their work and stated that he has a number of reprints of the works of Abanindranath Tagore and other artists in his personal collection.

Abanindranath Tagore (1871–1951) was the most esteemed artist of the Bengal School of Art, a group of artists that in many ways rivaled artist Raja Ravi Varma and promoted a new aesthetic of Indianness in the early twentieth century. Abanindranath was "discovered" by E. B. Havell, principal of the Government School of Art in Calcutta (1896–1905), who applauded his adoption of a Mughal style of painting and his rejection of the standards of western academic art (Guha-Thakurta 1992, 242).[2] In the early phase of his career, Abanindranath completed three paintings on the subject of Shah Jahan and the Taj Mahal. Of the three, *The Passing of Shah Jahan* (1902) earned him the most recognition and quickly came to be considered a masterpiece of Indian art. Tapati Guha-Thakurta has discussed this phase of Abanindranath Tagore's career in detail, noting that in defining himself as a modern Indian artist, Abanindranath sought to infuse the classical Indian poetic element of *bhāva,* or emotion, into the Mughal miniature style of painting. With particular reference to *The Passing of Shah Jahan* as the epitome of this new style, Guha-Thakurta writes:

> The architectural façade which frames the picture is most obviously Mughal in its painstaking replication of the rich inlay-work decoration on marble and the intricate railing patterns. The attention is, however, focused on the two small figures of the dying emperor and his daughter at his feet; and, then, drawn to the tiny image of the Taj Mahal in the distance, through the twist in the emperor's head and the direction of his gaze. The centrality of these images is intended, in turn, to convey the central theme of death and eternal separation, and the symbolism of the transitoriness of life *vis-à-vis* the immortality of art. (1992, 243)

The emphasis on bhāva in this painting was further emphasized by references to the legend of Shah Jahan in art circles. These references attempted to "explain" the painting through the romantic narrative that had become standard, focusing on the loss of Shah Jahan's beloved wife and his imprisonment within the Agra Fort. Sister Nivedita wrote one such narrative, published in the *Modern Review* in 1907, in which she articulated the sadness and the joy of Shah Jahan's final night, as illustrated by Abanindranath. Discussing first the sadness, Nivedita wrote:

> To joyous courtship succeeds long widowhood. On brilliant empire supervenes the seven-years' imprisonment. He, before whom the whole world bowed, is thankful and proud to win at last the long-sweet faith and service of a single-daughter prison-cell! . . . What were the memories and what the hopes that thronged the shadows in which Shah Jahan spent those last long years? (1961 [1907])

Nivedita next described those very memories that she imagines must have sustained Shah Jahan through his final night, emphasizing not eternal separation, as Guha-Thakurta sees it, but the joy of eternal reunion in the afterlife that would soon be his:

Ponder, beyond the bend, like some ethereal white-veiled presence, stands the Taj—*her* taj, her crown, the crown he wrought her. But to-night it is more than her crown. To-night, it is herself. To-night she is there, in all her old-time majesty and sweetness, yet with an added holiness withal. To-night, beyond the gentle lapping of the waters, every line of stately form speaks tenderness and peace and all-enfolding holiness, waiting for that pilgrim—with weary feet, bent back, and head so bowed, alas!—who comes, leaving behind alike palace and prison, battlefield and cell of prayer, to land on the quiet shore of the yonder side of death. (1961 [1907])

Other explanatory narratives of this painting followed. One notable one that focused on Shah Jahan's "dying scene" was written by the historian Jadunath Sarkar and published in the *Modern Review* in 1915:

Finally, while the sacred verses were being solemnly intoned, amidst the wail of the women and the sobs of his attendants, Shah Jahan, retaining full consciousness to the last and gazing on the resting-place of his beloved and long-lost Mumtaz Mahal, repeated the Muslim confession of faith. . . . A moment later he sank peacefully into his eternal rest. It was a quarter past seven in the evening. The body lay in the octagonal tower (Musammam Burj), where life had departed, in full view of the Taj Mahal, where he wished his mortal remains to mingle with those of his queen. (1915, 366)

Prior to Abanindranath Tagore's painting, Shah Jahan's final days had not been visualized. Mughal-era artists had painted many portraits of Shah Jahan, which were sketched by later artists, both Indian and European, and in the late eighteenth century western artists began to depict the Taj Mahal and its "sublime" qualities. But neither the portraits nor the landscapes contained narrative elements or attempted to convey substantial emotion.[3] Abanindranath's painting depicting the pathos of Shah Jahan's final days imprisoned in the Jasmine Tower and his last glimpse of the Taj Mahal, therefore, was a new innovation in Indian painting, one that corresponded to the increasing attention that the romantic narrative of the Taj Mahal and its creator were receiving in British India. *The Passing of Shah Jahan* received several awards: a silver medal at the Delhi Durbar Exhibition of Indian Arts and Crafts (1902–1903), where it was first exhibited, and a gold medal at the Congress Industrial Exhibition (1903). After Abanindranath received such recognition for this painting, other artists—both Indian and western—were quick to take up the same theme.

Abdur Rahman Chughtai (1897?–1975) created several Taj-themed paintings in his early career. Chughtai was loosely affiliated with Abanindranath and was influenced by the Bengal School of Art, but he was critical of the school's use of Muslim themes, for he felt that "the Bengali Movement in essence became a Hindu revival movement" (Chughtai 1987, 11). As a Muslim who traced his lineage to the architect who is said to have designed the Taj Mahal, Chughtai felt that he was the right artist to depict the great monuments of the Mughals and the legends surrounding them—in essence, to lay the foundation for a "revival of Muslim painting" (11).[4] Two of Chughtai's most acclaimed paintings are *Shah Jahan Looking at the Taj* (figure 28) and *Jahanara and the Taj* (ca. 1922), paintings that are clearly indebted to Abanindranath's earlier rendering of Shah's Jahan's final days. Like Abanindranath, Chughtai also studied Mughal miniature painting, and thus his paintings similarly evidence the "meticulous care with which he has drawn out the architectural details of the columns and their arches in the background" (Siraj-ud-din 1970). Chughtai's paintings also share a similar perspective, that of the expanse of water between the Agra Fort and the Taj Mahal as it is seen from within the Jasmine Tower. In *Shah Jahan Looking at the Taj,* as in Abanindranath's *The Passing of Shah Jahan,* this expanse of water serves to heighten the emotion of Shah Jahan's final days. Here the aged emperor stands, his back bowed under the unbearable weight of his final years, peering across the dark water at the Taj, presumably taking his last glimpse of it. Collapsed at the bedside is his daughter, Jahanara, waiting with the Holy Quran at the ready, perhaps in preparation for her father's death rites. The painting *Jahanara and the Taj* captures a later moment, shortly after Shah Jahan's death. Here it is Jahanara who stares out at the Taj Mahal across the water, while kneeling at her father's now empty bed. As in Chughtai's first painting, here too emotion is central to the image. Jahanara's loss is palpable: both of her parents will now be reunited in the great tomb across the water, but her father's death leaves her alone in the prison that is the Jasmine Tower and marks the end of a great era.

In many ways the cover and final panel of the *Shah Jahan* comic book make reference to these earlier images by Abanindranath Tagore and A. R. Chughtai: the skilled use of architectural details; the perspective, which positions the bed frame within the Jasmine Tower so that the body of water between the Agra Fort and the Taj Mahal is highlighted; and the emphasis on bhāva. Discussing Chughtai's paintings, James Cousins wrote that Chughtai retained the "mood and posture of the Persian tradition," but that his lines, his folds of drapery, and his decorative architectural backgrounds all "call the imagination away from the tyranny of the actual into free citizenship of the realm of romance" (1970). Like Abanindranath and Chughtai, Souren Roy studied Mughal portraits of Shah Jahan to develop his own profile of the emperor for this final image, and similarly acquainted himself with the relevant architectural details. Yet the artist's intent here as well was clearly to move beyond Mughal portraiture in order to convey some of the romantic sentiment of Shah Jahan's legend.

Thus in the final panel of the comic book, text and image together conclude on an overtly romantic note. Shah Jahan is shown lying on his prison bed in the Jasmine Tower, taking his last glimpse of the Taj Mahal. The text at the bottom of this panel tells us that "Shah Jahan died in 1666 at

Figure 28. *Shah Jahan Looking at the Taj,* painting by A. R. Chughtai. Courtesy of Osian's Connoisseurs of Art Ltd., Mumbai.

the age of seventy-four. He was buried beside his beloved Mumtaz Mahal" (31). It is a fitting end to the romantic legend of Shah Jahan, an end that reunites emperor and empress for all eternity after their lengthy separation. But it is also an end that leaves the reader with a very unheroic memory of Shah Jahan as a feeble, lovesick old man who was imprisoned by his own son. When the final panel of *Shah Jahan* is compared with the final panel of the *Shivaji* comic, the contrast is stark: Through the technique of narrative closure, Shivaji is immortalized as a powerful warrior-king, seated gloriously on his golden throne before his bowing courtiers, while Shah Jahan is immortalized as a pathetic has-been, dreaming of former days of glory while he lies dying.

Akbar the Accommodating and Aurangzeb the Puritan

The cover of the *Akbar* comic book features the Mughal emperor Akbar (r. 1556–1605) on horseback, commanding his armies to attack the Rajput stronghold of Chittor (figure 29). This was a decisive battle against the Rajput king Udai Singh that Akbar won in 1567, a victory that was quite important because in the wake of it many Rajput leaders submitted to Akbar's suzerainty. This cover is particularly interesting because it is an ideal example of Souren Roy's statement, previously cited, on the process of choosing the cover image: "if the story is about a historical king who won an important battle, then the cover should show that king, should depict something about that battle, and should depict the king's bravery in battle." We can tell from the cover alone, then, that one focus of the *Akbar* issue is this emperor's martial abilities—unlike the *Shah Jahan* issue.

The comic book begins with an episode that occurred when Akbar was just thirteen years old and had been newly crowned emperor after the sudden death of his father, Humayun (r. 1530–56). Seeking to take advantage of Akbar's youth and inexperience, an opposing chief named Hemu invaded Agra and then Delhi while Akbar was away in the Punjab. Guided by his chief minister, Bairam Khan, Akbar began to march back to Delhi to reclaim the city, while Hemu led his troops toward Akbar to engage him in battle. After an arrow struck Hemu in the eye, Hemu's men fled the battlefield, resulting in a victory for the Mughal forces in this battle, known as the Second Battle of Panipat (figure 30). In the last panel on page 7, the comic book informs the reader that "poor Hemu's headless body was displayed on a gibbet" in Delhi, in keeping with the "cruel practice in those days."

When asked about the making of the *Akbar* comic, Anant Pai stated that it was a good issue because it adhered to the rules of comic book storytelling in featuring Akbar as a hero from beginning to end, and he referred specifically to this panel:

> The story should have an element of surprise. The reader should constantly ask, "What will happen next?" and he shouldn't be able to predict the end. There must be a climax and then the victory of good over evil. Or, if evil wins, then the good one must not succumb. The good one may die, but he won't accept defeat. And after this climax the story should end quickly. Take the example of Akbar. After the Battle of Panipat, Hemu was defeated. Akbar was very young, just thirteen years old, and he ordered Hemu's headless body to be hung at the gate for all to see. This is disturbing, but it is a historical fact. It can't be avoided. Yet it need not be emphasized. So I chose to have this shown in long shot, not in close-up. That way, you see, Akbar stays a hero. He must be the hero of this issue from beginning to end.

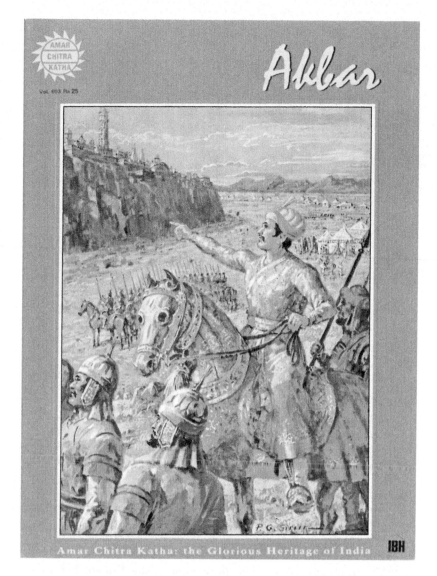

Figure 29. *Akbar,* no. 200 [reprint no. 603] (Bombay: India Book House Pvt. Ltd., 1979 [2000]), cover. From *Amar Chitra Katha,* with the permission of the publishers ACK Media, India.

But creating *Akbar* and writing this Mughal emperor as a comic book hero was not as simple as this makes it sound; this particular panel featuring Hemu's death was in fact the subject of significant controversy during the production process. According to Pai, the late Toni Patel, author of the *Akbar* script, insisted that a panel be included that depicted Hemu's headless body. When Pai vetoed this panel because of its violent content, Patel "was adamant that it be included," since it was "true, factual." So a compromise was ultimately reached: the hanging headless body would be shown, but only from a long shot and in shadows in the background—as it appears in the *Akbar* issue to this day. It is also noteworthy that in the panels on this page of the comic book Akbar does not give the command to behead Hemu and then display his body; in fact, on this page Akbar is an insignificant figure, appearing only in the middle of the second panel as

Figure 30. *Akbar,* no. 200 [reprint no. 603] (Bombay: India Book House Pvt. Ltd., 1979 [2000]), 7. From *Amar Chitra Katha,* with the permission of the publishers ACK Media, India.

a small shadow of his minister, Bairam Khan. When asked why he didn't want to depict this scene, Pai emphasized the need to minimize violent images in children's books:

> This is the motto that I work under: "One must tell the truth, one must tell what is pleasant; but don't tell what is unpleasant just because it is true." In Sanskrit this is "satyam bruyāt priyam bruyāt mā bruyāt satyam apriyam." You see, Indians have a generally good view of Akbar. He was a good king, very accommodating. Not in his youth, but he changed. You know, we promote integration through *Amar Chitra Katha.* So why show bad things about Akbar? Why not show that he was a good king? He had Muslim poets in his court who were devotees of Ram and Krishna. Aurangzeb, on the other hand, was not good. He killed his brothers and their children, too. On his father's—Shah Jahan's—birthday, he gave him the gift of Dara Shukoh's head! So Aurangzeb has not been featured.

These statements provide great insight into how the Mughals are represented in this comic book series and the internal debates that erupted around such representations during the production process. For Anant Pai, the central characters of the comics must be heroes, and that means that any violent actions or other repugnances they have committed must be minimized. To justify this editorial policy, Pai used the same Sanskrit maxim previously cited to justify the omission of goddess Kali drinking blood: "satyam bruyāt priyam bruyāt mā bruyāt satyam apriyam." For Toni Patel, however, reporting the facts—the "truth"—about the central characters' lives and portraying them accurately was more important than casting those characters in a pleasant light. But what is perhaps most telling is that this disagreement arose in the making of the historical comic books over the *Akbar* issue and not over any of the earlier issues about historical Hindu kings.

Producer No. 1 stated that all of the "gray episodes" of Shivaji's life were intentionally left out of the *Shivaji* issue in order to better portray this

Hindu king as a hero. This decision drew some external criticism, but it did not cause any internal disagreements among the producers of the comic books. Nor did the depiction of the beheading of Afzal Khan in *Shivaji* cause Anant Pai to invoke his policy regarding the depiction of violence (refer to figure 24). When asked further about how the "gray episodes" of historical characters' lives are overlooked, Producer No. 1 also cited the *Akbar* issue as the touchstone of this policy of telling the "pleasant truth," although his memory of the exact panel that was under debate is slightly different:

> When Toni Patel wrote the *Akbar* issue, she wanted to show how Akbar had his throne placed upon a platform that was built of decapitated human heads, you know, from battle. Human heads. Mr. Pai wouldn't allow this. But Toni Patel said she wanted to show character development, how Akbar was this way when he was young, but how when he was older he was the creator of the Din-i-Ilahi, and was so tolerant, so accommodating. So in the end there was a compromise reached, with an image that was not very graphic, and the character development remained. So you cannot have violence, cannot have sexuality, because the comics are for children.

What is particularly noteworthy about all of these insights into the production of the *Akbar* issue is the repeated emphasis on how "accommodating" and "tolerant" Akbar was. Despite the cover image, it would seem that Emperor Akbar is a hero not because of his great military victories—in fact, some of his military actions such as the beheading of Hemu are intentionally minimized—but because of his policy of accommodation or, in Anant Pai's words, because "he spread the word that all religions are equal."

As Akbar grows up, his accommodating qualities are increasingly stressed in the comic book. When he marries a Rajput Hindu princess, we are told that although "one reason for this alliance was to gain Hindu support, it was also an expression of the doctrine of religious tolerance, which Akbar increasingly practised" (20). The next several panels detail this doctrine of religious tolerance, which is said to be born of Akbar's "secular beliefs" (figure 31): Akbar appoints Hindu officers to command his military, he abolishes the *jizya* tax (the poll tax levied on non-Muslim subjects), and he allows Hindu festivals to be celebrated at his court. In these panels Akbar is counterposed with the orthodox Muslim mullahs, the "zealots" who "think there is only one path to heaven" and who "hated the enlightened policies of their ruler" (21). Like Aurangzeb in the *Shivaji* issue, here too orthodox Muslims are presented as the villains, drawn in the bottom panel with full beards, skullcaps, and deep scowls as they stand plotting together and proclaiming, "Akbar has given up the true religion!" and "He takes the advice of infidels!" On the other hand, Akbar's opponents in battle, the Rajput Hindus, are barely featured as Akbar and his men attempt to take the Chittor fort, tunneling into it in several panels and lobbing rocks at it in others. Only one close-up of the Rajput commander Jaimal is shown, where he is featured as a handsome, broad-shouldered soldier clad in armor who is prepared to die nobly defending the fort (28).

After his victory at Chittor, Akbar further consolidates his empire and is thus able to devote more time to spiritual matters. We are told that Akbar "invited people of all religions to hold discussions in his palace" but that he was dissatisfied with the sectarian bickering that resulted (31–32). Therefore, Akbar created his own spiritual path, Din-i-Ilahi (Divine Faith), a synthesis of religious beliefs from Islam, Hinduism, and other religions. The comic book ends with a reference to this new religion and comments that when Akbar died at the age of sixty-three, "he bequeathed to the future his ideal of a unified country of diverse religions and cultures" (32). This final panel of the *Akbar* issue features a noble bust of him in front of the Panch Mahal (Palace of Five Stories) at Fatehpur Sikri, the capital city built by Akbar in a style that combined both Islamic (Persian) and Hindu architectural elements.[5] It is a fitting memorial to an emperor who has been remembered as an accommodating leader and as a proponent of secular beliefs.

In this comic book, secular beliefs are paired with the doctrine of religious tolerance. As Anant Pai puts it, "Secularism means that you can't bring religion into politics." But in discussing his definition of secularism, he explains that religion and governance need not be strictly separated into public and private realms; rather, the government should allow for multiple religious beliefs to publicly exist side by side: "A Hindu can be secular if he respects Hinduism and other religions, too." Shivaji, he maintains, was a secular king because, although a devout Hindu, he had men of many religions and castes in his court and at his side in battle. Pai elaborated that Akbar was the only secular Muslim ruler in India:

> Akbar was secular, because there were Hindus at his court, like Birbal. And there were many Muslims in his court who respected and even worshipped Krishna. They composed devotional poetry to Krishna! Only Akbar was this way, though, not the other Mughals.

If Akbar is held up as a heroic exemplar of secular values here, then the Mughal emperor Aurangzeb (r. 1658–1707) is held up as the opposite—a long-bearded orthodox puritan, the ultimate villain. Pai contrasted Akbar with Aurangzeb, describing the former as "good" and thus deserving of a comic book issue that portrays him as a hero, and the latter as "not good" and thus not deserving of heroic portrayal. This is why Aurangzeb, the last of the Great Mughals, is the only one who has not had an *ACK* comic book title created in his name. Instead, Aurangzeb has had to settle for second billing, sharing a title with his eldest brother, Dara Shukoh (1615–59).

Figure 31. *Akbar*, no. 200 [reprint no. 603] (Bombay: India Book House Pvt. Ltd., 1979 [2000]), 21. From *Amar Chitra Katha*, with the permission of the publishers ACK Media, India.

The cover of the *Dara Shukoh and Aurangzeb* issue (no. 232, 1981) makes it clear that Aurangzeb is not the hero of this comic book, despite the fact that he was the brother who ultimately became emperor. Dara Shukoh takes center stage, riding his horse and waving to the assembled crowd. Aurangzeb is nowhere to be seen. Early in this issue the differing viewpoints of the two brothers are made clear: Dara Shukoh, eldest and favorite son of Shah Jahan, is described as "an ardent follower of the liberal Muslim saint, Mian Mir," whose doctrine he believes can unify Hindus and Muslims. Aurangzeb, on the other hand, feels that the one sure way to unify the people of India is through forced conversion, for in his opinion "there should be one state, one religion" (6). Throughout this comic the vast differences between the two brothers continue to be highlighted. While

Dara Shukoh spends his time translating the Hindu *Upaniṣad* scriptures into Persian, Aurangzeb is shown plotting Dara's downfall (15). When their father, Shah Jahan, becomes ill, Aurangzeb recognizes this as the opportunity he has been waiting for, and the ensuing war of succession occupies the second half of the comic book. Ultimately Aurangzeb emerged victorious from this war, but in this retelling of events the reader's sympathy is entirely with Dara, who fights bravely until the bitter end—as the hero should, according to the comic book format—while Aurangzeb, having just ordered his henchmen to murder Dara, smirks and says to himself, "Father will now see which of us is the greater person" (31). There is little room for doubt that the greater person of the two is Dara Shukoh, described in the introduction as "an idealist, a scholar, and a philosopher" whose "mission in life was to promote harmony among Hindus and Muslims."

In *Dara Shukoh and Aurangzeb,* the contrast drawn between the two brothers leaves the reader with the overall impression that the syncretistic, heterodox brother is the good one—the hero—while the *sharia*-oriented, orthodox brother is the bad one—the villain. The tragedy of this issue, of course, is that it is the villain, Aurangzeb, who emerges victorious and lives to enforce his puritanical, anti-Hindu reign upon the people of India. This contrast between the good Muslim and the bad Muslim is indebted to colonial historiography. While Shah Jahan came to be understood as a romantic and tragic figure when the British were consolidating their power in the colonial period, Dara Shukoh and Aurangzeb came to embody the tension between two opposing views of Islam, the heterodox and the orthodox. Colonial historians frequently described Dara Shukoh as the heir to his great-grandfather Akbar's syncretistic ideals, for as a Sufi scholar he sought to find a common denominator between Islam and Hinduism, as in his book *Majma al-bahrain* (*The Confluence of Two Oceans*). Aurangzeb, on the other hand, was usually characterized as having a stern, orthodox attitude—a "zealot" like those who had earlier challenged Akbar and whose *sharia*-oriented orthodoxy was blamed for the fall of the Mughal Empire. Hence Sir William Wilson Hunter described Aurangzeb as a "puritan Muhammadan monarch" in his overt attempt to distinguish British rule from Mughal despotism (Hunter 1903, 85).

As this characterization of Aurangzeb proliferated in the late nineteenth and early twentieth centuries, visual renderings of Aurangzeb's cruelty were created. Abanindranath Tagore, for instance, painted *Aurangzeb Examining the Head of Dara* in the early 1900s. Discussing this painting in some detail in *The Studio,* E. B. Havell wrote: "The story is told with great dramatic feeling. The artist makes us feel the curiously complicated character of Aurangzib; his cruelty, suspiciousness, and hypocrisy, combined with religious fanaticism and inflexibility of purpose" (1908, 115). Significantly, Anant Pai's earlier comment, that Aurangzeb has not been featured as a hero in this comic book series because he was so cruel as to give his father, Shah Jahan, "the gift of Dara Shukoh's head," is reminiscent of this emotional reading of Abanindranath's painting.

This characterization of Aurangzeb as a puritan persists in both western and Indian scholarship in the postcolonial period. For instance, the esteemed scholar of Islam in South Asia, Annemarie Schimmel, has explicitly and causally connected the partition of the Indian subcontinent in 1947, which resulted in the creation of Pakistan as an independent Muslim nation, with the religio-political tensions of the seventeenth century: "The tension inherent in the many-sided and colourful Indian Islam seems to be expressed best in the two sons of Shahjahan and Mumtaz Mahal . . . : Dara Shikoh the mystic and Aurangzeb the practical, orthodox minded ruler reflect those trends, which were to result in the partition of the Sub-continent in 1947" (1980, 2). Most emblematic of Aurangzeb's zealous behavior in many histories of Islam in South Asia, and in the *Dara Shukoh and Aurangzeb* comic book, is his effort to forcibly convert Hindus and other non-Muslims to Islam in his pursuit of one state with one religion. Although the belief that the majority of Indian Muslims were forcibly converted to Islam by foreign Muslim rulers—known as the "religion by the sword" theory—has been debunked by many scholars over the past several decades, the idea lives on in the popular reprints of many of these comic book issues, as in other popular media.[6]

Guru Tegh Bahadur (no. 114, 1976) provides another example wherein the issue of forced conversion is raised. This issue is a hagiography of the ninth Sikh guru, Tegh Bahadur (1621–75), who is approached by some Kashmiri Hindus. Their problem, we are told, is "the religious intolerance of the Mughal emperor, Aurangzeb" (24). One man explains, "Hindus in Kashmir are being severely repressed by Aurangzeb and their women-folk are being kidnapped," while a second man pleads with the guru for help, saying, "All Hindus are being forcibly converted to Islam" (24). Guru Tegh Bahadur writes to Aurangzeb with a challenge: If Aurangzeb can convert the guru to Islam, then the Kashmiri Hindus will also convert. But if he fails, then Aurangzeb must "give up his perverted policy of forcible conversion" (25). Aurangzeb is intrigued, in part because Guru Tegh Bahadur—a Sikh—is speaking on behalf of a group of Hindus, so he has the guru brought before him. When Aurangzeb asks the guru whether he will embrace Islam, he refuses, and Aurangzeb throws him in jail. There the emperor's men attempt—with the threat of force—to persuade the guru to convert. But he responds with a very modern-sounding statement about the secular nature of India: "India is a land of many races, religions, and cultures. It is wrong to impose one's religion on those who believe differently" (26).

Ultimately, Aurangzeb is unable to persuade the guru to convert to Islam, so he orders his beheading (figure 32). In this full-page panel, Guru

Tegh Bahadur is seated in the center of the image, where he is shown serenely awaiting his death with his hands folded in prayer and a tranquil look on his face. One stern-looking, long-bearded Muslim in fine Mughal robes and a skullcap stands to the guru's right, his finger pointed at him in a lecturing gesture—presumably haranguing him with a final offer to convert to Islam and thereby save his life. On the guru's left, a Muslim henchman approaches with a large sword, his face eager with anticipation (28). Here no dialogue balloons are necessary to identify the characters, for the reader is able to discern through the image alone who is righteous and who is not, who is heroic and who is villainous.[7]

In discussing the *Guru Tegh Bahadur* issue and the relationship between Sikhs, Hindus, and Muslims in India, Anant Pai launched into a discussion of the definition of Hinduism. In his opinion, a Hindu "is one who believes in the indestructibility of the soul—*atma*—and who believes in reincarnation based on karma." He explained that this means that Jainism and Buddhism are both Hindu sects (however, Jain and Buddhist teachings have very different philosophies about the soul, although both accept the doctrine of karma and rebirth). Pai then explained that for this reason Sikhs too are Hindus:

> There was even a tradition among Hindus to give the eldest son to Sikhism, so that he may fight for the country. So Sikhism is also a sect of Hinduism, otherwise why would Hindus do this? Also, when Aurangzeb was forcibly converting people to Islam, the Pandits of Kashmir went to Guru Tegh Bahadur to be saved. Tegh Bahadur wrote to Aurangzeb, saying that he is considered a *pir* among the Hindus of the north, and that if Aurangzeb could convert him, all the Hindus would follow in his footsteps. But if he could not, then Aurangzeb must leave all the Hindus alone. So you see, even Guru Tegh Bahadur considered himself a Hindu.

Rajinder Singh Raj, a Sikh who acts as the honorary consultant of Sikhism for India Book House and who has researched and scripted several *Amar Chitra Katha* issues about Sikh historical figures, had a different opinion on the subject of whether Guru Tegh Bahadur and other Sikhs are Hindus. He oversaw the production of *Guru Tegh Bahadur,* conducting the original research for the story, finding a Sikh artist, Ranjana, to do the illustrations, and checking the script for accuracy. When asked whether he considered Sikhs to be a sect of Hindus, he replied:

> Take the example of the Muslims in India. They were forced converts—90 percent of them are former Hindus, former backward class or tribal people. The Muslim invaders forced people to convert; they took away thousands of girls to other countries. But no one now says that these Muslims today are Hindu. The Sikhs have their own identity, like the Muslims. Their identity began in April 1699, when Guru Gobind gave the Sikhs the five symbols, the five Ks. This is where our rare identity comes from, and no other religion has that. Each symbol carries great significance. Without the *kirpan*—the sword—we would have been slaves. Without that symbol our identity would have vanished long

IT WAS TEGH BAHADUR'S TURN NEXT.

HE WAS BEHEADED. THE MUGHALS REFUSED TO GIVE HIS BODY TO HIS DEVOTEES.

Figure 32. *Guru Tegh Bahadur*, no. 114 [reprint no. 694] (Bombay: India Book House Pvt. Ltd., 1976 [1999]), 28. From *Amar Chitra Katha*, with the permission of the publishers ACK Media, India.

ago. . . . Without the weapon, Brahminic or Islamic culture would have eaten us up. Now we're established as a separate identity and community.

The statements of Anant Pai and Rajinder Singh Raj demonstrate how two very different concepts of religious identity underlie the production of the *Guru Tegh Bahadur* issue. The statement by Anant Pai echoes the definition of the term *Hindu* that has been put forward by proponents of Hindu nationalism, who claim that all religious traditions native to the Indian subcontinent are Hindu, including Jainism, Buddhism, and Sikhism, while imported religious traditions such as Christianity and Islam are not. The statement by Rajinder Singh Raj aligns with the now dominant Sikh position, carefully articulated in the late nineteenth and twentieth centuries, that Sikhs are not Hindus and that Sikhism is a separate world religion and not a sect within Hinduism.[8] The *Guru Tegh Bahadur* comic itself is ambiguous in that it does not clearly state that Guru Tegh Bahadur was a Hindu or that he was not a Hindu, only that Hindus, like Sikhs, venerated him as a guru. The final words of the issue state that the guru "is remembered with love and admiration by people of all creeds" (31). Careful attention has been paid to the wording of this issue to accommodate the multiple intentions of the editor, scriptwriter, and illustrator and to allow for different interpretations on the part of the audience.

Despite the differing opinions about Guru Tegh Bahadur's religious identity that arose in the production process, however, all involved parties agreed that Aurangzeb was the ultimate villain, for he—contrary to Guru Tegh Bahadur's best counsel—did everything in his power to tear down what his great-grandfather Akbar had built up and bequeathed to his heirs: the ideal of a unified, religiously plural country.

The Discourses of Secularism and Conversion

Throughout the *Amar Chitra Katha* comic book series, examples of religiously tolerant rulers abound who appear to conform to Anant Pai's definition of secularism as a form of political authority that allows for religious pluralism. In these issues, this very modern idea of a secular nation-state is cast backwards into the past in an attempt to demonstrate that India is indebted to neither the British nor the Mughals for its secular, democratic heritage, but to Hindu and Sikh heroes like Shivaji and Guru Tegh Bahadur. The introduction to *Ranjit Singh* (no. 49, 1974) describes this king as "one of the most broad-minded and secular rulers India has ever had." In this issue, Ranjit Singh (1780–1839) engages in one military campaign after another and gradually builds a large kingdom. Although Ranjit Singh is shown to be a devout Sikh, the comic reassures us that "Ranjit Singh was not establishing a Sikh kingdom, but a Punjab state in which Sikhs, Hindus, and Muslims enjoyed equal rights" (16). The page following this statement is divided into three panels and shows Ranjit Singh taking part in the Hindu festival of Dassehra in the first one, visiting his Muslim friends on Id in the second, and attending festivities with his Sikh family at the Golden Temple in Amritsar in the third. The following page then tells us that the members of Ranjit Singh's court also "reflected his secular nature" (18).

Similarly, the introduction to *Ahilyabai Holkar* (no. 74, 1975) informs the reader that this "pious Maratha queen," a Hindu, was "very orthodox in her religious beliefs but this never came in the way of her being a very efficient administrator." This comic book shows us many of the Hindu temples that Ahilyabai (r. 1766–95) financed during her reign, but also emphasizes that her rule was just, stable, and conducted with great respect for all religions. If, then, Hindu and Sikh rulers like Ahilyabai Holkar,

Ranjit Singh, and Shivaji can be both orthodox and secular, both pious and pluralistic, why is the case so different with Muslim rulers? Why are the "good" Muslim rulers the syncretistic, even heretical ones, and the "bad" Muslim rulers the orthodox, even puritanical ones? Can't a Muslim ruler also be both orthodox and secular?

Again and again in these comics, the Mughal emperors and other Muslims are cast as the villains in issues featuring Hindu and Sikh heroes, such as *Shivaji* and *Guru Tegh Bahadur*. But even in the comics featuring Muslim heroes, Muslims are still cast as the villains. Thus in *Dara Shukoh and Aurangzeb*, the hero is Dara Shukoh, the heterodox Muslim brother, while the villain is Aurangzeb, the orthodox Muslim brother and eventual Mughal emperor. In *Akbar*, the Mughal emperor Akbar is the heterodox hero, while the villains are the orthodox Muslim mullahs in his court. Even in *Shah Jahan*, where battles—and hence villains—are not the focus of this romantic issue, Aurangzeb is still cast as the unspoken villain, through images that dwell on the years that he kept his father locked up in his palace.

Together, these historical comic books convey the message that while Hindus and Sikhs can be secular rulers who generously and publicly tolerate other religions, Muslim rulers—with the notable exception of the great Mughal emperor Akbar—cannot. They also project a modern communal understanding of identity backwards in time by suggesting that Muslims are either foreigners who have invaded India or else Hindu natives of India who have converted to Islam under the threat of the sword. In this understanding of identity, Hindus and Muslims are seen as two distinct, religiously defined communities, where the Hindus (and Sikhs) are the rightful occupants of India, who must defend their land, community, and faith from the Muslim invaders.

However, court histories and other medieval sources demonstrate that in the premodern period it was not a nationalistic and religious concept of identity that was prevalent in the Indian subcontinent, but a variety of communities identified by locality, language, caste, occupation, and sect—what historian Romila Thapar has termed "segmented" identities (1989, 222).[9] But during the nineteenth century, communal narratives were constructed through the interaction of both colonial and indigenous initiatives that imagined Hindus to be a distinct, religiously defined community that is opposed to a separate Muslim community. For the British rulers, the idea that the Hindu (or "native") and Muslim ("convert" or "foreigner") peoples of India were volatile and fractious served to legitimize their power and intervention in the region. Leading Hindu and Muslim intellectuals, on the other hand, relied on religion in their efforts to forge a place for their respective communities within the burgeoning Indian nationalist movement. Hence Hindu authors like Bharatendu Harischandra

(1850–85) and Bankimchandra Chatterjee (1838–94) made ancient India the classical source of Indian modernity and the Muslim period the source of the decline of the "golden age" in their constructions of a modern Hindu identity. At the same time, Muslim figures like Sir Sayyid Ahmad Khan (1817–98) expounded on the Muslim *qaum,* or community, in India, while poets like Altaf Hussain Hali (1837–1914) and Muhammad Husain Azad (1830–1910) wrote patriotic Urdu verses about a Muslim identity that was both Indian and Islamic, in an effort to define a place for Muslims within Indian nationalism.[10]

Since the end of the colonial period and the partition of India and Pakistan in 1947, the communal conception of identity has only intensified, resulting in ongoing debates within India about secularism and conversion. Article 25(1) of the Indian Constitution, which sets forth the freedom of religion clause, says, "Subject to public order, morality and health and to the other provisions of the Part, all persons are equally entitled to freedom of conscience and the right freely to profess, practise and propagate religion." However, as P. N. Bhagwati, former chief justice of the Supreme Court of India, has pointed out, the word *secular* appeared in neither the original preamble to the Indian Constitution nor in this article guaranteeing freedom of religion (1993, 8). This is because at the time that the Constitution was being framed, there was widespread agreement that India should be a secular state but considerable disagreement about the exact meaning of the term *secular.* In the West, *secular* typically entails the separation of church and state, but during the Constitutional Assembly debates the argument was put forward that secularism in India should instead mean that the state tolerates and respects all religions (see Madan 1987). What is interesting is that in these same debates about religious freedom and the definition of secularism, the subject of conversion was repeatedly raised. The inclusion of the word *propagate* in Article 25 alarmed several members. One argued that in a secular state religion was a private affair and therefore should not be propagated; another argued that including the word *propagate* paved the way for the annihilation of Hinduism because proselytizing religions like Islam and Christianity would have an unfair advantage. Those who favored the inclusion of the word *propagate,* on the other hand, argued that Hindus, especially members of the Arya Samaj, did engage in the practice of conversion and that members of all religious communities should have this right in a secular state.[11]

Even after the ratification of the Constitution, debates over the definition of secularism and the proper place of conversion in a secular state continued. Numerous Lok Sabha bills, state acts, and Supreme Court cases attest to these ongoing debates. For example, the Orissa Freedom of Religion Act (1967) and the Madhya Pradesh Dharma Swatantrya Adhiniyam Act (1968) both invoke the language of religious freedom to place restrictions on the conversion of minors, women, and members of scheduled castes (Neufeldt 1993, 320–24). In 1976, the 42nd Amendment was enacted by Prime Minister Indira Gandhi, which formally added the word *secular* before the words *Democratic Republic* in the Indian Constitution. The next year, in 1977, Article 25 of the Indian Constitution was amended in a Supreme Court ruling that declared that the right to "propagate" religion did not, after all, extend to the right to convert. Thus even as India was increasingly being defined as a secular state, limits were being placed on the practices of proselytizing religions—specifically, Islam and Christianity. Discussing such amendments and acts, Gauri Viswanathan writes: "Ostensibly secular in motivation, the bills to ensure freedom of religious conscience were primarily intended to protect Hinduism against the incursions of other proselytizing religions, revealing the collusion of the state in the preservation of Hinduism" (2001, xiv).

The *Amar Chitra Katha* comic books on the Mughal emperors show the marked influence of colonial thought in the way that figures like Shah Jahan, Akbar, and Aurangzeb are still depicted and discussed today. But the repeated references to the subjects of secularism and conversion in the issues discussed in this chapter must also be understood within the larger context of the legislative, judicial, and public debates about religious freedom and the right to propagate that were ongoing in postcolonial India in the 1960s and 1970s as these comic books were created. These debates took place at a time when communal politics were continuing to gain momentum, and the *ACK* comics reflect the Hindu majoritarian community's efforts to broaden its scope by legally defining Hinduism as a secular and tolerant way of life, rather than as a religion per se (see Baird 1993), while simultaneously minimizing the influence of non-Hindu religions, especially Islam, which were considered a threat to the majority community because of their proselytizing nature.

The *Chaitanya Mahaprabhu* issue (no. 90, 1975) perhaps best illustrates this point. This comic retells many of the incidents in the life of Chaitanya (1486–1533), who would later be known as the founder of a sect of Hinduism known as Gaudiya Vaishnavism. Here Chaitanya is presented as a multifaceted hero. He is a leader of the people who preaches that "all men are equal," who teaches the citizens of Nabadwip not to yield to injustice, and who is described in the introduction as launching "the first-ever non-cooperation movement (satyagraha, as Gandhiji later called it)." Chaitanya is also a devout worshipper of the Hindu god Krishna who "not only stemmed the tide of conversion to Islam, but also provided a new life force to Hindu religion" by converting the whole town of Nabadwip to his form of Hinduism, including Kazi Barbahak, the Muslim administrator of the town, who tried to quash public displays of Hindu devotion. In this comic book, conversion to Hinduism is presented in a positive light as a spiritually fulfilling force for the individual and a socially uplifting force for society, and those who choose to convert do so of their own free will, with no threat of force. After Chaitanya has converted the town, he stands in one panel with his arms raised and eyes closed as if in prayer, laying his plans for the future: "It is time I renounced the world and carried my gospel beyond this town" (24). Here a Hindu, Chaitanya, is presented as a leader who is both broadminded and god-minded, simultaneously staunchly devout and secular, whereas Muslim leaders—like the Kazi and Aurangzeb—are not.

Conclusion: Seeming Fair and Secular

In 1985, an infamous Supreme Court decision revitalized the debate about secularism in India. In the Shah Bano case, the Supreme Court of India ruled that Ahmed Khan, a Muslim from the state of Madhya Pradesh, was required to pay maintenance to his ex-wife, Shah Bano, under Section 125 of the Criminal Code. Many Muslims protested this decision, arguing that Islamic law required that Ahmed Khan return the marriage settlement (*mehr*) to his wife and pay her maintenance (*iddat*) for three months only. As Muslim protests gained momentum, Prime Minister Rajiv Gandhi reversed his earlier support of the decision and introduced a new bill, the Muslim Women (Protection of Rights on Divorce) Bill, which stated that in accordance with Islamic law a Muslim woman is entitled to maintenance for the *iddat* period only. Rajiv Gandhi argued that this bill "would further secularism in India by ensuring religious communities of fundamental rights" (Khory 1993, 131). But many Hindus were outraged and argued that this was "pseudo-secularism" because this bill was a step backward from a uniform civil code that applied to all Indian citizens, regardless of their religion, and that it would further sunder India's unity.

The Shah Bano case was repeatedly brought up during my interviews with Anant Pai and other Hindus of his generation. While discussing the definition of Hinduism, Pai explained that Buddhists, Jains, and Sikhs had only recently begun to identify themselves as members of separate religions—that is, as religious minorities. This, he explained, was because "in its zeal to sound impartial the government has made many concessions to minorities." He continued:

> There is one famous Supreme Court case—the Shah Bano case. The Supreme Court constantly changes its ruling whenever the mullahs complain. You see, the government is not impartial, though it pretends to be. The so-called secularists, they are only interested in getting votes, getting the minority communities to vote for them. They are not interested in fixing the problems with the Constitution, with the system. So they cater to the minority communities. This is the problem with our system today.

This discourse of "so-called secularism" and "pseudo-secularism" demonstrates how many members of the Hindu majoritarian community have come to perceive themselves as being under attack in postcolonial India on multiple fronts: by proselytizing religions like Islam and Christianity that they believe seek to convert Hindus out of the fold; by liberal advocates of "pseudo"-secularism who they believe promote equal representation of religious communities despite the fact that Hinduism is the religion of a vast majority of Indians; and by politicians who they believe cater to religious minorities in exchange for votes. The government must not only be "fair and secular," Pai stated, it must also *seem* fair and secular: "You see, this is what I have to say about secularism. When there are two kids in the family, you must sound and seem just and fair." The government has failed at this, he continued, but "we at *ACK*, we make no distinction between the two children—we try to be fair."

In Pai's opinion, being fair and secular means recognizing that there are more Hindus in India than there are members of any other religion. Thus one must acknowledge the dominant position of Hinduism while also acknowledging the place of Islam and other minority religions in India. This, he feels, he has done in his comic book series by focusing primarily on historical Hindu heroes, with the addition of several issues featuring the Mughal emperors as Muslim heroes. But others have disagreed. There are a significant number of historical issues in this comic book series featuring twentieth-century Hindu "heroes" who battle colonial British "villains" for India's independence. In light of these issues, scholar Frances Pritchett has lamented that although the medieval Mughal emperors are portrayed "on the whole rather favorably," the lack of modern Muslim historical figures in this popular medium is a substantial oversight:

> On the "Makers of Modern India" list there are no Muslims to speak of either—no Dr. Zakir Husain, no Maulana Abul Kalam Azad, no Hakim Ajmal Khan, no Asif Ali, no Khan Abdul Ghaffar Khan, no Sir Sayyid Ahmad Khan. There is only *Thanedar Hasan Askari* (286), an issue devoted to an idiosyncratic, apolitical police inspector in Uttar Pradesh in the 1930s. . . . Apart from his name, there is nothing Muslim about him. (1995, 95–96)

But the most substantial criticism I encountered was raised by Yusuf Bangalorewala, a former artist for the *Amar Chitra Katha* series and one of the few Muslims to have worked for the company. He felt strongly that one of the "two children," to use Pai's analogy, was favored:

> *ACK* was launched for a large, pan-Indian audience by Hindus pretending to be secular. Aurangzeb and Muslim freedom fighters were sidelined, and gray-zone mystics such as Kabir and Dara Shukoh were chosen as representative of the Muslim hue. The Mughal and Muslim trimmings afforded India Book House a cloak of respectability in the eyes of the Muslim intelligentsia. But the first book was *Krishna,* and the main corpus forms a full course in Hinduism.

Although Yusuf was originally very enthusiastic about working for *ACK*, since he was a fan of the comic book genre, and although he remains proud of the issues he illustrated, especially the *Mirabai* (no. 36, 1972) issue about a medieval Hindu poet-saint, he decided to quit the company in the early 1990s. As communal violence escalated during this decade, Yusuf renewed his commitment to Islam, and in 1999 he threw away his original artwork and "stopped illustrating living beings, in accord with Islam."

Since the creation of the first historical *Amar Chitra Katha* comic books in the 1970s, the heroicization of historical Hindus and the vilification of historical Muslims has become more prevalent in Indian public culture. For instance, statues of medieval Hindu kings like Shivaji and Rana Pratap have been erected in many modern cities in the past several decades, but there are no heroic statues of any of the Mughal emperors, even at historical Mughal sites that are popular with tourists, such as the Taj Mahal and the Agra Fort. In Hindi films and Doordarshan TV serials from the 1980s forward, medieval and modern Muslims have often been portrayed as villains. In these media, as in the comics of the 1970s, Muslims are visually marked as villains through their long beards and their skullcaps, as well as their puritanical religiosity. Together, the statements of Anant Pai and Yusuf Bangalorewala attest to the irreconcilable differences that arose within the comic book production process in the attempt to portray Hindus and Muslims in a way that was both "fair and secular" in the *Amar Chitra Katha* series, and to the ongoing problems in defining secularism and Indianness in postcolonial India.

Mahatma Gandhi as a
Comic Book Hero

6

The earliest issues in the *Amar Chitra Katha* comic book series were myth-ologicals that cast characters such as the epic Hindu god-king Rama as a manly comic book hero, posed on the cover of the *Rama* issue (no. 15, 1970) with his chest muscles rippling and his bow and arrow at the ready to battle demons (plate 1). Historical issues were added to the series in 1971, beginning with *Shivaji* (no. 23, 1971), the tale of a seventeenth-century warrior-king from western India who was depicted as a fierce equestrian commander, wielding his sword and leading his troops into battle (figure 22). *Shivaji* and other historical issues produced throughout the 1970s featured medieval Hindu heroes who battled medieval Muslim villains. In the mid-1970s, this martial template was applied to a new type of historical hero: the modern Indian revolutionary who battled the British colonial rulers for India's independence.

One of the first issues to feature a modern hero was *Subhas Chandra Bose* (no. 77, 1975). Bose (1897–1945?) was a nationalist leader from Bengal who is famous for advocating militant resistance against the British and for founding the Indian National Army. On the cover of this issue, Bose is dressed in a military uniform and standing at attention. In the back-ground, several other soldiers hoist up India's tricolor flag, which waves prominently behind Bose's head and shoulders. The perspective is such that readers look up to Subhas Chandra Bose, who looms so large that he breaks out of the frame and can be depicted only from his thighs upward. Complementing this image, the introduction to this issue describes Subhas Chandra Bose as one of the "figures larger than life" of the national move-ment for independence in India.

Following *Subhas Chandra Bose,* other issues were printed in the late 1970s and throughout the 1980s featuring twentieth-century men who bravely fought the British, including *Chandra Shekhar Azad* (no. 142, 1977), *Bagha Jatin* (no. 156, 1978), *Bhagat Singh* (no. 234, 1981), *Rash Behari Bose* (no. 262, 1982), *Senapati Bapat* (no. 303, 1984), and *Khudiram Bose* (no. 364, 1986). In 1989, after twenty years of publishing success, the produc-ers of *Amar Chitra Katha* decided to release two issues on the world-renowned Indian politician and social activist Mohandas Karamchand

Oh, I can't say Gandhi was responsible for Jallianwala Bagh. You see, we can't say anything like that about Gandhi-ji! But like Subhas Chandra Bose said, when the ruler is so oppressive, how can we stick to nonviolence?

Anant Pai, personal interview

Gandhi (1869–1948), later known as the "Mahatma" (Great Soul). *Mahatma Gandhi I: The Early Days* (no. 414, 1989) focuses on Gandhi's childhood and education, his reform work in South Africa, and his return to India. *Mahatma Gandhi II: The Father of the Nation* (no. 416, 1989) highlights his work in India from 1919 until his death in 1948. But Gandhi, who is best known for his technique of nonviolent civil resistance, or *satyagraha,* presented a formidable challenge to the comic book creators. How to depict the Mahatma, the paragon of peace and nonviolence, as a hero in a visual medium that is notorious for its action and violence? Longtime comic book author Yagya Sharma explained the predicament:

> Gandhi was afraid of turning India into a violent society. You need maturity to be able to see the valor in nonviolent struggle. So the common man appreciates active characters more . . . and storytellers, too. This is because you cannot dramatize inaction. How do you put inaction with pictures, involve the child as a reader? But characters who are active, they make better stories.

For Sharma, a good comic script is one that adheres to *ACK*'s proven formula in which the hero fights great battles and ultimately wins or else dies bravely on the battlefield, as in *Rana Pratap* (no. 24, 1971) and *Prithviraj Chauhan* (no. 25, 1971), two issues about medieval Hindu kings who battled "invading Muslim armies":

> They are heroes because they stood up against a much larger power. They stood up against tremendous odds. Prithviraj Chauhan lost, but he fought bravely. This is what is important. And Rana Pratap, he did not meet his goal, but he did free Chittorgarh. So in a way he failed because he didn't free all of Rajasthan, but he also fought to his last. This is what makes them role models.

Gandhi, with his philosophy of nonviolence and his quest for Hindu-Muslim unity, does not fit into the same heroic mold as Shivaji, Rana Pratap, Prithviraj Chauhan, and other medieval Indian heroes in this series. Nowhere is this more apparent than in his death, for Gandhi did not die heroically, fighting an enemy on a battlefield; he was assassinated in 1948 in the Birla House garden in New Delhi as he walked to his evening ecumenical prayer meeting. Hence, while Rana Pratap and other heroes receive full-page panels lauding their ultimate sacrifice upon the battlefield, the scene of Gandhi's death is depicted in just one small panel in *Mahatma Gandhi II* (figure 33). The narrative text (in Hindi) at the top of this panel is brief: "But Gandhi's efforts to unite the people did not please everyone. At 5:10 PM on January 30, 1948—" (28).[1] The accompanying image shows an alarmed crowd circling the assassin as he shoots Gandhi, while the latter exclaims, "Hey Ram!" ("Oh, God!") as he falls to the ground.

Other historical Indian figures have also presented problems for the producers in the attempt to canonize them as national comic book heroes. Chapter 4 discussed the issue of narrative closure with regard to the

Shivaji issue, which ends with Shivaji's victorious coronation rather than his unheroic death due to illness six years later. Yagya Sharma noted that the ending of *Subhas Chandra Bose* was also particularly troublesome to script because of the disputed nature of his death and the need for a heroic ending to the comic book:

> Many people today believe that Subhas Chandra Bose may still be alive. When his plane crashed in 1945, there was no physical evidence of his death. So after independence in 1947, many thought that perhaps he was still alive, waiting for the right time to return to India. Of course, this raises a lot of problems, a lot of questions. But the minute you go and say that he's dead, there'll be an uproar. I mean, of course he died in the plane crash. But so many believed that he was still alive. And it is also part of storytelling, this ending. If we showed his death in the plane crash—well, that is just so undramatic for a hero. It is not at all like Rana Pratap fighting to his death. If Subhas Chandra Bose had died fighting, that would have been different. Storytelling needs a climax. What kind of a climax and resolution would it be if we just said, "And then he died in a plane crash"?

For these reasons, the producers decided to end *Subhas Chandra Bose* on a mysterious note. In a small final panel that features "Netaji" (Leader) Subhas Chandra Bose standing at attention in front of a plane, the last words read: "What became of Netaji on that fateful trip is a mystery. Is he dead? Does he live? There is no answer to these questions" (31).

The *Mahatma Gandhi II* issue also evidences some mystery about the circumstances of its protagonist's death. In this panel, the assassin is not the focus of the image—only his head and shoulders can be seen in the midst of the crowd, and he has no identifying marks to distinguish him. Nor is Gandhi the focus, although he is easily identified by his style of dress and glasses. Rather, the literal focal point of this image is the gun, which

Figure 33. *Mahatma Gandhi II: The Father of the Nation,* no. 416 (Bombay: India Book House Pvt. Ltd., 1989), 28. From *Amar Chitra Katha,* with the permission of the publishers ACK Media, India.

is placed at the very center of the image and is encircled by a large yellow halo. The last panels in this comic book conclude with the famous radio broadcast given by Prime Minister Jawaharlal Nehru in honor of Gandhi on the night of his assassination in which Nehru proclaimed, "The light has gone out of our lives, and there is darkness everywhere." Yet in this panel it appears as if it is not Gandhi that is that light but the gun itself. Visually, it is the act that is highlighted here, not the assassin or the victim. Textually, as well, this panel does not focus on the assassin: his name is nowhere mentioned, and thus he needs to be neither exculpated nor blamed. Here text and image are united in limiting the information presented to the reader. But why? W. J. T. Mitchell has argued that the text-image relation in mixed media is not merely a technical question but a site of tension or conflict, "a nexus where political, institutional, and social antagonisms play themselves out in the materiality of representation" (1994, 90–91). This chapter examines the depiction of Mahatma Gandhi in the *ACK* series in order to better understand the contested memory of Gandhi in postcolonial India and competing claims about who the proper heroes are of India's independence struggle.

A Leader of the Nation

The comic book is a sequential art form that combines textual and visual elements in a series of panels. In comic books, the relationship between text and image is a particularly important area of study, due to the wide variety of text-image relations found in this popular medium. Scott Mc-Cloud differentiates between seven types of text and image relationships: (1) word-specific panels in which pictures illustrate, but don't significantly add to a largely complete text; (2) picture-specific panels in which words do little more than add a soundtrack to a visually told sequence; (3) duo-specific panels in which both words and pictures send essentially the same message; (4) additive panels in which words amplify or elaborate on an image or vice versa; (5) parallel panels in which words and pictures seem to follow very different courses without intersecting; (6) montage panels in which words are treated as integral parts of the picture; and (7) interdependent panels in which words and pictures go hand in hand to convey an idea that neither could convey alone (McCloud 1993, 153–56). In Japanese manga, picture-specific panels are most common. In American comics, on the other hand, interdependent panels are typically held to be the ideal. In Indian comics, based as they are on the classic American comic book format, the interdependent panel is also typically held as the ideal.

In the *Amar Chitra Katha* comics, the narrative text runs across the top and/or bottom of the panels, and word balloons appear within the panels to convey dialogue. The artists are given pages with the panel divisions, the narrative text, and the scripted dialogue balloons already in place (refer to figure 7). Furthermore, the scriptwriters give the artists detailed written instructions that describe what to draw in each panel. Anant Pai maintains that this process was put into place to ensure that the images are accurate and match the text in an interdependent relationship. Contrasting *Amar Chitra Katha* with *Tinkle,* a fictive comic book series that India Book House began publishing in 1980 for children ages eight and younger, he explained:

> Well, with *Tinkle* we don't give very detailed visual directions to the artist. But the directions we gave for *ACK* were very detailed: we even gave the composition to the artist—who is on the left, who is on the right, that sort of thing. In *Tinkle* the artist only has to worry about matching the right character with the right dialogue bubble. But in *ACK* composition was very important. And we provided references to the artist. For example, what did the houseboat look like when Rabindranath Tagore and Vivekananda met? We were very careful, because these *ACK* are authentic. *Tinkle* we are not so careful with because it is for entertainment only.

Yagya Sharma agreed with Pai that visual instructions for the artist are important and that text and image should work together in a synergistic relationship:

> The visual directions to the artist tell him where the dialogue balloons go, which character is on which side, perspective, etc. In a film, the audio track can be different from the video track, because there is action, movement. In comics, however, there is no action, no movement. So the action must be described at times. I think the best way to put it is that there must be a synergy between text and image. The picture must match the text enough that they're not telling two different stories. And when it is not action but expression, then facial expression can say a lot, so sometimes no words are necessary.

Longtime comic book artist Pratap Mulick also stressed the interdependence of text and image:

> Sometimes it happens that text and image are different. The two should work together to tell the whole story. For instance, the image can show a fight, or a fight ending, and the text can say that after the fight the hero returned home. They are two different moments that can be told in the same panel then. Or else, the image can show action, and the text can provide information, thoughts, dialogue—things that can't be depicted easily.

Producer No. 2 agreed that it was crucial that the text and image should be well matched and equally weighted:

> It must all flow, move together—and fast! A slow pace isn't good for a comic book. A comic book shouldn't be too text-heavy. There should be a 50–50 blend of text and image. The script and the illustrations should melt into one another, and the reader shouldn't be able to understand one without the other.

However, precisely because the visual images in comic book panels do not necessarily exist in a one-to-one relationship with the verbal—even when that is the goal—they may have experiential or associative ties that work to produce meanings extending beyond the text. Quite often around the figure of Gandhi in particular the relationship between text and image grows more complicated than this interdependent ideal in three noteworthy ways. First, the "50–50 blend of text and image" discussed by Producer No. 2 is out of proportion in many panels, weighted heavily in favor of the textual. The *Mahatma Gandhi I* and *Mahatma Gandhi II* issues each contain twice as much verbiage as the average comic book in the series, featuring a dozen word-specific panels containing predominantly text with either no visual at all or pictures that serve only as illustrations without significantly adding to the text. For instance, in the two panels in *Mahatma Gandhi I* where the term *satyagraha* is first presented by Gandhi as a better alternative to *passive resistance* (19), the narrative text and thought balloons dominate, occupying two-thirds of the panels' space, while Gandhi is merely shown sitting at his desk in both panels.

Second, on several other occasions in the *Mahatma Gandhi I* and *Mahatma Gandhi II* issues, text and image do not "say" the same thing. For instance, the final panel of *Mahatma Gandhi I* demonstrates this complexity of text-image relations (figure 34). The narrative text in this last panel, which is about the Indian National Congress session that was held in Amritsar in 1919, states: "Gandhi was established and acknowledged as a leader of the nation" (31). The accompanying image features a large, orderly, motionless crowd with only a handful of people in the back chanting, "Mahatma Gandhi ki jai!" (Victory to Mahatma Gandhi). Down in the far right-hand corner is a stage with four tiny figures on it, so small that hardly any of their features can be made out. Of these miniscule figures, one of the seated ones is shirtless and appears to wear a white *dhoti* (loincloth). He is presumably Gandhi, our hero, although his identity is not otherwise explicit. The positioning of the reader here, to look down upon Gandhi as if from a great distance, in conjunction with the rather unmotivated crowd, encourages distance between the reader and the figure of Gandhi, rather than encouraging the view of him as a larger-than-life national figure. Thus although the concluding line of this comic book tells us that Gandhi is now a leader of the nation, the concluding image is more ambivalent about Gandhi's stature.

Throughout *Mahatma Gandhi I*—not just in the final panel—the reader is never positioned so as to look up to Gandhi. Even on the cover, where Gandhi is shown bravely burning his registration card in South Africa, he nonetheless appears no larger than the other people present. This perspective is quite unlike that used in most other comic books, wherein the hero is positioned as a figure to whom the reader can quite literally look up. As we have seen, Subhas Chandra Bose looms so large on the cover of his issue that he cannot fit into the frame. Even in the small final panel of

ON DECEMBER 29, AT THE INDIAN NATIONAL CONGRESS SESSION AT AMRITSAR, PRESIDED OVER BY MOTILAL NEHRU, A NEW SLOGAN BEGAN TO DOMINATE THE POLITICAL HORIZON.

MAHATMA GANDHI KI JAI!

GANDHI WAS ESTABLISHED AND ACKNOWLEDGED AS A LEADER OF THE NATION.

the issue, Subhas is still a figure for the reader to look up to as he stands at attention in front of the airplane. In *Subhas Chandra Bose,* text and image are united in the effort to convey the greatness of this hero. As previously cited, the introduction states that Netaji Subhas Chandra Bose is one of the "figures larger than life" of the national movement for independence in India. The introduction then compares Bose with Gandhi:

> Netaji Subhas Chandra Bose stands out as a dynamic, restless force in an era which had chosen the path of Gandhi, the path of peace and nonviolent non-cooperation. Bengal chose to voice its protest militantly, and Subhas Chandra Bose was a true son of Bengal.

This statement suggests that the disjuncture between text and image in the final panel of *Mahatma Gandhi I* is due to two competing theories of nationalism, two schools of thought about the proper place of violence in the struggle for independence—one of which is held up as being more heroic than the other. According to W. J. T. Mitchell, the real question to ask when confronted with image-text relations is not "what is the difference (or similarity) between the words and the images?" but "what difference do the differences (or similarities) make?" (1994, 90–91). The similarity of text and image in *Subhas Chandra Bose* works to promote this figure as a national leader, a larger-than-life figure in the national movement, while the difference between text and image in *Mahatma Gandhi I* calls into question this figure's alleged status as a leader of the nation.

Third, and most significantly, despite Gandhi's renown for his method of nonviolent protest, he is often associated with violent outbursts through text-image pairing and the sequencing of panels. According to *Mahatma Gandhi I,* he only came to be recognized as a "leader of the nation" immediately after the Jallianwala Bagh massacre. This infamous massacre occurred when the British brigadier-general Reginald Dyer ordered fifty

Figure 34. *Mahatma Gandhi I: The Early Days,* no. 414 [reprint no. 650] (Bombay: India Book House Pvt. Ltd., 1989 [2000]), 31. From *Amar Chitra Katha,* with the permission of the publishers ACK Media, India.

of his riflemen to open fire on the crowd that had assembled at Jallianwala Bagh in the city of Amritsar on April 13, 1919, killing hundreds or even thousands of Indians, depending on the source. In this comic book we are told that Gandhi "took his first major political step in India" by calling for a nationwide *hartal* (strike) on April 6, 1919, in protest over the Rowlatt Act (figure 35). The Rowlatt Act entailed two bills, written by Justice Sidney A. T. Rowlatt and introduced in the Imperial Legislative Council in February 1919, which were designed to allow the government to retain some of its wartime powers upon the advent of peace following World War I so as to better counteract revolutionary activity. Many Indians, however, saw these bills as a violation of their civil rights, and some even characterized them as the culmination of British tyranny and oppression.[2] The image that accompanies this text shows an empty street with all of the shops closed. At the bottom of this same panel we are told: "A nation coming peacefully to a halt was quite a spectacle" (29). But this spectacle of peaceful protest was not very long-lived, for the next panel informs us that after Gandhi was arrested on April 9, 1919, there were violent outbursts in Delhi, Amritsar, Ahmedabad, and Viramgam. Gandhi is shown deep in thought here, reflecting upon his "Himalayan miscalculation," his mistaken belief that the people would remain peaceful. In response to the violence, the narrative text at the bottom of this panel informs us that Gandhi called off his nationwide protest movement. The worst is yet to come, however, for in the very next panel an image of the Jallianwala Bagh massacre is presented, with General Dyer commanding his troops to fire on the left side of the panel, and Indians dying as they attempt to flee on the right side. The narrative text in this panel tells us that Dyer was angered by the violent outburst that had occurred in Amritsar and decided to punish the people:

> Then came April 13, Baisakhi, and the massacre at Jallianwala Bagh in Amritsar. An army officer, General Dyer, angered by the killing of some Englishmen in the city and the assault on an Englishwoman on the 10th by an excited crowd, wanted to punish the people. Under his orders sepoys [soldiers] fired on an unarmed crowd and killed more than a thousand* people and wounded more than three thousand. (30)

The asterisk in the text is footnoted at the bottom of the page, and the note reads: "The British gave the figures as 379 killed and over 1,200 wounded" (30). The sequencing of these three panels makes a causal association between the hartal, Gandhi, and the Jallianwala Bagh massacre. Other choices could have been made—for instance, in the second panel a more dynamic image of one of the violent outbursts discussed in the text could have been shown, in place of the static image of Gandhi in thought. But by depicting Gandhi in this way, he is connected with the massacre, despite the fact that he was not present in Amritsar when it occurred.

Mahatma Gandhi I next details the atrocities committed by the British during the period of martial law that they imposed following the massacre: compulsory roll call, public floggings, a crawling lane, air bombardments, and arbitrary arrests. Gandhi, we are told, was not allowed to go to Amritsar or anywhere in the northwestern Punjab region for several months. When he was finally allowed to visit Amritsar, large crowds welcomed him, and as the final panel informs us (figure 34), he was then established as a "leader of the nation." Gandhi, it would seem, could not have become a national leader without the Jallianwala Bagh massacre, an event that spurred Indians across the subcontinent to band together in order to protest the oppression of British rule. Yet the comic also suggests in a more subtle

Figure 35. *Mahatma Gandhi I: The Early Days*, no. 414 [reprint no. 650] (Bombay: India Book House Pvt. Ltd., 1989 [2000]), 29–30. From *Amar Chitra Katha*, with the permission of the publishers ACK Media, India.

fashion that the massacre would not have occurred at all, were it not for Gandhi and his "Himalayan miscalculation."

<table>
<tr><td>

The Jallianwala
Bagh Massacre: A
Turning Point

</td><td>

Although *Mahatma Gandhi I* was not published until 1989, the figure of Gandhi is repeatedly invoked throughout the *ACK* corpus, especially in connection with the Jallianwala Bagh massacre. One example is found in the *Rabindranath Tagore* issue (no. 136, 1977) about the Bengali poet and nationalist Rabindranath Tagore (1861–1941). In this large half-page panel we see several soldiers firing on a crowd in front of a long wall (figure 36). Those readers who are familiar with colonial Indian history would immediately recognize this as a depiction of the Jallianwala Bagh massacre. The lengthy narrative text at the top of this panel does not seek to explain the action—which is self-evident—but instead tries to place it within an ideological framework. It reads:

</td></tr>
</table>

> Rabindranath was deeply involved in his great experiments in education at Shanti Niketan. But he could not keep himself aloof from political happenings. The oppressive measures of the British had made Mahatma Gandhi give the call for hartal in 1919. Several hundred men and women had gathered at Jallianwala Baug, in the Punjab. Suddenly—(28)

The other two panels on the bottom of this page go on to highlight how Rabindranath Tagore renounced his knighthood in protest over this incident, suggesting that Rabindranath blamed the British for the massacre. Yet the combination of text and image in this top panel again makes a causal connection between British oppression, Mahatma Gandhi's call for hartal, and the massacre. In this way, the text provides the image with a meaning that it would not have had otherwise, by associating the massacre with the Mahatma, a figure who is not visibly present in the scene.

In other issues as well, text and image combine to make a similar connection between Gandhi and the violent massacre at Jallianwala Bagh. In *Bhagat Singh* (no. 234, 1981), the revolutionary hero Bhagat Singh (1907–31) is depicted as a twelve-year-old boy who is inspired by the protest over the Rowlatt Act and the events that unfold thereafter. In one panel we are told, "Under the leadership of Gandhiji, people throughout the country protested against the Rowlatt Act with demonstrations and meetings" (5). The image in this panel, however, does not send the same message that the text does. It does not just depict a protest in which people march, chant slogans, hold signs, and wave flags; instead, it builds upon these visual elements of protest, transforming the depiction into a violent scene by adding British police, armed with *lathis* (clubs), who beat the protestors. Together, this combination of text and image suggests a problem with Gandhi's philosophy: that nonviolence is only rewarded with violence.

Figure 36. *Rabindranath Tagore,* no. 136 [reprint no. 548] (Bombay: India Book House Pvt. Ltd., 1977 [1996]), 28. From *Amar Chitra Katha,* with the permission of the publishers ACK Media, India.

This is made even clearer in the next panel. The narrative text reads, "At one such meeting held at Jallianwalla Bagh, in Amritsar—" and the image shows British soldiers firing rifles and handguns into a heap of dying Indians (6). Here the incompleteness of the text forces the reader to look to the image to conclude the sentence, a technique that heightens the effect of this panel by causing the reader to pause and reflect upon it. Following the previous panel, this one builds upon the suggestion that peaceful meetings—the kind organized by Gandhi—only led to violent persecution.

For Bhagat Singh, Jallianwala Bagh is a holy place, a place that has been "anointed with the blood of patriots" (6) and therefore becomes a pilgrimage point. When he visits the site, Bhagat Singh collects some of the soil, just as a Hindu pilgrim would collect holy Ganges water, and takes it home with him so that it may inspire him to "sacrifice everything for the cause" (7). Jallianwala Bagh is clearly a central node in the history of colonial India as it is told in these comic books; the *Bhagat Singh* issue tells us that it was this massacre which "stirred the conscience of the nation" (7) and caused Gandhi to launch the noncooperation movement. Rajinder Singh Raj, co-author of this issue, explained that the Jallianwala Bagh massacre was so important because it united all Indians—Hindus, Muslims, and also Sikhs—in opposition to the British:

> It was important for India—it is after the massacre at Jallianwala Bagh in 1919 that many Indians began to recognize the need for independence, for an active movement to escape the British yoke. And it is important for my people—for Sikhs—also. Twenty years after Jallianwala Bagh, Shaheed Udham Singh took revenge for that massacre by shooting O'Dwyer.

Hence in addition to sparking national unity across multiple religious creeds, Jallianwala Bagh is also important to Raj because it suggests the ultimate failure of the nonviolent approach to the struggle for independence and the need for a more "active movement." The revolutionary Udham Singh (1899–1940) was present at the massacre and took his own revenge for it in London on March 13, 1940, when he shot Sir Michael O'Dwyer, who had been the lieutenant governor of the Punjab at the time of the massacre. Udham Singh was hanged for his act on July 31, 1940, but he has been immortalized by both Sikhs and non-Sikhs as an Indian martyr who was ready to sacrifice everything for the cause.[3]

Other incidents in *Bhagat Singh* reinforce the idea that the goal of independence could not have been attained by nonviolent means alone. In 1928, Bhagat Singh and other members of the Nav Jawan Bharat Sabha decided to join Lala Lajpat Rai's nonviolent procession in protest against the Simon Commission. The procession was met with a police lathi charge, however, and Lala Lajpat Rai (1865–1928) himself suffered severe injuries and died several days later. Bhagat Singh and his friend drive the moral home in one panel: "Lalaji's nonviolence was rewarded with fatal blows," says the friend. Bhagat Singh responds, "This government understands only one language—blood for blood" (17). With the lesson of the massacre and Lala Lajpat Rai's death fresh in his memory, Bhagat Singh rejected the nonviolent path. The following year, on April 8, 1929, he and a friend, Batukeshwar Dutt, threw a homemade bomb into the Legislative Assembly. The comic book depicts Bhagat Singh at his trial, contrasting his act with that of General Dyer:

> General Dyer killed hundreds of persons in Jallianwala Bagh. He was given lakhs of rupees as a reward by his countrymen. . . . In contrast, we throw a weak

bomb ensuring that no one is hurt. We are tried and given a life sentence. . . .
Our motive was not to kill, but to make our ideals heard and accepted. (25)

On March 23, 1931, Bhagat Singh was executed, becoming an instant martyr for Indian independence. It is this act of bomb throwing that Bhagat Singh has been most celebrated for from the 1930s to this day. Noting Bhagat Singh's popular appeal in calendar posters and bazaar art, Christopher Pinney argues that these pictorial affirmations of his violent actions contribute to a visual tradition of questioning the "relationship between what we might term 'official' and 'unofficial' nationalism" by suggesting the "indebtedness of official nationalism to revolutionary terrorism" (2004, 135). This tradition continues in the *ACK* comic books. Bhagat Singh is featured throwing the bomb on the cover of the comic book in his name, and the introduction provides an apologetic defense of his action:

> Bhagat Singh and his comrades were not blood-thirsty, trigger-happy terrorists. They were waging a war against a relentless colonial power. The odds were heavily against them. They were just a handful of selfless patriots and they had dared to take on the mighty British power.

Several other comic book issues invoke Mahatma Gandhi in connection with the Jallianwala Bagh massacre in a similar way to that seen in *Rabindranath Tagore* and *Bhagat Singh*. *Deshbandhu Chittaranjan Das* (no. 344, 1985) features the nationalist figure Chittaranjan Das (1870–1925) addressing crowds in the manner of Gandhi, whom he admired, and then discusses the aftermath of the passage of the Rowlatt Act, depicting crowds being lathi-charged, imprisoned, and "showered with bullets as in the shameful, mindless massacre of innocents ordered by General Dyer at Jallianwala Baugh in 1919" (14). Similarly, in *March to Freedom 3: The Saga of Indian Revolutionaries* (no. 360, 1986), Gandhi is again connected with the massacre in a sequence of panels that proceeds from peaceful crowds protesting the Rowlatt Act under Gandhi's leadership, to General Dyer and his troops opening fire during one such peaceful meeting in Jallianwala Bagh, to a close-up image (without text) of one man fleeing in terror and another falling over as a bullet strikes him (21). Finally, in the more recent *Story of the Freedom Struggle* (bumper issue no. 10), which was officially released by Prime Minister Atal Behari Vajpayee in 1997 on the fiftieth anniversary of India's independence, the same sequence of three panels from the *Mahatma Gandhi I* issue is reprinted, featuring the hartal, Gandhi in thought, and the massacre (50).

The Jallianwala Bagh massacre was even deemed a significant enough event in the history of modern India that it was given its own comic book, *Jallianwalla Bagh* (no. 358, 1986), despite the fact that this broke with the standard comic book formula, which centered the narrative on one person, written as a hero, and not on an event. The cover of this issue again features the scene of the massacre, with General Dyer in the foreground facing the crowd (his back to the reader), with his hand raised, frozen in the gesture of commanding his troops to fire. In the background the crowd panics and flees as bullets erupt. The introduction to this issue spells out the significance of this event:

> The sacrifice of the martyrs of Jallianwalla Bagh resulted in further intensification of the struggle for independence. It turned millions of loyal supporters of the British Raj into nationalists. The Jallianwalla Bagh massacre thus became an important landmark in India's struggle for freedom.

This issue opens with a debate about the significance of the Rowlatt Act among the people of Amritsar. One man says, "But who cares? It has nothing to do with me." A second man responds, "You are wrong, brother. Gandhiji says the Rowlatt Act is a symbol of national humiliation!" At this point the narrator's voice chimes in, stating: "People in Amritsar as in other parts of India looked to Gandhiji for guidance" (1). As the story unfolds, Gandhi is not visually depicted in any of the panels, although his name and his message of nonviolence are repeatedly invoked in the text. Dr. Saifuddin Kitchlew and Dr. Satyapal, both prominent citizens of Amritsar who organized protest meetings, are described as Gandhians and are depicted teaching their fellow citizens about Gandhi's message of nonviolence and his call for a hartal (2–3). The comic book recounts in great detail the incidents from April 6, the day of the hartal, to April 13, the day of the massacre, and then describes the British and Indian inquiry committees that were set up afterwards to investigate. One of the final panels mentions the "non-official enquiry committee, of which Gandhiji was an important member," and cites the committee's conclusion: "The Jallianwalla massacre was a calculated piece of inhumanity towards innocent and unarmed men, including children, and unparalleled in its ferocity in the history of modern British administration" (31).

By framing the story of the massacre with textual references to Gandhi, the textual narrative again provides the visual narrative with a level of meaning that it would not have had otherwise, associating the massacre with Mahatma Gandhi, a figure who is not visibly present in the *Jallianwalla Bagh* comic book. Moreover, this association again highlights the "problem" with Gandhi's nonviolent philosophy—that nonviolence on the part of Indians is only rewarded with violence on the part of the British—and thereby suggests the crucial need for an alternate path toward independence.

In his study of the Chauri Chaura riot of February 4, 1922, Shahid Amin has detailed how nationalist historiography has scripted Indian nationalism as "a massive undoing of Colonial Wrongs by a nonviolent and disciplined people" (1995, 2–3). In this process, he argues, a selective national amnesia has been applied to events that inconvenience this story—events like the Chauri Chaura riot, in which a crowd of Indian peasants burned down a police station, killing twenty-three policemen while chanting that Gandhi's *swaraj* (self-rule) had come. Amin demonstrates how this event was initially forgotten in nationalist lore, overlooked as an aberration, but was later rescripted as an event of nationalist violence that was "justified, forgiven, and made to seem normal by an inflated rhetoric of heroism within the description" (1995, 54–55). Only after it was rewritten in this way, he says, could Chauri Chaura be incorporated within the master story of the "Great Freedom Struggle."

The Jallianwala Bagh massacre, however, fit far more easily into the story of India's "Great Freedom Struggle": If Chauri Chaura was the aberration (in which Indians killed nonviolent colonial officers in a violent outburst), then Jallianwala Bagh was the norm (in which colonial officers killed nonviolent Indians in a violent outburst). The British, on the other hand, treated the massacre not as the norm but as a singular event that was the product of one misguided individual, General Dyer, and in doing so erased it from British history, much as the Chauri Chaura riot was erased from Indian history. Winston Churchill, for instance, called the Jallianwala Bagh massacre "an episode . . . without precedent or parallel in the modern history of the British Empire . . . an extraordinary event, a monstrous event, an event which stands in singular and sinister isolation" (Sayer 1991, 131).[4] Nonetheless, in India in the years since the massacre, Jallianwala Bagh has been heralded again and again as the "Colonial Wrong" par excellence. Thus in 1920 at the end of their investigation, the Indian members who made up the minority branch of the Disorders Inquiry Committee concluded:

> General Dyer wanted by his action at the Jallianwala Bagh to create a "wide impression" and "a great moral effect." We have no doubt that he did succeed in creating a very wide impression and a great moral effect, but of a character quite the opposite to the one he intended. The story of this indiscriminate killing of innocent people not engaged in committing any acts of violence but assembled in a meeting has undoubtedly produced such a deep impression throughout the length and breadth of the country, so prejudicial to the British Government, that it would take a good deal and a long time to rub it out. ("Majority and Minority Report of the Disorders Inquiry Committee [1920]" 1976, 193)

The massacre did indeed make a deep impression. By 1926 a lantern slide show on the massacre was being used by nationalist workers to demonstrate to Indians everywhere that they were "bound together because of their vulnerability to an illegitimate, foreign regime" (Trivedi 2003, 28–29); and this sentiment continued to echo during the next two decades throughout the struggle for independence. In 1961, more than a dozen years after India's independence, Prime Minister Jawaharlal Nehru remarked that the Jallianwala Bagh massacre marked "a turning point in Anglo-Indian relations," and Indian historians have made good use of this phrase ever since then.[5]

When asked what the Jallianwala Bagh massacre meant to him and why it was featured in so many *Amar Chitra Katha* comics, Anant Pai also characterized it as a turning point in modern Indian history:

> After 1857 Queen Victoria gave her declaration, and the Rule of Law was established from that day. Including Rabindranath Tagore, many intellectuals felt that the Queen's rule was very good, that it was much better than the East India traders and mercenaries had been. So they worked with the West to improve society. Like Rammohan Roy and the abolition of sati. Rammohan Roy worked with Bentick, you know? Many on the whole were happy about the Rule of Law, and 1919 was the turning point. Even Tagore returned his knighthood after this, after Jallianwala Bagh. It was after this slaughter of innocents that Indians on all levels—the intellectuals and the masses—increasingly worked toward independence.

Yet when asked whether he held Gandhi responsible in any way for Jallianwala Bagh, Pai replied with the quote that is cited at the outset of this chapter, stating that he couldn't say "anything like that" about Gandhi, then adding, "But like Subhas Chandra Bose said, when the ruler is so oppressive, how can we stick to nonviolence?" Aside from this subtle criticism of Gandhi and his strategy of nonviolence, Pai declined to comment further about Gandhi. This instance was significant, in that it was one of the rare occasions during my extended series of interviews with Pai when I encountered silence. His silence was a form of resistance to this line of questioning, of course, but in his refusal to say anything about Gandhi that might be seen as a negative and therefore controversial comment, he also refused to say anything positive about Gandhi as a modern Indian hero.

Others involved in the production of the comic books were more forthcoming with their opinions about the connection between Gandhi and Jallianwala Bagh. Producer No. 1 stated that in writing the *March to Freedom* series (nos. 348, 1986; 356, 1986; 360, 1986) he felt it was important to show how the armed struggle and the Gandhian movement were interwoven, one acting as a catalyst for the other. The Rowlatt Act, he stated, was a reaction to the armed struggle that had preceded it; Gandhi's noncooperation movement was a reaction to the Rowlatt Act; and Jallianwala Bagh followed from the noncooperation movement. He explained:

> Jallianwala Bagh is a very important point in Indian history. It is when the change from the Gandhian to the revolutionary movement occurred. Jallianwala Bagh followed Gandhi's noncooperation movement. But then after Jallianwala Bagh occurred, Gandhi left for twelve years. He was not sure that it was the right time for a noncooperation movement. He had some doubts. And during these twelve years revolutionary activity arose. So you cannot understand the freedom struggle, the noncooperation movement, or the revolutionary activity without understanding Jallianwala Bagh. In the *ACKs* we

present a very balanced story, I believe. We looked at sources from both sides to write the *Jallianwalla Bagh* issue.[6]

For this author, clearly, there is a cause-and-effect relationship between Gandhi, the Jallianwala Bagh massacre, and the revolutionary movement—a relationship that he has put much thought and effort into articulating for the comic book readers.

Other authors spoke less in terms of a causal relationship and more in terms of an oppositional one between the proponents of Gandhi's nonviolent path and the proponents of the revolutionary path—the "both sides" to which Producer No. 1 referred. Satyavrata Ghosh, a retired professor of political science and a former revolutionary, worked as a consultant on several of the *ACK* titles that featured revolutionaries. Outspoken about his desire to promote the heroes of the revolutionary path, Ghosh stated that it was his goal to "publicize the revolutionaries, the 'other stream,'" and not the "mainstream," which "in the name of so-called peace and nonviolence shut out the contribution of those who advocated violence in the freedom struggle." In an interview on All India Radio (AIR Bombay) on July 14, 1984, which is reprinted in his book *Indian Struggle for Freedom*, Ghosh set forth his opinion on this subject in greater detail:

> [T]he contribution by the Open Wing of the Freedom Movement has been magnified beyond all proportions so much so that children read and repeat that "Gandhiji gave us freedom." . . . [T]here have been broadly two streams in our freedom struggle—the more well-known one, somewhat over-publicised, of the open movement generally under the leadership of the Congress. There has also been the other stream, that of the revolutionary movement, much less known but no less potent as a contributing factor. . . . [I]f one were to observe carefully, each dose [of freedom] came in the wake of some revolutionary activities. The benefits, however, always went to the other wing of the Movement. (1988, 163–64)

Here we find an open expression of the tension that exists in these comics between the two paths to independence: the nonviolent path advocated by Gandhi and the violent path of the revolutionaries. Such statements provide some insight into the connection between Gandhi and the Jallianwala Bagh massacre that is found throughout the *ACK* comic book series. This connection serves two functions: It emphasizes the innocence of those who were killed by General Dyer in the massacre—the victims are repeatedly described as Gandhians who had embraced Gandhiji's message of nonviolence—and thereby heightens the brutality of Dyer's act and, by extension, of the entire colonial regime. But it also writes Gandhi as partly culpable for the massacre and thereby discredits his philosophy of nonviolent resistance.

Yet the *Amar Chitra Katha* comics refrain from directly criticizing Mahatma Gandhi. As Anant Pai stated, such negative things can't be said about Gandhi, a person who is revered the world over and is celebrated as the "Father of the Indian Nation." However, criticism of Gandhi's non-violent philosophy and his tactics, such as his fasts and ecumenical prayer meetings, can be found in many issues, without any direct reference to Gandhi himself. *Khudiram Bose* (no. 364, 1986), for instance, features the revolutionary Satyen Basu balling up his fist and proclaiming to a young Khudiram: "Prayer is not going to help us! Nor fasts! The only mantra that works is valour." The narrative text then tells us that Satyen Basu, "like other revolutionaries, believed that the British rule could be ended only by resorting to arms" (5). Instead of direct textual or visual criticism, it is the combination of text and image that conveys discomfort with Gandhi and the attentive sequencing of panels that transfers to Gandhi's shoulders some of the blame for outbursts of colonial violence. The one exception to this rule occurs in the *Senapati Bapat* issue (no. 303, 1984). Its introduction states:

> Though he believed in violence as a means to a noble end, he was not averse to peaceful methods but of course only if they worked. This was Senapati's greatest attribute—his catholicity of outlook and his openness of mind. He had the courage to criticise even Gandhiji if he thought him to be wrong, but the next moment, he would fast with the Mahatma if he considered the cause was good. The cause, not the man, was what mattered to Senapati—a high ideal he followed all through his life.

Senapati Bapat (1880–1967) was a revolutionary from Maharashtra who distributed manuals on the making of bombs among his colleagues. The British arrested him but then released him due to lack of evidence. It was at this point after his arrest, the comic book tells us, that Bapat "decided to try nonviolent methods" (23). In protest against the proposed construction of the Mulshi dam, which would displace local farmers and peasants, he delivered speeches, tore up railroad tracks, and served time in jail. When none of this met with any success, Bapat decided to try other tactics (figure 37): "But the struggle has to be kept alive—a violent struggle if need be!" Accompanied by a close-up shot of Bapat in thought, wearing a "Gandhi cap" while making this decision, the narrative text tells us that Senapati Bapat "decided to use a dramatic method to draw the attention of the government" and others to the peasants' cause (26). The next panel depicts this dramatic method in action: Bapat's men, armed with swords and lathis, await an approaching train whose path has been blocked. Bapat is featured in the foreground on the right half of the panel, a larger, more impressive figure than the locomotive on the left side. Still wearing his Gandhi cap, he is now armed with a revolver and marches confidently toward the train—so confidently that the reader can have no doubt about who will emerge victorious from the impending showdown. Here there is no tension between text and image. These two interdependent panels combine words and pictures to demonstrate the power of the revolutionary

SENAPATI BAPAT DECIDED TO USE A DRAMATIC METHOD TO DRAW THE ATTENTION OF THE GOVERNMENT AND THE PEOPLE TO THE INJUSTICE METED OUT TO THE FARMERS.

AGAIN, SENAPATI BAPAT INFORMED THE BUILDERS OF THE DAM OF HIS INTENTIONS. BARRICADES WERE PLACED BEFORE THE TRAIN COMING TO MULSHI.

path. Over the course of the next several panels, Bapat stops the train, shoots the train engineer in the leg, voluntarily proceeds to the police station to explain his act and turn himself in, and is sentenced to seven years in prison. The final panels make it clear that Bapat's violent act succeeds in drawing media attention to the peasants' cause, demonstrating that violent means can prove far more useful than nonviolent protest.

Gandhi cannot be depicted at the Jallianwala Bagh massacre because he was not in Amritsar when it happened. Gandhi was in Bombay for the hartal on April 6, 1919, and planned to leave the next evening for a brief visit to Delhi and travel to Amritsar thereafter (Gandhi 1983 [1948], 416). While en route, however, he was taken into police custody. Gandhi's growing popularity in Amritsar and other cities in the Punjab region alarmed British officials, who feared the possibility of rebellion. Gandhi was escorted

Figure 37. *Senapati Bapat,* no. 303 (Bombay: India Book House Pvt. Ltd., 1984), 26–27. From *Amar Chitra Katha,* with the permission of the publishers ACK Media, India.

Who Shot the Mahatma?

back to Bombay and was not allowed to enter the Punjab for over six months. Thus prior to the massacre, Gandhi had never been to Amritsar, had never met with local "Gandhian" leaders there, and had not helped organize any satyagraha activities there. Gandhi therefore explicitly denied all charges of culpability for the Jallianwala Bagh massacre. Although he did admit that it was a "Himalayan miscalculation" to call upon people to join the civil disobedience movement without first teaching them its deeper implications, Gandhi by no means felt that his call for a nonviolent protest against the Rowlatt Act was the cause of violence. On the contrary, Gandhi argued that his call for a hartal was "neither the cause nor the occasion of the upheaval," stating: "But for satyagraha, India would have witnessed scenes perhaps more terrible than it has passed through" (S. R. Singh 2000, 200).

For these reasons, it takes a substantial amount of text—of "telling"—to link images of the Jallianwala Bagh massacre with the figure of Mahatma Gandhi. As we have seen, the massacre forms the climax of *Mahatma Gandhi I: The Early Days:* the hartal and the massacre are discussed for nine panels at the end of the comic book and are ultimately followed by the final panel of the 1919 Congress session, where Gandhi became a "leader of the nation" (figure 34). The massacre is also the first thing mentioned in *Mahatma Gandhi II: The Father of the Nation,* where it is credited as the reason that Gandhi lost faith in the British and "turned a determined rebel against British rule in India" (1).

Although Gandhi rejected any causal connection to the violence of the Jallianwala Bagh massacre, his philosophy was deeply affected by it. Following the massacre, Gandhi began extensive outreach work, delivering speeches and writing articles to educate the common people about the integral relationship between *ahimsa* (nonviolence) and satyagraha.[7] But as Gandhi grew ever more popular with the masses, he also increasingly alienated himself from the Indian intelligentsia. Partha Chatterjee has argued that in rejecting the economic, cultural, and political structures of civil society, and in instead advocating a return to the simple self-sufficiency of "traditional" village life, Gandhi's ideology "operated from a standpoint that lay entirely outside the thematic of post-Enlightenment thought, and hence of nationalist thought as well" (1995, 100). This troubled many Indian nationalists, as did Gandhi's emphasis on womanhood as a civilizing force in human society (see Nandy 1980, 71–73). In the wake of the Chauri Chaura riot of 1922, as Gandhi urged moderation throughout the 1920s, these nationalists began to call for complete independence (*purna swaraj*) and increasingly rejected the tenets of Gandhism in favor of joining more militant Hindu nationalist organizations like the Hindu Mahasabha and the Rashtriya Swayamsevak Sangh (Bose and Jalal 1999, 145).

Nathuram Vinayak Godse (1912–49) was one such urban youth. A Chitpavan Brahmin from Pune, Godse was a member of the Maharashtrian Brahminic intelligentsia that advocated a staunch anti-British, pro-Hindu form of nationalism. Indeed, Ashis Nandy argues that by his cultural inheritance as a Chitpavan Brahmin from an orthodox Hindu city in Maharashtra, Godse was naturally a potential opponent of Gandhi; he also points out that all of the known unsuccessful attempts to kill Gandhi occurred in Maharashtra (1980, 77). In the late 1920s Godse participated briefly in Gandhi's civil disobedience movement, but soon found the ideology of the Hindu Mahasabha and the Rashtriya Swayamsevak Sangh (RSS) more appealing. Over the years, Godse became increasingly outspoken about his disagreements with Gandhi's philosophy. He used his newspaper, *Hindu Rashtra,* to articulate how Gandhism was emasculating Hindus and to urge Hindus to actively defend their nation rather than passively abide while it was harmed by the British and the Muslims.[8] The partition of India and Pakistan on the occasion of independence in 1947 was the final straw. Blaming Gandhi for the partition, Godse and several conspirators began planning to assassinate him. On January 30, 1948, the assassination was carried out: Godse approached Gandhi while he was going to conduct his evening prayers at the Birla House in Delhi. Godse first bowed down before Gandhi, purportedly demonstrating his respect for the services that Gandhi had rendered to the nation, and then shot him three times in the chest. Godse then calmly called for the police and turned himself in.

An hour after the assassination, an All India Radio broadcast informed listeners across India of the shooting, saying only: "Mahatma Gandhi was assassinated in New Delhi at twenty past five this afternoon. His assassin was a Hindu." Immediately thereafter, anti-RSS and anti-Brahmin riots broke out throughout the area of modern-day Maharashtra as people protested the killing of the Mahatma.[9] It was not long, however, before some began to hail Godse as a hero in Maharashtra and beyond.

During his trial, Godse described his action as a duty that he had to perform for the sake of the nation:

> Gandhiji failed in his duty as the Father of the Nation. He has proved to be the Father of Pakistan. It was for this reason that I as a dutiful son of Mother India thought it my duty to put an end to the life of the so-called Father of the Nation who had played a very prominent part in bringing about the vivisection of the country—our Motherland. (Nandy 1980, 83)[10]

This speech has come to be celebrated within some Hindu nationalist circles, especially in the western state of Maharashtra, where it plays a significant role in the revisioning of the freedom struggle. Nathuram Godse's brother, Gopal Godse, has written several books about his brother's act.

One of them, *May It Please Your Honour,* centers upon the speech given by Nathuram Godse as his defense plea at his trial. First published in 1977, this book came into the limelight in 1998 when a play based on it was staged in Bombay. The two-act play by Pradeep Dalvi, *Me Nathuram Godse Boltoy* (This Is Nathuram Godse Speaking), enacts Godse's defense plea and thereby explores the assassination of Gandhi and the trial of Godse from Godse's point of view. Audience members inside the packed theater reportedly cheered when the actor playing Godse victoriously proclaimed his reasons for killing the Mahatma, while outside the theater hundreds of protestors demanded the cancellation of the play, which they felt denigrated Gandhi and glorified violence (Koppikar 1998; Dasgupta and Koppikar 1998). The controversial play was banned by the government of Maharashtra in 1998, and the book that inspired it was banned the following year. In the past few years, however, these rulings have been overturned, and then those reversals have been overturned, and still the court battle rages on. Other expressions of appreciation of Godse and his infamous act have been as controversial as the play—such as the yearly gathering in Pune on November 15, the anniversary of Godse's execution, when his followers perform acts of worship before his portrait and his shirt, which was splattered with Gandhi's blood.[11]

Nathuram Godse, as his followers remember him, is in many ways the sort of historical character that is scripted as a revolutionary hero in the *Amar Chitra Katha* comic books. Like the Maharashtrian revolutionary hero Senapati Bapat, Godse embraced the revolutionary path only after trying and rejecting Gandhi's nonviolent approach. The *Senapati Bapat* comic tells us that before his showdown with the locomotive, Bapat informed the dam builders of his intentions, and after shooting the engineer in the leg, Bapat surrendered to the police and explained the reasons for his actions, stressing that he had only injured the driver, not killed him (27). Stories of Godse's act as told by his followers similarly stress his efforts to minimize violence. In order to avoid injuring anyone other than Gandhi, Godse allegedly pushed Gandhi's grandniece, Manu, aside before firing his gun. Like Bapat, Godse immediately surrendered to the police, and during his trial he eloquently justified the violence. Like Senapati Bapat, Bhagat Singh, and other revolutionary heroes featured in the *ACK* comic books, Nathuram Godse is remembered by his followers as a courageous, active, articulate, and ethical man who was willing to take whatever action was necessary in order to defend his nation.

Given the contested status of both Mahatma Gandhi and Nathuram Godse in postcolonial India, how then are the comic book creators to deal with the assassination? In order to retain their wide mass-market appeal, they depict Gandhi's assassin neither as a hero (no matter how closely his story resembles that of other revolutionary heroes) nor as a villain. Instead, they attempt to mediate between both sides by limiting the information presented to the reader, as when the assassination is depicted in *Mahatma Gandhi II* (figure 33). In this panel, the literal focal point of this dramatic image is the gun, which is placed at the center of the image and encircled by a large yellow halo. Visually the act is highlighted, not the assassin or the victim. The text also diverts attention from the assassin by not naming Godse. Here text and image work together, but not in the "interdependent" sense in which they work to move the narrative forward. Instead, they work together to stall the narrative, to limit the information presented to the reader. By focusing on the act rather than the actor, the unnamed assassin is neither exculpated nor blamed. The assassination is a mere statement of fact, and it is up to the reader to draw his or her own moral conclusions, to decide whether to mourn or celebrate. Yet, because of this attempt to mediate between both sides, the ending of this comic book deviates from the standard heroic formula, wherein the hero either emerges victorious in the end or dies a noble death actively fighting in battle with the villain. Just who is the hero here, and who is the villain?

G. D. Birla (no. 382, 1987) is another comic book issue that depicts the scene of Gandhi's death (plate 10). In this panel, the disassociation between the act of killing Gandhi and the actor is even clearer. The text states: "The relationship between Gandhi and Birla was so close that Gandhi stayed at Birla House while in Delhi. Ironically it was here that he was murdered" (29). In the image, only two figures can be identified: Gandhi occupies the right side of the panel and is beginning to bleed from the three bullets that have just lodged in his chest. Gandhi's grandniece Manu is a smaller figure in the bottom center of the image, where she has fallen to the ground, presumably after being pushed aside by Godse. The assassin is not depicted. Instead, the assassin's gun occupies the entire left side of the image, and the perspective is such that we readers watch the bullets leave the barrel and strike the Mahatma from an angle that positions us next to the shooter. This is an angle that subtly discourages us from identifying with the victim, Gandhi, or with his followers, who fade into the background of the image behind him. Instead, in a way that is reminiscent of many video games, this angle places us at the forefront of the action and alongside the shooter, as if we readers are the assassin's accomplices or co-conspirators, looking down at the gun just after pulling the trigger.

The assassination as it is depicted in *Mahatma Gandhi II* contains many more descriptive elements than this panel in *G. D. Birla*. For instance, we read that it occurred at exactly 5:10 PM on the evening of January 30, 1948, and we see that Gandhi is in a well-manicured garden, and that he is surrounded by both loyal followers in "Gandhi caps" and a larger, amorphous crowd. In these descriptive details the panel in *Mahatma Gandhi II* calls to mind other detailed visual renderings of the assassination, including the beginning and ending scenes of British director Richard Attenborough's 1982 film *Gandhi*.[12] Whereas the reader remains a passive witness of the act here, the panel in *G. D. Birla* focuses more on the action by minimizing descriptive details and positioning us as more active participants in the narrative action. Yet despite this significant difference between these two renderings of Gandhi's death, the message of these two panels is ultimately the same. In both, the compositional focal point is the gun. Furthermore, in each panel a yellow halo with lines radiating outward surrounds the gun and the bullets that pierce Gandhi's chest. In American comics such action lines (or "zip ribbons") are often used to indicate dynamic movement, to "depict action with drama," and as Scott McCloud points out, over time they have become "so stylized as to almost have a life and physical presence all their own" (1993, 111–12). Here, in these two panels the action lines and the yellow halo do indeed convey dramatic action: They highlight the violent path of the bullets as they erupt from the gun and rip into Gandhi's chest, making the gun and bullets take on a life of their own, as the active subject of these images. In both panels, therefore, the focus is clearly upon the violent act of the assassination itself, not the assassin or the victim. Who shot the Mahatma?

Conclusion: Massacre and the Mahatma

What is perhaps most startling about this panel in the *G. D. Birla* issue depicting the assassination of Gandhi is how disconnected it is with the rest of the storyline. Ghanshyam Das Birla (1894–1983) was a prominent industrialist and philanthropist and a close follower of Gandhi. The comic is careful to point out the disagreements between Birla and Gandhi, devoting two full pages (27 and 28) to their differences over Gandhi's concept of cottage industries and Birla's belief in the need for large-scale industrialization. The first panel on page 29 then mentions that Gandhi's civil disobedience movement was gaining momentum and shows Gandhi marching with many followers in line behind him. The second panel, on the bottom left, mentions that Gandhi represented the Indian National Congress at the Second Round Table Conference in 1931, while Birla was a representative of the Indian business community. The third and final panel of this page depicts Gandhi's assassination. On the next page, the narrative returns to its proper subject, Birla, highlighting both his worldly position and his spiritual prowess.

Why is this image of the assassination even included in the *G. D. Birla* issue? The assassination of Gandhi is only tangentially related to the storyline, connected through the insertion of the narrative explanation that the assassination "ironically" happened at the Birla House. Yet placed as it is in the lower right-hand corner at the very end of a two-page spread about Birla's relationship with Gandhi, this panel taints all of the previous panels on these two pages. Now the disagreements that Birla had with Gandhi over economic progress take on a more ambiguous quality. Are they merely friendly debates? Or are they more sinister, symptomatic of the increasing disapproval of Gandhi's ideology, even amidst his loyal followers and friends? Although readers are ultimately positioned to share the responsibility for Gandhi's death in the final panel of this spread through our position alongside the shooter, the text and image together implicate Birla as well. The "hero" of this particular issue, Birla, is nowhere to be seen in the assassination panel. In fact, all of Gandhi's followers, aside from his fallen grandniece, have been pushed into the distant background, becoming mere spectators, faceless and nameless. Where are his loyal followers now, when they are needed? Here the use of the word *ironically* in the narrative text also raises questions about Birla's loyalty, for this choice of wording points out that it was precisely where Gandhi should have been most protected—at the home of his good friend Birla—that he was murdered.

The repetition of images of Gandhi's assassination in the *ACK* comic book series, like the repetition of images of the Jallianwala Bagh massacre, is significant, suggesting that the assassination is also a nodal point in the history of modern India—especially as that history is recounted by the comic book producers, the majority of whom are Hindu Brahmins based in Maharashtra, where there is a legacy of promoting martial Indian heroes like Shivaji and Senapati Bapat. Images of the assassination in the *G. D. Birla* and *Mahatma Gandhi II* issues work—like the images of the Jallianwala Bagh massacre—to again suggest a problem with Gandhi's philosophy: that nonviolence is ultimately rewarded with violence. Yet whereas the images of the Jallianwala Bagh massacre required an excess of text in order to "explain" them—to causally connect the massacre with both Gandhi and the British—the images of Gandhi's assassination require the moderation of text in order to break the causal connection between Godse and the event. Eliminating the shooter's identity, of course, is one way of reducing the possibility of controversy, of remembering the act of the assassination without passing judgment on the actor either positively, by declaring him a revolutionary hero, or negatively, by declaring him a criminal villain. But it also is a form of collective amnesia, one that extends beyond these comic books and seriously impacts how the life and death of Gandhi are remembered in modern India.

Historian Krishna Kumar has discussed the passage on Gandhi's assassination in the National Council of Educational Research and Training (NCERT) textbook of modern Indian history for class eight, noting how confusing the passage is for its intended audience due to its recalcitrance. Kumar writes:

> If a text were aimed at communicating to children the story and also the significance of Gandhiji's murder, it could not possibly avoid delving into the web of details about Hindu-Muslim conflict, the politics of partition and the politics of Hindu revivalist organizations, and Gandhiji's own frustration in the final months of his life. These details, howsoever briefly one might discuss them, are necessary for anyone who wishes to make sense of Gandhiji's assassination. (1996, 15)

Instead, the textbook—like the comic books—only mentions that "some people" did not like Gandhi's message of love and brotherhood, yet refuses to explain who those people were and what their motivations were or, more specifically, to name Gandhi's assassin. Concluding his discussion of the textbook, Kumar argues that despite the authors' intention to teach history from a secular (or "received") perspective, such textbooks often end up furthering a communal (or "rival") perspective instead:

> The vague, incomplete knowledge we found in the NCERT textbook about an event of modern Indian history as major as Gandhiji's murder can be counted on to leave children all the more eager than they anyhow are to accept the "rival" perspective. In cruel brevity, the "rival" perspective blames Gandhiji for his own murder. It denies that his killer was a fanatic inspired by the institutionalized ideology of Hindu revivalism. It suggests that Gandhiji's disappearance from the political scene was not such a bad thing after all since he was lionising the Muslim community and Pakistan. (1996, 17)[13]

Like Kumar, I too have found that these instances of collective amnesia, even when meant to minimize communal conflict, can at times have the opposite effect. When discussing the *ACK* comic books with college-age readers in urban India and the North American diaspora, many who were not already familiar with Nathuram Godse and his act had assumed that it was a Muslim who shot Gandhi. During one group interview with a dozen second-generation Indian college students in the United States, one young man who admitted to gaining most of his knowledge of India from these comic books further stated that this was the reason for much of the ongoing Hindu-Muslim strife in postcolonial India. Several others present nodded in agreement; fortunately, one student in the group did recall Nathuram Godse's name and spoke up to set the record straight.

The *ACK* comic books have no end of praise for Hindu and Sikh revolutionary figures who died fighting for India's freedom from the British, like Khudiram Bose, Chandra Shekhar Azad, and Bhagat Singh. The comics repeatedly pair references to their patriotism with textual and visual references to their manliness. The introduction to *Chandra Shekhar Azad*, for instance, tells readers:

> The activities of Azad and his associates contributed in no small measure to the awakening of the Indian masses—a task which the national leaders of the day were trying to achieve through a peaceful means. Azad had a strong physique, plenty of common sense and patriotic zeal. The British described him as a terrorist. But he considered himself a freedom fighter.

Similarly, *Bhagat Singh* ends by quoting Prime Minister Jawaharlal Nehru: "The lesson which we should learn from Bhagat Singh is to die in a manly and bold manner so that India might live" (30). Throughout these comic books, a connection is repeatedly made between manliness, patriotism, and the revolutionary path. This is the formula for a modern Indian hero.

The nonviolent path, on the other hand, is associated with both a lack of manliness and a lack of patriotism, and it is Gandhi who was the most outspoken proponent of the nonviolent path. Throughout the *Amar Chitra Katha* series, by causally connecting Gandhi with the Jallianwala Bagh massacre and by dwelling on Gandhi's own violent death, the nonviolent path is repeatedly shown to be untenable, to constantly meet with violence, and therefore to be the path of a false hero, for the "Father of the Nation" did not and would not die bravely fighting for his country, but his assassin would and did.

Conclusion: The Global Legacy of Amar Chitra Katha

We used to drive to the temple for holidays and other special occasions. It was an hour away, and sometimes I didn't want to go. I'd rather stay home and play games with my friends outside, or play video games, you know. But my parents bribed me: If I went and was good, they would give me a comic book to read on the way back. I guess as a kid I didn't really understand why we worshipped those gods in the temple, what they meant. But I remember reading the *Hanuman* comic in the car one time and finding a connection with Hinduism. Hanuman is like the Indian version of Superman. He has these special powers, and he tries to do good with them.

A reader

In 1990, the producers of *Amar Chitra Katha* released two new issues that radically differed from their successful comic book formula: *An Exciting Find* (no. 430) and *Indus Valley Adventure* (no. 432). In these issues our "heroes" are Vijay and Durga, a boy and girl who go on holiday with their grandfather, an amateur archaeologist, to Harappa, the ancient city of ruins in the northwestern region of the Indian subcontinent. They are completely bored with their grandfather's history lesson until they uncover a time machine that takes them back to the year 2000 BCE, when the Indus Valley civilization thrived. There they learn all about this ancient civilization by walking through its markets, playing with the local children, and attending a public sacrificial ritual before returning to their own time. Author Yagya Sharma described these comics, which he had envisioned as the first in a larger sequence of themed issues, as among his best scripts:

> I said, let's try using the common people as the central figures. Then we could write history from a completely different perspective. I thought we could look at the period from Harappa up to Akbar. Stopping at Akbar, because he was the last glorious king in India. And starting with Harappa because at that time there was a lot of new information coming out about that civilization. Lots of research was needed, a different kind of research, to write from this perspective. So we began with the *Indus Valley Adventure*.[1] We planned two or three others on the Indus Valley, with these same characters, and then we were going to move on to the Vedic period. But I had to leave. I could not make enough of a living just writing the comic book scripts. So I took another position. Possibly they couldn't find the right author to write these scripts. It takes a lot of imagination to create new characters out of nothing and to tell the story from this sort of perspective. It is an unusual perspective. Perhaps the perspective was just too unusual. Perhaps it didn't appeal.

Artist Yusuf Bangalorewala illustrated *An Exciting Find,* and he also described it as the best work he had done for the *ACK* series:

> My best work for *Amar Chitra Katha* from a technical point of view was *An Exciting Find,* an adventure of a twin brother and sister duo who are transported back 4,500 years [*sic*] right into the Indus Valley or Harappan civilization. Did Anant Pai show you this book? They published just a few copies that were available for around six months. After that there were no reprints. Maybe it

failed to sell owing to an ugly cover. But in my opinion the inside stuff made it the most well illustrated, adventurous, exciting, and thrilling book for Indian children during that period. It was done with a Rotring pen with a full ink reservoir to last two or three pages, unlike *Mirabai* or *Tansen,* which were done with a bare crow quill nib dipped every twenty seconds into an ink pot! I did this classy book just before I did *Jawaharlal Nehru,* around 1988 or 1989.

The author and the artist of these issues both stress the originality of the story line and the artwork. Yet *An Exciting Find* and *Indus Valley Adventure* did not sell well. Anant Pai agreed with Sharma that the perspective was just too unusual for *ACK's* readers: "We received a few positive letters. But we received many more letters of complaint, requesting that we bring back the old heroes." Thus the other scripts that had originally been envisioned as part of this sequence were abandoned.

Most *ACK* readers were simply not interested in reading about time machines or other fictionalized novelties, nor were they interested in reading about "common people." Instead, they wanted to read about their Indian heritage, to envision it, to believe in it, to take comfort in it. They wanted formulaic heroes like the mythological god-king Rama, the historical warrior-king Shivaji, and the modern freedom fighter Bhagat Singh: heroes who battled their foes and either emerged victorious or else died bravely in the process. For the readers of these comics, this is the very formula for Indianness. And this is true not only of the Indians who read these comic books in India but also of the transnational Indians who read these comic books throughout the world today.

The *Amar Chitra Katha* series seemed to be dying out in the early 1990s. Sales of *Jawaharlal Nehru* (no. 436, 1991), about India's first prime minister, another issue that broke with the successful formula in its overly biographical and academic tone, were very disappointing: only 24,000 copies sold, nowhere near the break-even mark of 40,000 copies (Doctor 1997, 38). Anant Pai and the other *ACK* producers decided that it was time to pull the plug and stop creating new issues. If *ACK* has weathered this storm and even made a comeback in recent years—creating new issues, reprinting bestsellers, and moving into new media like television, animation, and the internet—this resurgence is due largely to its ever-broadening base of global Indian readers. The reader quoted above is a former student of mine who grew up in the United States, born to parents who had emigrated from northern India. He too finds the *ACK* formula appealing in its lineup of formulaic mythological and historical Indian superheroes who try "to do good," like the Hindu monkey-god Hanuman, who fights the evil demon-king Ravana by Rama's side in the *Rāmāyaṇa* epic. But his statement also alludes to the significance of this series for Indians, and especially Hindus, who now live outside of India.

The Pleasures of Reading Comic Books in the Indian Diaspora

As discussed in the introduction, there are many interrelated and often overlapping pleasures associated with reading *ACK* comic books in India: the pride entailed in reading indigenous comics featuring uniquely Indian heroes and stories; the patriotism that is inspired by reading comics about India's brave historical heroes; the lighthearted humor that is encountered in some issues; the pleasure of the comic book medium itself in its short and colorful format; the comfort taken from the formulaic pattern of storytelling; and the pleasure that Hindus specifically take in learning more about their religion through the mythological comics. Understanding these pleasures is key to understanding why these comic books have come to occupy such a cherished place in the lives of so many of their readers in India. For transnational or nonresident Indians (NRIs) who have emigrated from India to other countries and those born to émigré parents, these comic books are associated with two other pleasures that are unique to those readers in the Indian diaspora: first, the pleasure of maintaining a connection with the Indian "homeland" by reading about its historical eras and leaders; and second—for Hindus in particular—the pleasure of learning to articulate what Hindus believe in an environment where Hinduism is not the majority religion and where a perceived vacuum of resources about Hinduism is often keenly felt. One NRI whose parents immigrated to Canada from the state of Uttar Pradesh in northern India summarized this succinctly in his statement about what these comics meant to him:

> I was born and raised in Edmonton, Canada. Both of my parents are from the U.P. (Faizabad and Gonda). As we did not have any relatives here when I was growing up, I relied almost exclusively on *ACK* for learning about Hinduism and the history of India.

Like my methods for studying the consumption of *ACK* in India, my methods for studying the consumption of these comics beyond India were also wide-ranging. I have had many conversations with students of Indian heritage in the United States; I spent a month in 2002 in Great Britain speaking with NRIs there about the comics; I have visited Hindu temples and Indian community centers in the United States to learn about their youth education programs and their usage of *ACK* comics in such programs and in their libraries; and I have spoken with Indian grocery store owners in the United States who stock these comics on their shelves in addition to imported Indian grocery items, household products, and films. Once again, while all of this helped to form a picture of what these comics mean to their NRI readers, much of my insight into the significance of *ACK* for readers in the diaspora comes from those who sought me out after learning about my research. After *India Abroad* articles on my research were published (Joshi 2003; Saptharishi 2007), many readers in North

America contacted me to express their love for these comics, and some even generously offered to share their comic book collections:

> I am in Austin, and one of my friends in Virginia read about you in *India Abroad* newspaper, about your research project. They have lot of books of *Amar Chitra Katha* cartoon storybooks similar to Aesop Fables and want to send you if you need them and can use them.

In addition to North American NRIs, Indians living around the globe have contacted me—from Australia to Brazil to Kuwait to London to Singapore to Tanzania—demonstrating just how widespread the readership of *ACK* is. They stress that they have often had to explain facets of Indian culture to others in their community who are not familiar with it and who may even have absorbed negative stereotypes about India and Indians. The *ACK* comic books, with their many issues on ancient, medieval, and modern Indian heroes, helped them to develop a sense of pride about Indian history and civilization and thus about their own Indian heritage. Certainly this was the case for one reader of Indian heritage in Brazil, who mentioned that he buys the comics to share with his Brazilian girlfriend as a way of countering common misperceptions about India:

> *ACK* conveys to her a different India from what many Christian missionaries in Latin America paint: full of poverty, hunger, superstition, and ignorance. While I understand that *ACK* is a distorted version of reality, it is needed to balance the worldview created by missionary education in the western world. . . . My European and Latin American friends have been amazed at a nonacademic comic book that is so interesting and engaging that children actually read it.

The vast majority of NRI readers who contacted me were Hindus who explained that the comic books also helped them to better understand what it means to be a Hindu and to articulate what Hindus believe and why. To understand this point, it is useful to take a closer look at the American diaspora community—the Indian diaspora with which my research has been most involved—as an example. The immigration of Hindus and other religious groups from India to the United States occurred in two phases. The first phase consisted of the early immigrants who came from the northwestern part of the Indian subcontinent (the Punjab region) to California and other areas along the West Coast that were in need of agricultural laborers. This migration took place from the mid-nineteenth century until new U.S. immigration laws were passed in 1917 and 1924 that discriminated against Asians (including Indians). The second phase consisted of the new immigrants who began to arrive after the passage of the 1965 Immigration and Naturalization Act, which reversed the previous immigration laws and initiated preferential admission of Asians who were considered highly skilled. Karen Isaksen Leonard has shown that whereas the first phase of

South Asian immigrants to America "acted essentially on their own, either carrying out private religious acts or discarding their religions," the second phase of immigrants was very different in that they sought to retain their religious identities and establish visible and permanent places for Hinduism and other South Asian religions in their new homeland by founding religious organizations, building Hindu temples and community centers, and importing religious specialists and ritual items (1997, 107). These Indian immigrants were typically well educated professionals who came to America to pursue advanced educational opportunities and professional employment. Furthermore, most of these immigrants initially planned to return to India. However, as time passed and these immigrants married and had children, they began to settle down. They bought homes, enrolled their children in schools, applied for permanent residency, and built Indian community centers and Hindu temples.

Several recent studies of Hinduism in America have discussed the rise of a Hindu temple tradition beginning in the 1970s. The Sri Lakshmi Temple in Ashland, Massachusetts, celebrated its grand opening in 1986 and its formal consecration in 1990, but plans for this temple began in 1978 when a group of Hindu immigrants living in New England decided they were in need of a permanent religious edifice in their new homeland. Discussing this process, Diana Eck writes:

> In the 1970s new Indian immigrants to Boston, most of them professionals who had come during their student years, took jobs and settled in New England. They all intended to return to India eventually. Then they began to have children, and before long their children were in grade school. By now, these young families were putting down deeper roots in America and beginning to look toward a future here. They realized that their children would have no cultural or religious identity as Hindus at all unless they themselves began to do something about it. . . . These Hindus were engineers and doctors, metallurgists and biochemists, not temple builders. In fact, many of them had not been actively religious at all in India. Had they returned to Madras or Bangalore, they would never have become involved in the building or administration of a temple. But here in America their education as Hindus took on a new and practical form. (2002, 88–89)

The earliest full-scale Hindu temples built in America (as distinguished from converted warehouses, churches, or other preexisting spaces) were dedicated in the 1970s, such as the Sri Maha Vallabha Ganapati Devasthanam Temple in the Flushing neighborhood of Queens in New York City and the Sri Venkateswara Temple in Penn Hills, Pennsylvania. In the decades since then, middle-class professionals have built Hindu temples in urban areas across the United States (see Waghorne 2004; Dempsey 2006). The communities behind all of these temples share the concern that without such formal spaces for practicing Hinduism, their children would grow up denuded of their religious heritage. In India, without ever going to the temple, a child could absorb many of the beliefs and practices of Hinduism through annual festivals, life-cycle ceremonies performed within the home, and the telling of mythological stories in various media. But in the American context, few such opportunities existed to learn about Hinduism outside of the temple. Additionally, parents who had not received any formal religious training often found themselves at a loss when called upon to explain Hindu beliefs or practices to their children or to non-Hindu neighbors and co-workers, and so they desired a formal establishment that would aid them in articulating their religious beliefs and educating their children. Discussing this sentiment in the context of her conversations with Hindus at the Sri Venkateswara Temple in Penn Hills, Vasudha Narayanan writes:

> It is always difficult to perceive oneself clearly and to articulate one's faith and tradition to oneself, the community and to one's children, especially if one has had no formal training or education in the field. But such is the predicament of a Hindu here; having grown up in India, soaking up the Hindu religious experience, does not make one a specialist in it. And yet, we are forced to articulate over and over again what it means to be a Hindu and an Indian to our friends and to our children, and one feels ill-equipped for the task. Frequently, all that one remembers of a festival in India is the food that was prepared for it; one was never called upon to explain Deepavali or Sankaranti, and least of all, "Hinduism." (1992, 172)

The significance of the *Amar Chitra Katha* comics for Hindus living in the American diaspora should be understood in this context. These comic books first began to be produced in 1967, just as the second phase of immigration to America had begun. As more and more titles were released throughout the 1970s, and as these immigrants started their own families, they found in these comics a handy tool with which to educate their children and themselves about Hindu mythology and Indian history. Thus whereas many readers of these comics in India already know the story being told before they read the comic, and therefore take pleasure in seeing that story retold in the comic book medium, readers in the diaspora have a very different experience, for they take pleasure not only in the medium itself but also in learning a new story of a new Indian hero. Many families reported that when they made visits to India over winter or summer holidays they would buy a set of all of the available comics to take back to America with them; other families reported that grandparents or aunts and uncles still living in India would ship the comics to their grandchildren or their nieces and nephews on birthdays and on festival occasions. In a format that was relatively cheap to purchase and transport overseas and that was concise, accessible, and interesting to children, these comics introduced the Hindu pantheon, explained Hindu mythology, and provided an overview of Indian history through its legendary leaders.

Those Hindus who were born in America to Indian émigrés or came to America as children repeatedly stressed that these comics were tremendously influential in teaching them Hinduism; in the words of one reader, it was from the *ACK* comics that he learned "all the values of Hinduism—Hindu *devas* [gods], *dharma* [religious and social duty], morality, family values, roles of men and women, and the glory of ancient Indian culture." Similarly, a young man of Indian heritage living in Texas stated, "I didn't really buy into worship like most devout Hindus, though I didn't want to offend my parents trying to be different either. I'd strongly think my moral yardsticks can be attributed to comics like *ACK* instead of those visits to the temple or religious instruction."

Many of these children were disinterested in temple visits, often because they felt self-conscious about seeming different from other children in their neighborhoods and schools. Frequently, they didn't know how to explain to themselves or to their non-Hindu friends why Hindus went to worship "those gods in the temple and what they meant." For the reader quoted at the outset of this chapter, Hindu beliefs and practices only began to make sense when he read the *Hanuman* (no. 19, 1971) comic book. Suddenly he knew the mythological stories associated with one of the gods that was featured in the temple his family visited, and he knew why Hanuman was worshipped. Whereas he had previously thought it was silly, even somewhat embarrassing, that Hindus worshipped animals, he volunteered the next year to play the role of Hanuman when his temple reenacted the *Rāmāyaṇa* epic, and as an adult he remains a devotee of this monkey-god.

In the American context, *ACK* comic books have been part and parcel of the Hindu temple experience. With the mission of educating the community about their Hindu faith and their Indian heritage, American Hindu temples were built not only as places of worship but also as community centers where annual festivals and special events such as weddings could be celebrated, where cultural traditions such as Indian dance and musical concerts could be performed, and where youth education programs could take place. Most temples were constructed with rooms designed for such activities, often including a classroom and library. Many parents who immigrated to America and raised their children with these comics reported that they donated them to their local Hindu temple after the children grew up; and Hindus who grew up in America often reported that they read these comics with their Indian-heritage friends at the temple library or in youth education classes. One young man who grew up in the Bay Area in California, for instance, reported that he loved the comics because *ACK* "tells stories about Hindu culture and it teaches about good qualities that one should have. And it doesn't have stories only about one god, but many gods." When asked where he read these comics, he reported that he "read so many of them at the library of my local temple, the Shiva-Vishnu Temple of Livermore, California."

The Shiva-Vishnu Temple was incorporated as a Hindu community and cultural center in 1977, and it has an active youth and education department with regular class offerings for both children and adults, as well as a learning center that contains among other items an "almost full set of *Amar Chitra Katha* books for the children—all bound in sets of 3 to 5."[2] The Shiva-Vishnu Temple has a dual worship focus: both the gods Shiva and Vishnu are enshrined within the temple, along with their respective entourages, including Vishnu's wife, the goddess Lakshmi, and Shiva's wife, the goddess Parvati. With its dual focus and sanctums to multiple deities, this temple stands apart from traditional temples in India, which are typically dedicated to either Shiva or Vishnu, but not both. Historically in India these gods have more often acted as sectarian rivals than as interfaith brothers, but outside of India, in places where Hindus are but a small minority, Hindus from various regional, linguistic, and sectarian backgrounds have often joined together to create a sacred space where Shaiva, Vaishnava, and Shakta gods all have representation in an effort to unify the Hindu community and make all members feel welcome.[3] Thus this reader's comment that he likes the *ACK* comics precisely because they feature the stories of multiple Hindu gods has important theological significance, for it points to one way that Hinduism is changing in the diaspora: the now prevalent doctrine that "Truth is One, paths are many." In the effort to unify the many Hindu traditions into one Hinduism, and also to counter charges of idolatry in countries where image worship is often regarded with suspicion, Hindus now regularly proclaim in temple bulletins and philosophical sermons that in Hinduism there are many images or "idols" of gods, but all are symbols of the One True God (Eck 2002, 86; Narayanan 1992, 165). Therefore, Shaivas, Vaishnavas, and Shaktas should learn to recognize one another as co-religionists who are united in their devotion to God. Throughout the transnational Hindu community, the *ACK* series helps to unite Hindus across the various sectarian divides— the many paths—by featuring issues that explain the mythology of Rama, Krishna, Shiva, Durga, and other Hindu deities.

Commenting on the predominant position of *Amar Chitra Katha* comic books and the "controlled diet" of simplified creeds such as "Truth is One, paths are many" in temple Hinduism as it is practiced in America, Vasudha Narayanan sounds a cautionary note:

> The influence of these articles in the [temple] bulletins should not be underestimated; unlike a person in India, where newspapers and regular television programming carry glimpses of varied rituals and synopses of religious discourses, these articles may be the only regular "religious education" the readers of the bulletin get. By appearing in this bulletin, the articles also

seem authoritative. Thus we may have an entire generation of young Hindus growing up in this country, educated on the myths recounted by *Amar Chitra Katha*—where again, *one* story line is presented and is ratified as "true" unlike the oral tradition, which may present alternative versions of a story—and on symbolic meanings of temples, deities, and rituals. The effects of this controlled diet will have to be judged in future years. (1992, 168–69)

Indeed, *ACK* comics often attain an even greater significance in the religious lives of their transnational readers than in the religious lives of their readers in India, where these comic books are just one source among many for learning about Hindu beliefs and practices. I first realized how important *ACK* was in the American diaspora when I was a teaching assistant at the University of Texas at Austin, where many students of Indian heritage enrolled in the undergraduate courses on South Asian religion and culture. Frequently, these comics were the primary means by which these students had learned Hindu mythology. Thus in one course on the Indian epics, as we read the ending of an English translation of the Sanskrit *Rāmāyaṇa* epic by Valmiki, in which Rama banishes his pregnant wife, Sita, to the forest based on unfounded rumors of her infidelity, one student protested that this ending was wrong, exclaiming vociferously that the epic ends when Rama and Sita return victoriously to their kingdom and are crowned king and queen. As I explained that that was the end of the sixth book of the epic, but there was also a seventh book in which Sita is banished and raises her twin sons alone in exile at Valmiki's forest hermitage, the student grew quiet and withdrew from the conversation in contemplation. Later that week, he brought in his *Valmiki's Ramayana* (bumper issue no. 10001, 1992) and showed me its ending (plate 8): a final full-page panel featuring Rama and Sita being crowned king and queen. Although I tried to use this as a "teaching moment" to instruct my student about the many different renditions of the Indian epics that have been composed over the centuries, in the end this student taught me about the significance of these comic books. For him, clearly, the *ACK* version of the *Rāmāyaṇa* epic featuring Rama as a superhero who encounters his foes, defeats them in battle, and then rules Ayodhya happily ever after was the only version of the epic that mattered: it was the "true" version of Valmiki's *Rāmāyaṇa*.

A Closed Canon of Indian Heroes?

In 1991, when Anant Pai and the other *ACK* producers decided to stop creating new issues and focus only on reprinting bestsellers, a curious thing happened. Despite the well-known hardships that the entire print industry in India was encountering at this time and the obvious financial reasoning behind this decision, a persistent rumor arose that the creators had to stop making these comic books because there were no more Indian heroes left. When asked if there were other figures that they felt should be featured in the comic book series, reader after reader explained that there weren't any figures left to include. "All of the major characters have already been done," said one reader in Bombay. "That is why they stopped making new issues." Another asked, "Who else could they feature? It has all been done—the great saints, the kings, the freedom fighters, all the heroes of India!" While a few readers did wish for new issues on contemporary political leaders and Hindu swamis—and a few requested an *ACK* comic version of *Lord of the Rings*—the general consensus among the readers I interviewed was that the comic book series had completely represented all of India's immortal heroes, mythological and historical. Other readers replied: "I'd be surprised if they left any facet of Indian mythology, history untouched"; "*ACK* has done all the stories from all over India, and a couple folk tales from other countries as well"; "*Amar Chitra Katha* adequately represents all of India as we get to know about the folk tales, saints, and freedom fighters from the different parts of India"; and "There are so many worshippable demigods and gods, but personally I know *Amar Chitra Katha* has virtually exhausted all of them." For these readers, the national canon of gods, kings, and other heroes was complete—no other regional Hindu gods and goddesses, no other religious figures from India's other religious traditions, no other men and women from any historical period need be added.

The case studies of the mythological and historical issues presented in the preceding chapters have shown that the *Amar Chitra Katha* comic book series is a form of public culture wherein ideologies of religion and national identity are actively created and re-created amid ongoing debate. We have seen how the artists, authors, and editors involved in the creative process have debated several significant questions during the making of these Indian comic books: What textual and visual resources are considered authentically Indian? What is the place of science and faith in postcolonial India? Which Hindu gods and goddesses are central to Hinduism? Who is the ideal Indian woman? What roles do Muslims and other non-Hindus play in Indian history and society? And who should be remembered as heroes of the struggle for India's independence? But as Christopher Pinney warns, we must also pay attention to the limits of such debates, for in public culture there is also "ample evidence of erasure, of the elevation of particular dominant norms, alongside an ongoing debate about the nature of personal, community, and national identity" (2001, 9). These case studies have also shown the limits of these debates. For instance, throughout the making and remaking of the first issue, *Krishna* (no. 11, 1969), and the debates over the propriety of depicting miracles, no one challenged the assumption that all Indian children needed to learn Krishna's story. And despite the new emphasis on authenticity during the production of *Tales of Durga* (no. 176, 1978), everyone agreed to the need to sanitize goddess Kali to make her more appealing. These issues demonstrate not only the centrality of Hinduism to this Indian comic book series but also that it is a modern, middle-class, upper-caste, predominantly Vaishnava strand of Hinduism. In the 1970s, when debates arose about the depiction of women and Muslims that resulted in an alternative feminine ideal and in the portrayal of some Muslim emperors as heroes, an emphasis was nonetheless maintained on the heroines' ultimate self-sacrifice and on the evils of Muslim orthodoxy. During the making of *Shivaji* (no. 23, 1971), we saw that care was taken to portray him as a warrior-king that both Brahmins and non-Brahmins could look up to. Yet artists, authors, and editors agreed to the depiction of him as a manly defender of Maharashtra and the larger Hindu nation. The portrayal of Gandhi in various comics in conjunction with references to the Jallianwala Bagh massacre likewise demonstrates the preference for a more militant form of nationalism, as well as regional and caste influences, in the presentation of this modern Indian icon. Overall, these case studies demonstrate that hegemonic conceptions of Hinduism and national Indian identity do not exist passively but are actively created amid ongoing debate.

And yet this debate is in many ways limited to the production process. Whereas readers do actively participate in these debates about religion and nation by deciding which comic books to buy and which to bypass and by writing letters to the comic book producers, one factor that significantly hampers the possibility of ongoing discussion about what it means to be Hindu and Indian is the context in which the *ACK* comics are consumed by the majority of their readers. In India, they are now used in urban English-medium schools as an alternative to textbooks. As one principal in Bombay stated, "Up through the ninth standard we teach for life; in the tenth standard we teach for examinations." She went on to explain that in preparing students for this transition, the *Amar Chitra Katha* comic books are a useful tool:

> In fact, we have made the *Freedom Struggle* [bumper issue no. 10, 1997] comic book compulsory reading for the ninth standard. In the tenth standard they have to do a paper on the Freedom Struggle, so this gives them some background, some ability to visualize the important figures ahead of time. And it is not as heavy as the textbooks they will have to read in tenth standard for their exams and their papers. And we give *Amar Chitra Katha*s out as awards to our students at various functions.

Other principals of English-medium schools in Bombay and elsewhere confirmed that they too regularly use these comic books as a part of their curriculum and stock both the historical and the mythological issues in their libraries. In discussing the function of South Asian education systems, Krishna Kumar writes that educating children is not only about teaching them a love of reading or math or science. It is also about transforming them into good national subjects:

> [S]ystems of education are oriented towards cultivating the characteristics of loyal citizens in children, in preference to the development of their intellectual or contemplative capacities. As far as teaching about the past is concerned, schools in different systems perform the job of socializing the young into an approved national past ... the school uses the officially approved knowledge of the nation's past to inspire and prepare children for fulfilling the roles expected of them as obedient citizens. (2001, 20–21)

When educators present the *ACK* comic books to children as an authentic source of information about India that they should memorize, then the possibility for greater debate about and alternative visions of what it means to be Indian is largely foreclosed. Likewise, in the diaspora where the *ACK* comic books are used in youth education classes and stocked in libraries at Hindu temples, and are again presented to children as an authentic source of information about India and Hinduism, the possibility for greater debate about what it means to be Indian and Hindu is again largely foreclosed.

In the past several years, however, a few who grew up on a steady diet of *Amar Chitra Katha* comics in India and around the globe have begun to rethink the vision of Indianness that is presented in this series and that they so identified with as children. In New Delhi, Rukmini Sekhar has started a new Indian comic book series called *Vivalok Comics*. Sekhar acknowledged her indebtedness to *ACK*, which she fondly recalled reading as a child, but stated that in her comics she and her co-producers try to "draw out the undercurrents and subtleties of mythology, to use comic books for rigorous inquiry." For instance, in their *Godavari Tales* issue (not numbered, 2003), a very different version of the *Rāmāyaṇa* epic is presented in the short story entitled "Sita Banished." Whereas the *Rama* and *Valmiki's Ramayana* comics by *ACK* deploy the strategy of narrative closure to end with a happily-ever-after scenario depicting Rama and Sita being crowned king and queen of Ayodhya, "Sita Banished" begins where these comic books end and focuses on the final book of the epic, a part of the epic that has been central to many women's retellings of this epic for centuries, in which Rama banishes Sita.[4] It ends with a final panel in which Sita is shown wandering alone in the forest (figure 38), while the narrative text concludes, "Since he was king, he banished Sita to the forest. That too when she was carrying her first child! So ... what do you make of Rama's decision?" (41). This version of the *Rāmāyaṇa* dwells on the moral ambiguities of the epic, calling into question not only the justness of Rama's behavior toward Sita but also the dominant version of the epic that presents Rama as a flawless god-king, an ever-victorious superhero.

In the United States, New York–based artist Chitra Ganesh has created her own comic book, *Tales of Amnesia* (2002), as well as a number of large single-panel prints by using digital manipulation, collage, and other techniques to alter the narratives of *Amar Chitra Katha* comic books and

Figure 38. *Godavari Tales,* not numbered (New Delhi: Viveka Foundation, 2003), 41. From the *Vivalok Comics* series, with the permission of the publisher Viveka Foundation, New Delhi, India.

thereby infuse them with new meaning. In this work, Ganesh questions the definition of Indianness presented in *ACK* by raising queer issues and feminist critiques and by making more subtle commentaries upon life in the Indian diaspora. In her own words, she engages "familiar narrative and pictorial conventions to draw the viewer into a tale of disintegration and discomfort." For the cover of *Tales of Amnesia,* she has adapted the splash page from the *Hanuman* (no. 19, 1971) *ACK* issue, transforming the mythological monkey-god into a half-monkey, half-human *junglee* (wild or barbaric) girl who defies social norms. In these pages she depicts lesbian sexuality, draws connections between the plight of women in premodern India and Indian women in the diaspora, and pairs fractured bodies with jarring text segments. When asked what led her to *Amar Chitra Katha* and prompted her to consider using these comics in her own artwork, Ganesh replied:

> I read these comics as a kid, and it was in large part the way I learned about Indian myth, history, and religion. A few years ago, my girlfriend sent me a package when I was away at a residency with a few of these books. From that point on, this work grew out of revisiting and dissecting stories of the *Amar Chitra Katha,* a popular religious comic used to disseminate "authentic" Indian culture to the subcontinent and diaspora. I interrupt the original tales by inserting dissonant dialogue into stories, and fracturing the coherence of bodies that inhabit them. Bodies split open, double, and otherwise transform as history and fantasy merge. In the process, I want to unsettle traditional narrative structures and activate the comic's potential as a subversive form.

Overall, however, the vast majority of the readers of *Amar Chitra Katha* cherish this comic book series for its heroic presentation of India's historical and mythological leaders. For these readers, Rama remains the archetypal Indian superhero (plate 8): seated magnificently on his throne, he is immortalized as the ever-victorious god-king who defeated the demon-king Ravana, rescued his lovely and long-suffering wife, Sita, and returned to Ayodhya to begin his ideal reign. In addition to Hindu deities like Rama and Krishna, the series includes issues on celebrated Hindu warrior-kings such as Shivaji and Rana Pratap and colonial era freedom fighters such as Bhagat Singh and Subhas Chandra Bose. All of these figures are transformed into heroes by adhering to the successful *ACK* formula: They encounter their foes, be they mythological demons or medieval Muslim kings or colonial British officers, engage them in fierce battles, and either emerge victorious or die bravely in the process. For the majority of the readers of *ACK*, this Indian comic book series presents a national canon of gods, kings, and other heroes that they regard as both authentic and complete.

As a form of public culture that has reached into the everyday lives of millions of middle-class Indian children over the past four decades, *Amar Chitra Katha* has had a substantial impact on their concepts of Hinduism and Indianness. But the influence of *ACK* extends even beyond its significant reading audience. These Indian comic books draw on a long tradition of Indian visual and literary culture, and they have been especially influenced by the Indian nationalist period in the late nineteenth and early twentieth centuries when popular texts and images (including paintings, god posters, and bazaar art) were employed in the struggle for independence from British colonial rule. If, as Arjun Appadurai and Carol Breckenridge have argued, each new media technology in South Asia "has distinctive capabilities and functions, and each interacts in a different way with older modes of organizing and disseminating information" (1995, 7), then it is also important to acknowledge the ways in which newer media in India in turn draw on comic books. The production of *ACK* comic books began in 1967, before satellite television had become entrenched in urban India, and these comic books have had a direct, though little-recognized, influence on this medium in India. Sales of the comic books boomed from the 1970s to the mid-1980s. But in the mid-1980s and early 1990s, television suddenly became available throughout urban India as hundreds of transmitters were erected (Mankekar 1999, 5). In the mid-1980s, televised entertainment serials were introduced on Doordarshan, the state-run network, and the most successful one of this time was Ramanand Sagar's *Ramayan,* which aired from January 1987 until July 1988 and captured an estimated daily viewership of 40 to 60 million, with the most popular episodes being viewed by 80 to 100 million people (Lutgendorf 1995, 223). *Amar Chitra Katha* and Doordarshan were competing for the same audience, and Doordarshan appeared to be winning. Throughout the late 1980s *ACK* sales slid, until the producers finally stopped making new issues in 1991.

But focusing only on the competition between these two media for India's middle-class audience causes us to overlook the interconnections between these media. Philip Lutgendorf has commented on the "homogenization" he sees between the comic books and the *Ramayan* TV series, noting that "visually speaking, the characters and settings of the Sagar serial look much like those of the *Amar Chitra Katha* comic books" (1995, 246). This is particularly true in the final hourlong episode (no. 78), which aired on July 31, 1988, and ended the series with Rama's coronation in a way that seems directly indebted to the comic book: seated magnificently on his throne with Sita at his side, Rama is immortalized as the ever-victorious god-king and ideal ruler. *ACK* author Yagya Sharma had an explanation for this visual and narrative homogenization that occurs in *Ramayan* and also B. R. Chopra's TV series *Mahabharat,* which aired from September 1988 until July 1990:

> I have a story to tell you about that. You see, when the *Mahabharat* TV serial was being made—this was over ten years ago—I had a friend who was a cameraman on the set. And he told me that they often brought the *ACK Mahabharata* series onto the set and used it as reference material—for the dress, the buildings, and also for the episodes, the content. It is Kamala Chandrakant who deserves the credit for this. She was thorough and very, very careful with regards to authenticity. For every event that occurs in the *ACK Mahabharata*—the 42-volume set!—there is an actual *sloka* [verse] on that event in Sanskrit in the *Mahabharat* epic.

Television producers have repeatedly turned to the *Amar Chitra Katha* series as reference material for costume design, set production, and subject matter. When making the live-action serial based on the *Amar Chitra Katha* comic books that aired on UTV in 1998, producer Zarina Mehta stated that the idea seemed plausible to her because the comic books are quite cinematic already, particularly in the way that they "alternate action with a lot of drama and emotion," which makes their adaptation to the television medium a relatively simple process. Mehta was inspired to undertake this project because she credits these comic books with helping her as a Parsi to learn Indian mythology, and she wanted to bring that Indian heritage to a new generation:

> The comics taught me a lot. I read them all when I was younger, and they inspired me to learn more about these things. In fact, I still have all of them somewhere around here. The comics were quite popular with many Indian children when I was growing up, Hindus and also non-Hindus, like me. They are the reason that we know India's mythology, the reason we can visualize it and remember it. So we thought a TV serial based on these comics could help

bring India's history and mythology to a new generation. And I really enjoyed producing the show. It was great fun.

During the making of this series, the Sagars, who produced *Ramayan,* and the Chopras, who produced *Mahabharat,* each co-produced some of the *ACK* TV episodes, furthering the homogenization between these two media in their respective visions of who India's heroes are, what they look like, and how their stories should be told.

Like these television serials, dozens of Indian films have also been produced in the past quarter century featuring the same Indian heroes that were canonized in *ACK* and demonstrate the marked influence of these comic books in the ways that these heroes are envisioned and their stories are told in the filmic medium. Creators of new animated cartoons and children's internet productions in India are also now turning to *ACK* for inspiration. Thus not only have *Amar Chitra Katha* comic books been instrumental in establishing a national canon of heroes that defines what it means to be Hindu and Indian for millions of middle-class readers in India and throughout the transnational Indian diaspora. These comics have also been instrumental in disseminating that definition of Hinduism and Indianness through other popular Indian media.

Notes

Introduction

The names of all comic book readers and some comic book producers are protected in this book for their privacy. The names of comic book producers, when given, are used with their generous permission.

1. For lists of superhero traits in U.S. comics, see Oropeza 2005, 5, and Reynolds 1992, 12–16. According to Oropeza—who lists seven common superhero traits including parents who are not present—some lists contain more traits, some less, and not every superhero will have all the traits, but there are "enough 'family resemblances' among the heroes to warrant such a list."

2. The Clay Sanskrit Library has put out a seven-volume English translation of the Sanskrit *Rāmāyaṇa* epic, and many abridged versions exist. For an excellent discussion of the changing devotional understanding of Rama over time, see Lutgendorf 1991.

3. India Book House published *ACK* from 1967 until 2007. In 2007, *ACK* was purchased by the start-up company ACK Media.

4. For readers who are unfamiliar with the partition of the Indian subcontinent and with modern Indian history more generally, a good overview is provided by Metcalf and Metcalf 2006.

5. For further information on Nehru, see Tharoor 2004.

6. In addition to Metcalf and Metcalf 2006, also see Jaffrelot 2007 for further information on Hindu nationalism.

7. Other sources on new visual media and Hindu worship include Gillespie 1995 and Lutgendorf 2003 on television and film, and Inglis 1995, Jain 2007, Pinney 2004, and Smith 1995 on bazaar art or god posters.

8. On this "distinct gaze" in early Indian cinema, see Rajadhyaksha 1993, 68–69.

9. Also on the efficacy of god posters, see Jain 2007, 269–313.

10. For theoretical introductions to the study of media, religion, and culture and discussions of the state of this field, see Albanese 1996, Clark 2002, Clark and Hoover 1997, Hoover and Venturelli 1996, and Mitchell

and Marriage 2003. Among the recent scholarship on media, culture, and Abrahamic or "western" religions, see Detweiler and Taylor 2003 (on Christianity) and Hafez 2000 (on Islam).

11. A groundbreaking work on comics in the 1970s was Dorfman and Mattelart 1975. The 1970s also saw the publication of several important studies of the ideology of comics by French scholars, including Souchet 1975, and comparative studies between film and comics, including Lacassin 1972. For a theoretical introduction to the study of comics, see Lombard, Lent, Greenwood, and Tunc 1999. A few recent and excellent studies of comics include Carrier 2000, McAllister, Sewell, and Gordon 2001, Oropeza 2005, and Varnum and Gibbons 2001. Among the recent studies of comics and culture on a global scale, see Douglas and Malti-Douglas 1994, Kinsella 2000, Lent 2001, Rubenstein 1998, and von Alphons Silbermann and Dyroff 1986.

12. In addition to those sources already mentioned in the discussion above, also see K. Johnson 2003, Mishra 2001, and Vasudevan 2001.

13. Again, in addition to those sources already mentioned in the discussion above, a few noteworthy exceptions are Dalmia 1997, Mankekar 1999, and Rajagopal 2001.

14. Pritchett 1995 provides a valuable overview of the themes in the *Amar Chitra Katha* series; Hawley 1995 focuses on the portrayal of the bhakti poet-saints in *ACK* in an important essay; Lent 2004 discusses the historical methods employed in *ACK*'s production process; and Chandra 1997 provides insight into the marketing of *ACK*. Also see McLain 2005, 2007, and 2008.

1. The Father of Indian Comic Books

1. The biographical information provided here on Anant Pai is compiled from interviews the author conducted with him in Bombay in 2001 and 2002. Also see Gangadhar 1988.

2. Anant Pai did not have specific figures for *Krishna* alone, but he said he believed these were conservative numbers.

3. For an interesting account of one Indian reader's discovery of the revision of the *Krishna* comic book, see

Desai 2003. Desai characterizes the revision as a betrayal and "a most audacious publishing con."

4. For a discussion of Krishna's childhood miracles, see Hawley 1983; for an account of Hindus who go on pilgrimage to relive the miracles associated with Krishna, see Haberman 1994.

5. On the readership of Japanese manga, see Schodt 1997, 12–27; on criticisms of U.S. comic books and the implementation of the comics code, see Nyberg 1998 and Heins 2002.

6. On the impact of the American anti-comics movement in Asia, see Lent 1999, who focuses on the controversies over comics in the 1950s and succeeding decades in the Philippines, Taiwan, South Korea, and Japan.

7. For further information on advertising in this comic book series, see Chandra 1997.

8. These numbers are reported in Sharma 1994. The Amar-Vikas newsletter editor confirmed these figures when I spoke with him at the comic book studio in Bombay in 2001.

9. See also Rajagopal 2001, 72–120, 326n48.

10. For press coverage of these and related events, see "Amarchitra Katha Goes Digital" 1998, Gangadhar 2001, Gulab 1998, Kadapa-Bose 1998, and "Uncle Pai's Fun-Filled Stories Launched on CDs, Cassettes" 2001. I thank Zarina Mehta for sharing some of the UTV episodes with me.

11. Falk 2005, for instance, distinguishes between four teaching traditions within Hinduism: Brahmins (priests), sadhus (renouncers), bhaktas (devotees), and samajists (modern reformers and revivalists). Also see Llewellyn 2005 and Dalmia and von Stietencron 1995.

12. On Vaishnavism as the dominant trend within Hinduism, see Dalmia 1995 and 1997. On contesting the equation of Vaishnavism with Hinduism, see Narayanan 2000 and Ilaiah 2005.

13. On the history textbook controversy, see *Saffronised Substandard* 2002. A few of the many news articles that I clipped include Habib 2002, "Joshi Agrees to Put School Textbooks to 'Holy Test'" 2001, Khan and Sachdeva 2001, and Minwalla 2001.

2. Long-Suffering Wives and Self-Sacrificing Queens

1. On U.S. comic book consumption patterns, see Pustz 1999. On Wonder Woman and her legacy, see Robinson 2004. For a political reading of Captain America in the American context, see Jewett and Lawrence 2003.

2. For an English translation of Kalidasa's play and also the story of Shakuntala as told in the *Mahābhārata*, see W. J. Johnson 2001.

3. The first *ACK* comic book to feature a historical heroine was *Mirabai* (no. 36, 1972), which was followed by *Padmini*. Mirabai was a sixteenth-century poet-saint who

was so consumed by her love for the god Krishna that she ignored her wifely duties and caused much strife in her in-laws' home. For an excellent discussion of how her story has been transformed in the *Mirabai* comic to present her as both a faithful wife and a faithful devotee, see Hawley 1995.

4. For further discussion of the western reception of *Sacontala, or The Fatal Ring*, see Thapar 1999, esp. 197–217.

5. At this time, many proponents of race science argued that the colonized "natives," although originally of Aryan stock, were racially inferior because of the long history of blood mixing between Aryans and indigenous Dravidians in the Indian subcontinent since the classical period. See Trautmann 1997, esp. 165–216.

6. For further information on Varma, see Guha-Thakurta 1992, Mitter 1994, Neumayer and Schelberger 2003, Parimoo 1998, and Sharma 1993. On photography and painting in India, see Pinney 1997a and Shinde 1998.

7. On Varma's tours, see Venniyoor 1981, 27, 34, and Mitter 1994, 201–2. On the "Aryan" physiognomy of Varma's heroines, see G. Kapur 2000, 163, and Uberoi 1990, WS44.

8. I have put the terms *modern* and *traditional* in quotes here because both Indian aesthetics, of course, were newly articulated products of colonial modernity. On these rivaling claims to Indianness in art, see Guha-Thakurta 1992, 185–225.

9. On the withering of the aura, see Benjamin 1968, 217–51.

10. On the history of female impersonators and actresses on the Indian stage, see Adarkar 1991 and K. Hansen 1998.

11. A photograph of Bal Gandharva as Shakuntala can be seen in Nadkarni 1988, 59. This photograph immediately calls to my mind the heroine in Ravi Varma's painting *Arjuna and Subhadra*. Others have commented on the similarities between photographs of Gandharva and Varma's paintings, including Kannal 1998, 37–38, and K. Hansen 1998, 2296.

12. On the difficulties experienced by one of the first film actresses in India, Ramalabai Gokhale, who played the part of Mohini in Phalke's *Bhasmasur Mohini* (1914), see Bahadur and Vanarase 1980, 22–25.

13. Kathryn Hansen 1998, 2296–97, makes this valuable point in her article "Stri Bhumika: Female Impersonators and Actresses on the Parsi Stage."

14. For instance, Lebra-Chapman 1986 discusses many literary works about the Rani of Jhansi that were banned, and Pinney 1999 discusses the banning of lithographic images of the goddess Kali that were interpreted by the British as seditious political allegories.

15. But also see Kathryn Hansen's persuasive argument that the more conservative (or Moderate) nationalists typically favored the pativratā, while the more radical

(or Extremist) nationalists typically favored the vīrāṅganā ideal. K. Hansen 1992, 39.

3. Sequencing the Tales of Goddess Durga

1. For more on Pai's insistence that his comics are truthful and accurate, see Lent 2004, 62–67.

2. On moment-to-moment and other types of panel transitions, see McCloud 1993, 70–80.

3. As discussed in chapter 2, the heroes of these comics are fair-skinned, "Aryanized" men and women; as seen in *Tales of Durga*, the villains of the mythological issues are dark-skinned, stout men and women with wide lips and noses. Also, although *tejas* is translated as "light" in the comic book, it is a far more powerful concept; see Whitaker 2000.

4. Much effort has gone into trying to identify the iconographic details of these various Durga Mahiṣāsuramardinī images with narratives from the *Devī Māhātmya* and other oral and written texts in the effort to try to trace the spread of the Brahminical Sanskrit tradition. See Coburn 1991, 13–18, Divakaran 1984, Erndl 1993, 22, Harle 1963, von Stietencron 1983, and Williams 1982, 5.

5. The only scholar to speculate about the existence of such an image, to my knowledge, is Divakaran 1984, who discusses the pairing of a Mahiṣāsuramardinī relief with one of Vishnu asleep on his serpent bed in the seventh-century Pallava Dynasty rock-cut Mahiṣāsuramardinī cave at Mahabalipuram.

6. See, for instance, the collection of images in Larson, Pal, and Smith 1997, Neumayer and Schelberger 2003, and Pinney 2004.

7. On Durga Puja rituals, see Kinsley 1986, 106–15, Hudson 1999, and Harlan 1992, 52–90.

8. Mahendra Mittal's *Maa Durga* (n.d.) is an illustrated text, not a comic book, but it provides a useful contrast with *Tales of Durga*. *Maa Durga* is also based on the *Devī Māhātmya*, but it includes the frame story and the first story of the classical scripture. On page 10, as Brahma praises the Goddess, she appears in a vision before him.

9. On the feminine principle in the *Devī Māhātmya* and as compared with other scriptures, see Pintchman 1994, esp. 119–22.

10. For further discussion of this, see Humes 2000, 139.

11. This maxim is derived from the Hindu code of law, the *Manusmṛti* (4.138). Hawley, who interviewed Anant Pai in 1989, reports that Pai related this maxim to him as well. Hawley 1995, 115–18. My thanks to Patrick Olivelle for pointing out that this maxim is a reference to Manu; for more on this law code, see Olivelle with Olivelle 2005.

4. The Warrior-King Shivaji in History and Mythology

1. Here I am indebted to the discussion of pictorial narrative in Winter 1985.

2. For example, the colonial quest to identify the historical Buddha has resulted in the lasting dominance of narrative issues in the study of early Buddhist art in India. Leoshko 2003, 15, notes that an example of this is the recently renewed debate over a possible aniconic phase. For this debate, see Huntington 1990, Dehejia 1992, and Huntington 1992.

3. The print by the unknown Dutch artist can be viewed in Neumayer and Schelberger 2003, plate 133. Varma's portrait of Shivaji is unfortunately no longer extant.

4. On Tilak and the Ganapati festival, see Barnouw 1954, Cashman 1975, 75–97, and Kaur 2000.

5. For an account of the Shivaji festivals in the Deccan, see Samarth 1975, 20–57; on the reception of Shivaji outside of western India, see the essays in Kulkarnee 1975; also Rai and Puri 1980.

6. For more on Shivaji's disputed caste status, see O'Hanlon 1985, 19–25, Apte 1974, and Sharma 1974.

7. Although beyond the scope of this chapter, it is worth noting that many Muslims were also offended by the nationalist narrative of Shivaji. Daud 1980 [1935] argued that "Maharashtra has not produced a more cruel and atrocious person than Sevaji" (187). This book created a sensation in Maharashtra in the 1930s and 1940s and was banned by the Indian government in 1945.

8. O'Hanlon 1985, 175–79, reports that Phule's ballad received harsh reviews in the literary journal *Vividhadnyan Vistar* in July 1869 and in *Dnyanodaya* on August 16 and September 1, 1869. For the subaltern versions of the stories of Rama, Bali/Vali, and other Hindu gods and demons, see Ilaiah 2005, 71–101.

9. On the complexity of the term *Maratha* and Maratha identity, see O'Hanlon 1985, 15–21, Gordon 1994, 182–208, and Deshpande 2004.

10. Also see the discussion of the recycling of images within the artistic lineages of god poster artists in Inglis 1995.

11. Section 295(A) of the Indian Penal Code prohibits deliberate and malicious acts intended to outrage religious feelings of any class by insulting its religion or religious beliefs. On the Valmiki Sabha's protest of the *Valmiki* comic book, see Leslie 2003, 12–17. Leslie writes that "the popularity of this comic-book series surely bears some responsibility for the spread of the legend and thus for the continued attribution of a wicked past to the divinized poet-saint, Valmiki" (13).

12. On the destruction of the Babri Masjid in 1992 and the Hindu nationalist effort to build a temple to Rama in its place, see van der Veer 1994; on the Bombay riots of 1992–93, see T. Hansen 2001, 121–59.

13. In addition to state-sponsored statuary, the "Chhatrapati Shri Shivaji Maharaj" 30-rupee postal stamp (released by the Indian government in 1980), which shows Shivaji descending the stairs of the Pratapgarh fort en route to meeting Afzal Khan, is one example of the attention given to the Shivaji narrative by nationalist politicians. So also is the renaming of streets and public buildings after Shivaji in Bombay and elsewhere, as discussed by T. Hansen 2001.

14. Pinney 1997b, 863–66, discusses a new poster of Shivaji slaying Afzal Khan that was created by artist Rajan Musle and published by S. S. Brijbasi in Bombay in 1994, noting that this popular image is unsigned because both the artist and the publisher are aware that it is likely to "trigger some communal feelings"; the same artist created an image of muscular Rama in 1994, following the destruction of the Babri Masjid in Ayodhya in 1992.

15. On the significance of Shivaji's coronation, see the edited volumes published in celebration of the third centennial anniversary of the coronation: Apte 1974 and Kulkarnee 1975. Many of the essays in these volumes adhere to the belief that Shivaji's coronation marks the beginning of secular rule in India.

5. Muslims as Secular Heroes and Zealous Villains

1. For other Indian criticisms of the *ACK* series, also see Adajania 1993, Kumar 1983, Mannur 2000, and Pal 1987.

2. For more on Havell's role, also see Havell 1908 and Havell 1980 [1908], esp. 260–73; on Abanindranath Tagore and the Bengal School, see Guha-Thakurta 1992, 226–312, and Sen 1961.

3. For a discussion of some of these portraits and landscapes, see Pal et al. 1989.

4. Partha Mitter notes that Abanindranath Tagore had hoped to promote the Bengal School style of art in the northwest through A. R. Chughtai, and that Chughtai paid homage to Abanindranath. However, other sources, most notably Chughtai's son, dispute this relationship. See Mitter 1994, 335–36, and Chughtai 1976. On Chughtai's claim to be related to the architect of the Taj Mahal, see Chughtai 1976; on the plausibility of this claim, see Leoshko 1989, 70.

5. Discussing the Panch Mahal and other buildings that share a courtyard at Fatehpur Sikri, Brand and Lowry write: "As a group, the buildings in and around this courtyard form a passage of architecture unique in Islamic India, and display perfectly the experimentation and yearning for new forms that characterize Akbar's personality during the Fatehpur-Sikri years" (1985, 48–50). For a further discussion of north Indian architecture and Hindu-Muslim identities, see Asher 2000.

6. For scholarship challenging the "religion by the sword" theory, see Eaton 1985, Ernst 1992, 155–86, Hardy 1979, and Lawrence 1984.

7. For another example of a comic book featuring Sikhs being forcibly pressed to convert to Islam under Aurangzeb's orders, see *Guru Gobind Singh* (no. 32, 1972), which shows two of Guru Gobind Singh's sons being bricked alive between two walls because they refused to convert.

8. For a foundational Hindu nationalist definition of the term *Hindu*, see Savarkar 1969 [1923]. On Sikh religious identity, see Barrier 1992 and Das 1995.

9. For further discussions of medieval identity politics, see Talbot 1995a, esp. 719–21, Ernst 1992, esp. 22–29, and Chattopadhyaya 1998.

10. On the role of the British in the construction of Hindu-Muslim communalism, see Pandey 1989 and Viswanathan 2001, esp. 161–70. On Hindu authors and Indian nationalism, see Dalmia 1997, Kaviraj 1998, and Sarkar 1996. On Hali and Azad, see Pritchett 1994 and Minault 1986; on Muslims and Indian nationalism, see Jalal 2000.

11. On these debates, see the discussion of Tajamul Husain's and Lokanath Misra's arguments by Neufeldt 1993, 318–20, and Viswanathan 2001, xi–xx; and on the practice of conversion—or "reconversion"—by the Arya Samaj, see K. Jones 1995.

6. Mahatma Gandhi as a Comic Book Hero

1. This is cited from the original English edition of the comic book, but the image comes from a rare 1994 Hindi edition of the comic purchased in Rajasthan in 1999. Although the *Mahatma Gandhi I* issue is regularly reprinted in English, *Mahatma Gandhi II* is not. In the 1980s and 1990s, many of these English-language comic books were translated into Hindi and other Indian languages. *Mahatma Gandhi I* and *II* were both printed in Hindi-language editions, but in smaller quantities than many other titles in the series.

2. Gandhi observed that the Rowlatt Act was the symptom of a deep-seated disease and an open challenge that Indians must not succumb to if they desired to prove their "capacity for resistance to arbitrary or tyrannical rule." See Kumar 2000, 20.

3. On the significance of Jallianwala Bagh in the Sikh Punjabi community, see Mohinder Singh 2000.

4. In addition to Sayer 1991, another good discussion of the historiography of the Jallianwala Bagh massacre is Narain 1998.

5. Cited in Datta and Settar 2000, vii. In his autobiography, Nehru recalls riding on the same train with General Dyer, the "hero of Jallianwala Bagh," in 1919 after Dyer had testified before the Hunter Committee. Nehru comments that he was shocked by Dyer's brash justification of the firing. See Nehru 1958 [1936], 43–44.

6. Gandhi actually suspended his noncooperation movement in 1922 after the Chauri Chaura riot occurred,

not after the Jallianwala Bagh massacre; this statement may reflect some of the collective amnesia discussed by Amin 1995.

7. For further discussion of this, see Chatterjee 1995 [1986] and Bose and Jalal 1999.

8. Nandy 1980 notes that Godse's writings were "punctuated by references to the British and Muslims as 'rapists,' and Hindus as their raped, castrated, deflowered victims" (86). For further biographical information on Godse, see Malgonkar 1978.

9. For a detailed account of these riots, see Patterson 1988.

10. For further discussion of Godse's trial speech, see also Godse 1977 and "Nathuram Godse: Why I Shot Gandhi" 1978.

11. See Dasgupta and Koppikar 1998. Also, the showing of painter Kunal Kishor's "cartoon-cum-poster" exhibition on Nathuram Godse in Patna on May 19, 2003, the anniversary of Godse's birth, generated more controversy.

12. *Gandhi* begins with the assassination, alternating shots between Godse holding his gun and Gandhi falling, and ends by returning to the scene of the assassination and the cremation of Gandhi. Attenborough's film was in turn influenced by Henri Cartier-Bresson's photos of Gandhi just before his assassination and of the cremation. See Cartier-Bresson 2001 [1987] and Srivatsan 2000. Although Anant Pai had not seen *Gandhi* when I interviewed him, a few others involved in the production of the comic books had.

13. On the recent controversy over the complete exclusion of the assassination of Gandhi in the latest NCERT textbooks, see "Govt on the Mat over Textbooks" 2002.

Conclusion

1. *An Exciting Find* (no. 430) was actually the first issue in the series, and *Indus Valley Adventure* (no. 432) was the second.

2. "Youth and Education" at the Shiva-Vishnu Temple in Livermore, Calif.: http://livermoretemple.org/hints/library/temple/in_the_beginning.htm.

3. For discussions of such "eclectic" temples and the new Hindu theologies that accompany such changes in sacred space, see Eck 2002, 80–141, Falk 2005, 295–321, Jacob and Thaku 2000, and Waghorne 2004, 171–230.

4. For scholarship on women's retellings of the *Rāmāyaṇa* epic, see Kishwar 2001, Nilsson 2001, and Rao 1991.

Bibliography

Abbott, Lawrence L. 1986. "Comic Art: Characteristics and Potentialities of a Narrative Medium." *Journal of Popular Culture* 19, no. 4: 155–76.

Adajania, Nancy. 1993. "Myth and Supermyth." *Illustrated Weekly,* April 10–16, 34–35.

Adarkar, Neera. 1991. "In Search of Women in History of Marathi Theatre, 1843–1933." *Economic and Political Weekly,* October 26, WS87–WS90.

Albanese, Catherine L. 1996. "Religion and Popular Culture: An Introductory Essay." *Journal of the American Academy of Religion* 59, no. 4: 733–42.

Alpers, Svetlana. 1976. "Describe or Narrate? A Problem in Realistic Representation." *New Literary History* 8: 15–41.

"Amarchitra Katha Goes Digital." 1998. *Organiser,* November 29, 18.

Amin, Shahid. 1995. *Event, Metaphor, Memory: Chauri Chaura, 1922–1992.* Delhi: Oxford University Press.

Anand, M., and M. Rajshekhar. 2000. "Moral of the Story." *Businessworld,* October 2, 52–54.

Appadurai, Arjun, and Carol A. Breckenridge. 1995. "Introduction: Public Modernity in India." In Carol A. Breckenridge, ed., *Consuming Modernity: Public Culture in a South Asian World,* 1–20. Minneapolis: University of Minnesota Press.

Apte, B. K., ed. 1974. *Chhatrapati Shivaji: Coronation Tercentenary Commemoration Volume.* Bombay: University of Bombay.

Asher, Catherine B. 2000. "Mapping Hindu-Muslim Identities through the Architecture of Shahjahanabad and Jaipur." In David Gilmartin and Bruce Lawrence, eds., *Beyond Turk and Hindu: Rethinking Religious Identities in Islamicate South Asia,* 121–48. Gainesville: University Press of Florida.

Bahadur, Satish, and Shyamala Vanarase. 1980. "The Personal and Professional Problems of a Woman Performer." *Cinema Vision India* 1, no. 1 (January): 22–25.

Baird, Robert D. 1993. "On Defining 'Hinduism' as a Religious and Legal Category." In Robert D. Baird, ed., *Religion and Law in Independent India,* 41–58. New Delhi: Manohar.

Barnouw, Victor. 1954. "The Changing Character of a Hindu Festival." *American Anthropologist,* n.s., 56, no. 1 (February): 74–86.

Barrier, N. G. 1992. "Vernacular Publishing and Sikh Public Life in the Punjab, 1880–1910." In Kenneth Jones, ed., *Religious Controversy in British India: Dialogues in South Asian Languages,* 200–226. Albany: State University of New York Press.

Barry, Ann Marie Seward. 1997. *Visual Intelligence: Perception, Image, and Manipulation in Visual Communication.* Albany: State University of New York Press.

Begley, Wayne. 1979. "The Myth of the Taj Mahal and a New Theory of Its Symbolic Meaning." *Art Bulletin* 61: 7–37.

Benjamin, Walter. 1968. *Illuminations.* New York: Schocken Books.

Bernier, F. 1968 [1891]. *Travels in the Mogul Empire AD 1656–1668.* Trans. A. Constable. New Delhi: S. Chand.

Bhagwati, P. N. 1993. "Religion and Secularism under the Indian Constitution." In Robert D. Baird, ed., *Religion and Law in Independent India,* 7–21. New Delhi: Manohar.

Bordwell, David. 2006. *The Way Hollywood Tells It: Story and Style in Modern Movies.* Berkeley: University of California Press.

Bose, Sugata, and Ayesha Jalal. 1999. *Modern South Asia: History, Culture, Political Economy.* Delhi: Oxford University Press.

Brand, Michael, and Glenn D. Lowry. 1985. *Akbar's India: Art from the Mughal City of Victory.* New York: Asia Society Galleries.

Brilliant, Richard. 1984. *Visual Narratives: Storytelling in Etruscan and Roman Art.* Ithaca, N.Y.: Cornell University Press.

Carrier, David. 2000. *The Aesthetics of Comics.* University Park: Pennsylvania State University Press.

Cartier-Bresson, Henri. 2001 [1987]. *Henri Cartier-Bresson in India.* Boston: Bulfinch Press.

Cashman, Richard I. 1975. *The Myth of the Lokamanya: Tilak and Mass Politics in Maharashtra.* Berkeley: University of California Press.

Chakravarti, Uma. 1990. "Whatever Happened to the Vedic *Dasi*? Orientalism, Nationalism, and a Script for
the Past." In Kumkum Sangari and Sudesh Vaid, eds.,
Recasting Women: Essays in Indian Colonial History,
27–87. New Brunswick: Rutgers University Press.

Chakravarti, Uma, and Kumkum Roy. 1988. "In Search of
Our Past: A Review of the Limitations and Possibili-
ties of the Historiography of Women in Early India."
Economic and Political Weekly, April 30, WS2–WS10.

Chakravarty, Sumita S. 1993. *National Identity in Indian
Popular Cinema (1947–1987).* Austin: University of
Texas Press.

Chandra, Moti. 1973. *Costumes, Textiles, Cosmetics, and
Coiffure in Ancient and Mediaeval India.* Delhi: Orien-
tal Publishers on behalf of the Indian Archaeological
Society.

Chandra, Nandini. 1997. "Market Life of Amar Chitra
Katha." *Seminar,* May, 25–30.

Chatterjee, Partha. 1993. *The Nation and Its Fragments:
Colonial and Postcolonial Histories.* Princeton:
Princeton University Press.

———. 1995 [1986]. *Nationalist Thought and the
Colonial World: A Derivative Discourse?* Minneapolis:
University of Minnesota Press.

Chatterjee, Ramananda. 1907. "Ravi Varma." *Modern
Review,* January. Reprinted as appendix I in R. C.
Sharma, ed., *Raja Ravi Varma: New Perspectives,*
144–46. New Delhi: National Museum, 1993.

Chattopadhyaya, Brajadulal. 1998. *Representing the
Other? Sanskrit Sources and the Muslims.* New Delhi:
Manohar.

Chughtai, Abdullah Rahman. 1987. *Beauty and Power:
A Survey of Art in Pakistan.* Lahore: Chughtai
Museum Trust.

Chughtai, Arif Rahman. 1976. *Artist of the East: Abdur
Rahman Chughtai.* Lahore: Chughtai Museum Trust
and Nisar Art Press.

Clark, Lynn Schofield. 2002. "The Protestantization of Research on Media and Religion." In Stewart M. Hoover
and Lynn Schofield Clark, eds., *Practicing Religion in
the Age of Media: Explorations in Media, Religion, and
Culture,* 7–34. New York: Columbia University Press.

Clark, Lynn Schofield, and Stewart M. Hoover. 1997. "At
the Intersection of Media, Culture, and Religion: A
Bibliographic Essay." In Stewart M. Hoover and Knut
Lundby, eds., *Rethinking Media, Religion, and Culture,*
15–36. Thousand Oaks: Sage.

Coburn, Thomas B. 1984. *Devi-Mahatmya: The Crystal-
lization of the Goddess Tradition.* Delhi: Motilal
Banarsidass.

———. 1991. *Encountering the Goddess: A Translation of
the Devi-Mahatmya and a Study of Its Interpretation.*
Albany, N.Y.: SUNY Press.

Coomaraswamy, Ananda K. 1907. "The Present State of
Indian Art." *Modern Review,* August. Reprinted as

Appendix III in R. C. Sharma, ed., *Raja Ravi Varma:
New Perspectives,* 154–55. New Delhi: National
Museum, 1993.

Cousins, James H. 1970. Foreword to Razia Siraj-ud-din,
ed., *Chughtai's Paintings.* 2d ed. Lahore: Print Printo
Press.

Dalmia, Vasudha. 1995. "'The Only Real Religion of the
Hindus': Vaisnava Self-Representation in the Late
Nineteenth Century." In Vasudha Dalmia and Hei-
nrich von Stietencron, eds., *Representing Hinduism:
The Construction of Religious Traditions and National
Identity,* 176–210. New Delhi: Sage.

———. 1997. *The Nationalization of Hindu Traditions:
Bharatendu Harischandra and Nineteenth-Century
Banaras.* Delhi: Oxford University Press.

Dalmia, Vasudha, and Heinrich von Stietencron. 1995.
*Representing Hinduism: The Construction of Religious
Traditions and National Identity.* New Delhi: Sage
Publications.

Danna, Elizabeth. 2005. "Wonder Woman Mythology: He-
roes from the Ancient World and Their Progeny." In
B. J. Oropeza, ed., *The Gospel According to Superheroes:
Religion and Popular Culture.* New York: Peter Lang.

Das, Veena. 1995. "Counter-Concepts and the Creation
of Cultural Identity: Hindus in the Militant Sikh
Discourse." In Vasudha Dalmia and Heinrich von
Stietencron, eds., *Representing Hinduism: The Construction of Religious Traditions and National Identity,*
358–68. New Delhi: Sage.

Dasgupta, Swapan, and Smruti Koppikar. 1998. "Nathuram
Godse on Trial Again." *India Today,* August 3, 22.

Datta, V. N., and S. Settar, eds. 2000. *Jallianwala Bagh Massacre.* Delhi: Indian Council of Historical Research.

Daud, Saiyid Tafazzul. 1980 [1935]. *The Real Sevaji.*
Karachi: Indus Publications.

Dehejia, Vidya. 1992. "Aniconism and the Multivalence of
Emblems." *Ars Orientalis* 21: 45–66.

———, ed. 1999. *Devi: The Great Goddess: Female Divinity
in South Asian Art.* Washington, D.C.: Arthur M.
Sackler Gallery.

Dempsey, Corinne G. 2006. *The Goddess Lives in Upstate
New York: Breaking Convention and Making Home at
a North American Hindu Temple.* New York: Oxford
University Press.

Desai, Chetan. 2003. "The *Krishna* Conspiracy." *International Journal of Comic Art,* Spring, 325–33.

Deshpande, Prachi. 2002. "Brave Warriors, Damsels in
Distress: Nation, Region, and Gender in Marathi His-
torical Fiction." Paper presented at the 31st Annual
Conference on South Asia, University of Wisconsin,
Madison.

———. 2004. "Caste as Maratha: Social Categories, Colo-
nial Policy, and Identity in Early Twentieth-Century
Maharashtra." *Indian Economic and Social History
Review* 41, no. 1: 7–32.

Detweiler, Craig, and Barry Taylor, eds. 2003. *A Matrix of Meanings: Finding God in Pop Culture*. Grand Rapids, Mich.: Baker Academic.

Dharap, B. V., and Narmada Shahane. 1980. "Birth of a Film Industry." *Cinema Vision India* 1, no. 1 (January): 16–25.

Divakaran, Odile. 1984. "Durga the Great Goddess." In Michael W. Meister, ed., *Discourses on Siva: Proceedings of a Symposium on the Nature of Religious Imagery*, 271–88. Philadelphia: University of Pennsylvania Press.

Doctor, Vikram. 1997. "The Return of the Mythological Heroes." *Businessworld*, June 7, 38–39.

Dorfman, Ariel, and Armand Mattelart. 1975. *How to Read Donald Duck: Imperialist Ideology in the Disney Comic*. Trans. David Kunzle. New York: International General.

Douglas, Allen, and Fedwa Malti-Douglas. 1994. *Arab Comic Strips: Politics of an Emerging Mass Culture*. Bloomington: Indiana University Press.

Douglas, James. 1893 [1883]. *Bombay and Western India*. 2 vols. London: Sampson Low, Marston.

Dryden, John. 1971. *Aureng-Zebe*. Ed. Frederick M. Link. Lincoln: University of Nebraska Press.

Dwyer, Rachel. 2000. *All You Want Is Money, All You Need Is Love*. London: Cassell.

Dwyer, Rachel, and Divia Patel. 2002. *Cinema India: The Visual Culture of Hindi Film*. London: Reaktion Books.

Eaton, Richard. 1985. "Approaches to the Study of Conversion to Islam in India." In Richard C. Martin, ed., *Approaches to Islam in Religious Studies*, 106–23. Tucson: University of Arizona Press.

Eck, Diana L. 1998. *Darśan: Seeing the Diving Image in India*. 3d ed. New York: Columbia University Press.

———. 2002. *A New Religious America: How a "Christian Country" Has Become the World's Most Religiously Diverse Nation*. San Francisco: HarperOne.

Eisner, Will. 1985. *Comics and Sequential Art*. Tamarac, Fla.: Poorhouse Press.

Erndl, Kathleen. 1993. *Victory to the Mother*. New York: Oxford University Press.

Ernst, Carl W. 1992. *Eternal Garden: Mysticism, History, and Politics at a South Asian Sufi Center*. Albany: State University of New York Press.

Extracts from the Home Department. 1898. Public A., nos. 345–76, May. Reprinted as appendix I in Narayan H. Kulkarnee, ed., *Chhatrapati Shivaji: Architect of Freedom*, 227–338. Delhi: Chhatrapati Shivaji Smarak Samiti, 1975.

Falk, Nancy Auer. 2005. *Living Hinduisms: An Explorer's Guide*. Belmont, Calif.: Thomson Wadsworth.

Freitag, Sandria B. 2001. "Visions of the Nation: Theorizing the Nexus between Creation, Consumption, and Participation in the Public Sphere." In Rachel Dwyer and Christopher Pinney, eds., *Pleasure and the Nation: The History, Politics, and Consumption of Public Culture in India*, 35–75. New Delhi: Oxford University Press.

"Future Generation Should Know Country's Heritage and Culture." 2000. *Free Press Journal*, August 24, 3.

Gandhi. 1982. Directed by Richard Attenborough. RCA/Columbia TriStar Home Video. Film.

Gandhi, Mohandas K. 1983 [1948]. *Autobiography: The Story of My Experiments with Truth*. New York: Dover.

Gangadhar, V. 1988. "Anant Pai and His Amar Chitra Kathas." *Reader's Digest [of India]*, August, 137–41.

———. 2001. "Story Time with Uncle Pai." *Free Press Journal*, December 30, 10.

Ghosh, Satyavrata. 1988. *Indian Struggle for Freedom*. Delhi: B.R. Publishing.

Gillespie, Marie. 1995. "Sacred Serials, Devotional Viewing, and Domestic Worship: A Case-Study in the Interpretation of Two TV Versions of the *Mahabharata* in a Hindu Family in West London." In Robert C. Allen, ed., *To Be Continued . . . : Soap Operas around the World*, 354–80. New York: Routledge.

Godse, Gopal. 1977. *May It Please Your Honour: Statement of Nathuram Godse*. Pune: Vitasta Prakashan.

Gordon, Stewart. 1994. *Marathas, Marauders, and State Formation in Eighteenth-Century India*. Delhi: Oxford University Press.

"Govt on the Mat over Textbooks." 2002. *Times of India*, November 27, 1.

Grant Duff, James. 1826. *A History of the Mahrattas*, vol. 1. London: Longman, Rees, Orme, Brown, and Green.

Guha, Ranajit. 1989. "Dominance without Hegemony and Its Historiography." In Ranajit Guha, ed., *Subaltern Studies VI*, 210–309. Delhi: Oxford University Press.

Guha-Thakurta, Tapati. 1986. "Westernisation and Tradition in South Indian Painting in the Nineteenth Century: The Case of Raja Ravi Varma (1848–1906)." *Studies in History* 2.2: 165–95.

———. 1991. "Women as 'Calendar Art' Icons: Emergence of a Pictorial Stereotype in Colonial India." *Economic and Political Weekly*, October 26, WS91–WS99.

———. 1992. *The Making of a New 'Indian' Art: Artists, Aesthetics, and Nationalism in Bengal, c. 1850–1920*. Cambridge: Cambridge University Press.

———. 1995. "Visualizing the Nation: The Iconography of a 'National Art' in Modern India." *Journal of Arts and Ideas*, nos. 27–28 (March): 7–40.

Gulab, Kushalrani. 1998. "Illustrated History of India." *Asian Age*, September 13, 23.

Haberman, David L. 1994. *Journey through the Twelve Forests: An Encounter with Krishna*. New York: Oxford University Press.

Habib, Irfan. 2002. "It's Going to Be More Mythology than History" (guest column). *Times of India*, February 3, 12.

Hafez, Kai. 2000. *Islam and the West in the Mass Media:*

Fragmented Images in a Globalizing World. Cresskill, N.J.: Hampton Press.

Hansen, Kathryn. 1992. "Heroic Modes of Women in Indian Myth, Ritual, and History: The Tapasvini and the Virangana." In Arvind Sharma and Katherine K. Young, eds., *The Annual Review of Women in World Religions* 2: 1–62. Albany: State University of New York Press.

———. 1998. "Stri Bhumika: Female Impersonators and Actresses on the Parsi Stage." *Economic and Political Weekly,* August 29–September 4, 2291–2300.

Hansen, Thomas Blom. 2001. *Wages of Violence: Naming and Identity in Postcolonial Bombay.* Princeton, N.J.: Princeton University Press.

Hardy, Peter. 1979. "Modern European and Muslim Explanations of Conversion to Islam in South Asia: A Preliminary Survey of the Literature." In Nehemia Levtzion, ed., *Conversion to Islam.* New York: Holmes and Meier.

Harlan, Lindsey. 1992. *Religion and Rajput Women: The Ethic of Protection in Contemporary Narratives.* Berkeley: University of California Press.

———. 2003. *The Goddesses' Henchmen: Gender in Indian Hero Worship.* New York: Oxford University Press.

Harle, James C. 1963. "Durga, Goddess of Victory." *Artibus Asiae* 26, no. 3–4: 237–46.

Havell, E. B. 1908. "The New Indian School of Painting." *Studio* 44 (July): 107–17.

———. 1980 [1908]. *Indian Sculpture and Painting: With an Explanation of Their Motives and Ideals.* New Delhi: Cosmo Publications.

Hawley, John Stratton. 1983. *Krishna, The Butter Thief.* Princeton, N.J.: Princeton University Press.

———. 1995. "The Saints Subdued: Domestic Virtue and National Integration in Amar Chitra Katha." In Lawrence Babb and Susan Wadley, eds., *Media and the Transformation of Religion in South Asia,* 107–34. Philadelphia: University of Pennsylvania Press.

———. 2001. "Modern India and the Question of Middle-Class Religion." *International Journal of Hindu Studies* 5, no. 3: 217–25.

Heins, Marjorie. 2002. *Not in Front of the Children: "Indecency," Censorship, and the Innocence of Youth.* New York: Hill and Wang.

Hoover, Stewart M., and Shalini S. Venturelli. 1996. "The Category of the Religious: The Blindspot of Contemporary Media Theory?" *Critical Studies in Mass Communication* 13, no. 3: 251–65.

Hudson, Dennis. 1999. "The Ritual Worship of Devi." In Vidya Dehejia, ed., *Devi: The Great Goddess: Female Divinity in South Asian Art.* Washington, D.C.: Arthur M. Sackler Gallery, 73–98.

Humes, Cynthia Ann. 2000. "Is the Devi Mahatmya a Feminist Scripture?" In Alf Hiltebeitel and Kathleen Erndl, eds., *Is the Goddess a Feminist? The Politics of South Asian Goddesses.* New York: New York University Press, 123–50.

Hunter, Sir William Wilson. 1903. *The India of the Queen and Other Essays.* London: Longmans, Green.

Huntington, Susan. 1990. "Early Buddhist Art and the Theory of Aniconism." *Art Journal* 49: 401–8.

———. 1992. "Aniconism and the Multivalence of Images." *Ars Orientalis* 22: 111–56.

Ilaiah, Kancha. 2005 [1996]. *Why I Am Not a Hindu.* Calcutta: SAMYA.

Inglis, Stephen. 1995. "Suitable for Framing: The Work of a Modern Master." In Lawrence Babb and Susan Wadley, eds., *Media and the Transformation of Religion in South Asia.* Philadelphia: University of Pennsylvania Press, 51–75.

Jacob, Simon, and Pallavi Thaku. 2000. "Jyothi Hindu Temple: One Religion, Many Practices." In H. R. Ebaugh and J. Saltzman Chafetz, eds., *Religion and the New Immigrants: Continuities and Adaptations in Immigrant Congregations.* Walnut Creek, Calif.: AltaMira Press, 229–42.

Jaffrelot, Christophe. 2007. *Hindu Nationalism: A Reader.* Princeton, N.J.: Princeton University Press.

Jain, Kajri. 2000. "The Efficacious Image: Pictures and Power in Indian Mass Culture." *Polygraph,* no. 12: 159–85.

———. 2007. *Gods in the Bazaar: The Economies of Indian Calendar Art.* Durham: Duke University Press.

Jalal, Ayesha. 2000. *Self and Sovereignty: Individual and Community in South Asian Islam since 1850.* New York: Routledge.

Jamison, Stephanie W. 1996. *Sacrificed Wife, Sacrificer's Wife.* Oxford: Oxford University Press.

Jewett, Robert, and John Shelton Lawrence. 2003. *Captain America and the Crusade against Evil: The Dilemma of Zealous Nationalism.* Grand Rapids, Mich.: W. B. Eerdmans.

Johnson, Kirk. 2003. *Television and Social Change in Rural India.* Thousand Oaks: Sage Publications.

Johnson, W. J. 2001. *Kalidasa: The Recognition of Sakuntala.* New York: Oxford University Press.

Jones, Kenneth W. 1995. "The Arya Samaj in British India, 1875–1947." In Robert D. Baird, ed., *Religion in Modern India.* 3d ed. New Delhi: Manohar, 26–54.

Jones, Sir William. 1789. *Sacontala, or The Fatal Ring.* London.

"Joshi Agrees to Put School Textbooks to 'Holy Test.'" 2001. *Times of India,* December 9, 1.

Joshi, Monika. 2003. "Remember Amar Chitra Katha Comics? Now, Someone's Doing a PhD on Them!" *India Abroad,* February 7, A1, A8.

Joshi, Sanjay, and Rajni Bakshi. 1983. "ACKs: Distorted History or Education?" *Telegraph,* November 13, 8.

K., Kavitha. 1995. "Comic Release." *Deccan Herald,* May 20, page 1 of the "Open Sesame" insert.

Kadapa-Bose, Surekha. 1998. "Uncle Pai's Classics." *Week,* September 13, 46.

Kannal, Deepak. 1998. "Ravi Varma and the Marathi Aesthetic." In Ratan Parimoo, ed., *The Legacy of Raja Ravi Varma, the Painter.* Baroda: Maharaja Fatesingh Museum Trust, 36–39.

Kapur, Anuradha. 1993a. "Deity to Crusader: The Changing Iconography of Ram." In Gyanendra Pandey, ed., *Hindus and Others: The Question of Identity in India Today.* New York: Viking, 74–109.

———. 1993b. "The Representation of Gods and Heroes: Parsi Mythological Drama of the Early Twentieth Century." *Journal of Arts and Ideas,* nos. 23–24 (January): 85–107.

Kapur, Geeta. 2000. *When Was Modernism? Essays on Contemporary Cultural Practice in India.* New Delhi: Tulika.

Kaur, Raminder. 2000. "Rethinking the Public Sphere: The Ganapati Festival and Media Competitions in Mumbai." *Polygraph* 12: 137–58.

Kaviraj, Sudipta. 1998. *The Unhappy Consciousness: Bankimchandra Chattopadhyay and the Formation of a Nationalist Discourse in India.* Delhi: Oxford University Press.

Khan, Sakina Yusuf, and Sujata Dutta Sachdeva. 2001. "The Fine Print: Has the 'Talibanisation' of Education Begun?" *Times of India,* November 25, 1 and 7.

Khory, Kavita R. 1993. "The Shah Bano Case: Some Political Implications." In Robert D. Baird, ed., *Religion and Law in Independent India.* New Delhi: Manohar, 121–37.

Kinsella, Sharon. 2000. *Adult Manga: Culture and Power in Contemporary Japanese Society.* Richmond: Curzon.

Kinsley, David. 1986. *Hindu Goddesses: Visions of the Divine Feminine in the Hindu Religious Tradition.* Delhi: Motilal Banarsidass.

Kishwar, Madhu. 2001. "Yes to Sita, No to Ram: The Continuing Hold of Sita on Popular Imagination in India." In Paula Richman, ed., *Questioning Ramayanas: A South Asian Tradition.* Berkeley: University of California Press, 285–308.

Koppikar, Smruti. 1998. "Mee Nathuram Godse Boltoy: Hype and Hysteria." *India Today,* July 27, 77.

Kulkarnee, Narayan H., ed. 1975. *Chhatrapati Shivaji: Architect of Freedom.* Delhi: Chhatrapati Shivaji Smarak Samiti.

Kulkarni, Mangesh. 1997. "Politics of Historiography: The Illustrated Weekly Case in Retrospect." *Secularist,* November–December, 125–34.

Kumar, Kamalini. 1983. "Confused Ideals in Fantasy Land." *Telegraph,* May 8, 7.

Kumar, Krishna. 1996. *Learning from Conflict.* New Delhi: South Asia Books.

———. 2001. *Prejudice and Pride: School Histories of the Freedom Struggle in India and Pakistan.* New Delhi: Viking by Penguin Books.

Kumar, Ravinder. 2000. "The Jallianwala Bagh Tragedy, the Rowlatt Satyagraha, and the Character of the Nationalist Struggle in India: Some Reflections." In V. N. Datta and S. Settar, eds., *Jallianwala Bagh Massacre.* Delhi: Indian Council of Historical Research, 16–24.

Lacassin, Francis. 1972. "The Comic Strip and Film Language." *Film Quarterly* 26, no. 1: 11–23.

Laine, James W. 2003. *Shivaji: Hindu King in Islamic India.* New York: Oxford University Press.

Laine, James W., with S. S. Bahulkar. 2001. *The Epic of Shivaji.* Hyderabad: Orient Longman.

Larson, Gerald James, Pratapaditya Pal, and H. Daniel Smith. 1997. *Changing Myths and Images: Twentieth-Century Popular Art in India.* Exhibition catalog. Bloomington: Indiana University Art Museum.

Lawrence, Bruce B. 1984. "Early Indo-Muslim Saints and Conversion." In Yohanan Friedmann, ed., *Islam in Asia,* vol. 1. Boulder, Colo.: Westview Press, 109–45.

Lebra-Chapman, Joyce. 1986. *The Rani of Jhansi: A Study of Female Heroism in India.* Honolulu: University of Hawaii Press.

Lent, John A. 1999. "Comics Controversies and Codes: Reverberations in Asia." In John A. Lent, ed., *Pulp Demons: International Dimensions of the Postwar Anti-Comics Campaign.* Madison, Wisc.: Fairleigh Dickinson University Press, 179–214.

———, ed. 2001. *Illustrating Asia: Comics, Humor Magazines, and Picture Books.* Honolulu: University of Hawaii Press.

———. 2004. "India's *Amar Chitra Katha*: 'Fictionalized' History or the Real Story?" *International Journal of Comic Art,* Spring, 56–76.

Leonard, Karen Isaksen. 1997. *The South Asian Americans.* Westport, Conn.: Greenwood Press.

Leoshko, Janice. 1989. "Mausoleum for an Empress." In Pratapaditya Pal et al., *The Romance of the Taj Mahal.* London: Thames and Hudson; Los Angeles: Los Angeles County Museum of Art, 53–87.

———. 2003. *Sacred Traces: British Explorations of Buddhism in South Asia.* Burlington: Ashgate.

Leslie, Julia. 1994. "Recycling Ancient Material: An Orthodox View of Hindu Women." In L. Archer, S. Fischler, and M. Wyke, eds., *Women in Ancient Societies: An Illusion of the Night.* Basingstoke: Macmillan, 233–51.

———. 2003. *Authority and Meaning in Indian Religions: Hinduism and the Case of Valmiki.* Burlington: Ashgate.

Link, Frederick M. 1971. Introduction to John Dryden, *Aurang-Zebe.* Lincoln: University of Nebraska Press.

Llewellyn, J. E., ed. 2005. *Defining Hinduism: A Reader.* London: Equinox.

Lombard, Matthew, John A. Lent, Linda Greenwood, and Asli Tunc. 1999. "A Framework for Studying Comic

Art." *International Journal of Comic Art,* Spring/
Summer, 17–32.

Lukács, Georg. 1970. "Narrate or Describe." In Arthur D.
Kahn, ed., *Writer and Critic and Other Essays.* New
York: Grosset and Dunlap.

Lutgendorf, Philip. 1991. *The Life of a Text: Performing the
Ramcaritmanas of Tulsidas.* Berkeley: University of
California Press.

———. 1995. "All in the (Raghu) Family: A Video Epic in
Cultural Context." In Lawrence Babb and Susan Wad-
ley, eds., *Media and the Transformation of Religion in
South Asia.* Philadelphia: University of Pennsylvania
Press, 217–53.

———. 2003. *"Jai Santoshi Maa* Revisted: On Seeing a
'Hindu' Mythological Film." In S. Brent Plate, ed.,
*Representing Religion in World Cinema: Mythmaking,
Culture Making, Filmmaking.* New York: Palgrave/
St. Martin's, 19–42.

Madan, T. N. 1987. "Secularism in Its Place." *Journal of
Asian Studies* 46, no. 4: 747–59.

"Majority and Minority Report of the Disorders Inquiry
Committee (1920)." 1976. Reprinted as *Punjab Dis-
turbances 1919–20, Volume Two: British Perspective.*
New Delhi: Deep Publications.

Malgonkar, Manohar. 1978. *The Men Who Killed Gandhi.*
Delhi: Macmillan.

Mani, Lata. 1990. "Contentious Traditions: The Debate
on *Sati* in Colonial India." In Kumkum Sangari and
Sudesh Vaid, eds., *Recasting Women: Essays in Indian
Colonial History.* New Brunswick: Rutgers University
Press, 88–126.

———. 1998. *Contentious Traditions: The Debate on Sati
in Colonial India.* Berkeley: University of California
Press.

Mankekar, Purnima. 1999. *Screening Culture, Viewing
Politics: An Ethnography of Television, Womanhood,
and Nation in Postcolonial India.* Durham: Duke
University Press.

Mannur, Anita. 2000. "'The Glorious Heritage of India':
Notes on the Politics of Amar Chitra Katha." *Book-
bird: A Journal of International Children's Literature* 38,
no. 4: 32–33.

McAllister, Matthew, Edward Sewell Jr., and Ian Gordon,
eds. 2001. *Comics and Ideology.* New York: P. Lang.

McCloud, Scott. 1993. *Understanding Comics: The Invisible
Art.* New York: Kitchen Sink Press.

McDermott, Rachel Fell, and Jeffrey J. Kripal, eds. 2003.
*Encountering Kali: In the Margins, at the Center, in the
West.* Berkeley: University of California Press.

McLain, Karline. 2005. "Lifting the Mountain: Debating
the Place of Science and Faith in the Creation of a
Krishna Comic Book." *Journal of Vaishnava Studies* 13,
no. 2: 22–37.

———. 2007. "Who Shot the Mahatma? Representing

Gandhian Politics in Indian Comic Books." *South
Asia Research* 27, no. 1: 57–77.

———. 2008. "Holy Superheroine: A Comic Book Interpretation of the Hindu *Devi Mahatmya* Scripture."
Bulletin of the School for Oriental and African Studies
71, no. 2 (June/July): 297–322.

Metcalf, Barbara D., and Thomas R. Metcalf. 2006. 2d ed.
A Concise History of Modern India. Cambridge:
Cambridge University Press.

Minault, Gail, trans. 1986. *Voices of Silence: English Translations of Khwaja Altaf Hussain Hali's Majalis un-nissa
and Chup ki dad.* Delhi: Chanakya Publications.

Minwalla, Shabnam. 2001. "Students Won't Accept
Pathetic Attempts at Saffronisation." *Times of India,*
December 30, 3.

Mishra, Vijay. 2001. *Bollywood Cinema: Temples of Desire.*
New York: Routledge.

Mitchell, Jolyon, and Sophia Marriage, eds. 2003. *Mediat-
ing Religion: Conversations in Media, Religion, and
Culture.* New York: T&T Clark.

Mitchell, W. J. T. 1994. *Picture Theory.* Chicago: University
of Chicago Press.

Mittal, Mahendra. n.d. *Maa Durga: The Holy Saga of Maa's
Powers and Miracles.* Delhi: Manoj Publications.

Mitter, Partha. 1994. *Art and Nationalism in Colonial India,
1850–1922.* Cambridge: Cambridge University Press.

Modleski, Tania. 1982. *Loving with a Vengeance: Mass-
Produced Fantasies for Women.* New York: Routledge.

Monier-Williams, Sir Monier. 1855. *Sakoontala, or The Lost
Ring.* Hereford: Stephen Austin.

———. 1887. *Sakoontala, or The Lost Ring.* 5th ed. London.

Mulvey, Laura. 1975. "Visual Pleasure and Narrative
Cinema." *Screen* 16, no. 3 (Autumn): 6–18.

Nadkarni, Dnyaneshwar. 1988. *Balgandharva and the
Marathi Theatre.* Bombay: Roopak Books.

Nair, P. K. 1980. "Silent Films in the Archive." *Cinema
Vision India* 1, no. 1 (January): 104–13.

Nandy, Ashis. 1980. *At the Edge of Psychology: Essays in
Politics and Culture.* Delhi: Oxford University Press.

Narain, Savita. 1998. *The Historiography of the Jallianwala
Bagh Massacre, 1919.* Surrey: Spantech and Lancer.

Narayanan, Vasudha. 1992. "Creating the South Indian
'Hindu' Experience in the United States." In Ray-
mond Brady Williams, ed., *A Sacred Thread: Modern
Transmission of Hindu Traditions in India and Abroad.*
Chambersburg, Pa.: Anima Publications, 147–76.

———. 2000. "Diglossic Hinduism: Liberation and Len-
tils." *Journal of the American Academy of Religion* 68,
no. 4: 761–79.

"Nathuram Godse: Why I Shot Gandhi." 1978. *Onlooker,*
November 16–30, 22–25.

Nehru, Jawaharlal. 1958 [1936]. *Jawaharlal Nehru, an
Autobiography.* London: Bodley Head.

Neufeldt, Ronald W. 1993. "To Convert or Not to Convert:

Legal and Political Dimensions of Conversion in Independent India." In Robert D. Baird, ed., *Religion and Law in Independent India*. New Delhi: Manohar, 313–31.

Neumayer, Erwin, and Christine Schelberger. 2003. *Popular Indian Art: Ravi Varma and the Printed Gods of India*. New Delhi: Oxford University Press.

Nilsson, Usha. 2001. "Grinding Millet but Singing of Sita: Power and Domination in Awadhi and Bhojpuri Women's Songs." In Paula Richman, ed., *Questioning Ramayanas: A South Asian Tradition*, 137–58. Berkeley: University of California Press.

Nivedita, Sister. 1907. "The Function of Art in Shaping Nationality." *Modern Review*, February. Reprinted as appendix II in R. C. Sharma, ed., *Raja Ravi Varma: New Perspectives*, 150. New Delhi: National Museum, 1993.

———. 1961 [1907]. "Notes on Paintings," in P. Sen, ed., *Abanindranath Tagore: Golden Jubilee Number*, 107. Calcutta: Indian Society of Oriental Art.

Nyberg, Amy Kiste. 1998. *Seal of Approval: The History of the Comics Code*. Jackson: University Press of Mississippi.

O'Brien, Charles. 2005. *Cinema's Conversion to Sound: Technology and Film Style in France and the U.S.* Bloomington: Indiana University Press.

O'Hanlon, Rosalind. 1985. *Caste, Conflict, and Ideology: Mahatma Jotirao Phule and Low Caste Protest in Nineteenth-Century Western India*. Cambridge: Cambridge University Press.

———. 1992. "Issues of Widowhood: Gender and Resistance in Colonial Western India." In Douglas Haynes and Gyan Prakash, eds., *Contesting Power: Resistance and Everyday Social Relations in South Asia*, 62–108. Berkeley: University of California Press.

O'Rourke, Meghan. 2004. "Nancy Drew's Father: The Fiction Factory of Edward Stratemeyer." *New Yorker*, November 8, 120–29.

Olivelle, Patrick, with Suman Olivelle. 2005. *Manu's Code of Law: A Critical Edition and Translation*. New York: Oxford University Press.

Omvedt, Gail. 1976. *Cultural Revolt in a Colonial Society: The Non-Brahman Movement in Western India, 1873–1930*. Bombay: Scientific Socialist Education Trust.

Oropeza, B. J., ed. 2005. *The Gospel According to Superheroes: Religion and Popular Culture*. New York: Peter Lang.

Pai, Anant. 1987. Letter to the editor, published in *Express Magazine*, November 29.

———. 2000. "Mythology in Pictures." *Gentleman*, February, 38–40.

Pal, Bulbul. 1987. "Angry Young Men and Weepy Women." *Express Magazine*, November 22, letters section.

Pal, Pratapaditya, Janice Leoshko, Joseph M. Dye III, and Stephen Markel. 1989. *The Romance of the Taj Mahal*. London: Thames and Hudson; Los Angeles: Los Angeles County Museum of Art.

Pandey, Gyanendra. 1989. "The Colonial Construction of 'Communalism': British Writings on Banaras in the Nineteenth Century." In Ranajit Guha, ed., *Subaltern Studies VI*, 132–68. Delhi: Oxford University Press.

Parimoo, Ratan, ed. 1998. *The Legacy of Raja Ravi Varma, the Painter*. Exhibition catalog. Baroda: Maharaja Fatesingh Museum Trust.

Patterson, Maureen. 1988. "The Shifting Fortunes of Chitpavan Brahmans: Focus on 1948." In D. W. Attwood, M. Israel, and N. K. Wagle, eds., *City, Countryside, and Society in Maharashtra*. University of Toronto: Centre for South Asian Studies, 35–58.

Perret, Marion D. 2001. "'And Suit the Action to the Word': How a Comics Panel Can Speak Shakespeare." In Robin Varnum and Christina Gibbons, eds., *The Language of Comics: Word and Image*. Jackson: University Press of Mississippi, 123–44.

Phule, Jotirao G. 1991. *Gulamagiri: Slavery in the Civilised British Government under the Cloak of Brahmanism*. Trans. P. G. Patil. Bombay: Education Dept., Govt. of Maharashtra for Mahatma Jotirao Phule Death Centenary Central Committee.

Pinney, Christopher. 1997a. *Camera Indica: The Social Life of Indian Photographs*. London: Reaktion Books.

———. 1997b. "The Nation (Un)Pictured? Chromolithography and 'Popular' Politics in India, 1878–1995." *Critical Inquiry* 23 (Summer): 834–67.

———. 1999. "Indian Magical Realism: Notes on Popular Visual Culture." In G. Bhadra, G. Prakash, and S. Tharu, eds., *Subaltern Studies X*, 201–33. New Delhi: Oxford University Press.

———. 2001. "Introduction: Public, Popular, and Other Cultures." In Rachel Dwyer and Christopher Pinney, eds., *Pleasure and the Nation: The History, Politics, and Consumption of Public Culture in India*, 1–34. New Delhi: Oxford University Press.

———. 2004. *Photos of the Gods: The Printed Image and Political Struggle in India*. London: Reaktion Books.

Pintchman, Tracy. 1994. *The Rise of the Goddess in the Hindu Tradition*. Albany: State University of New York Press.

"PM to Unveil Shivaji Statue." 2004. *Times of India*, September 29. Online at http://timesofindia.indiatimes.com/articleshow/421320.cms.

Pritchett, Frances W. 1994. *Nets of Awareness: Urdu Poetry and Its Critics*. Berkeley: University of California Press.

———. 1995. "The World of *Amar Chitra Katha*." In Lawrence Babb and Susan Wadley, eds., *Media and the Transformation of Religion in South Asia*, 76–106. Philadelphia: University of Pennsylvania Press.

Pustz, Matthew J. 1999. *Comic Book Culture: Fanboys and True Believers.* Jackson: University Press of Mississippi.

Radway, Janice A. 1991 [1984]. *Reading the Romance: Women, Patriarchy, and Popular Literature.* Chapel Hill: University of North Carolina Press.

Rai, Lala Lajpat, and R. C. Puri, trans. 1980. *Shivaji, the Great Patriot.* New Delhi: Metropolitan.

Rajadhyaksha, Ashish. 1993. "The Phalke Era: Conflict of Traditional Form and Modern Technology." In Tejaswini Niranjana, P. Sudhir, and Vivek Dhareshwar, *Interrogating Modernity: Culture and Colonialism in India,* 47–82. Calcutta: Seagull.

Rajagopal, Arvind. 2001. *Politics after Television: Hindu Nationalism and the Reshaping of the Public in India.* Cambridge: Cambridge University Press.

Ranade, M. G. 1900. *Rise of the Maratha Power.* Bombay: Punalekar.

Rao, Velcheru Narayana. 1991. "A *Ramayana* of Their Own: Women's Oral Tradition in Telegu." In Paula Richman, ed., *Many Ramayanas: The Diversity of a Narrative Tradition,* 114–36. Berkeley: University of California Press.

Ravi Varma: The Indian Artist. 1903. Allahabad: Indian Press.

Rawlinson, H. G. 1915. *Shivaji the Maratha: His Life and Times.* Oxford: Clarendon Press.

Reynolds, Richard. 1992. *Super Heroes: A Modern Mythology.* Jackson: University Press of Mississippi.

Richman, Paula, ed. 1991. *Many Ramayanas: The Diversity of a Narrative Tradition in South Asia.* Berkeley: University of California Press.

———, ed. 2001. *Questioning Ramayanas: A South Asian Tradition.* Berkeley: University of California Press.

Robinson, Lillian S. 2004. *Wonder Women: Feminisms and Superheroes.* New York: Routledge.

Role of Chitra Katha in School Education. 1978. Bombay: India Book House Education Trust.

Rubenstein, Anne. 1998. *Bad Language, Naked Ladies, and Other Threats to the Nation: A Political History of Comic Books in Mexico.* Durham: Duke University Press.

Saffronised Substandard: A Critique of the New NCERT Textbooks—Articles, Editorials, Reports. 2002. New Delhi: Sahmat.

Saklani, Juhi. 1998. "The Magic Lantern Man." *India Magazine of Her People and Culture,* March, 7–13.

Salunkhe, A. H. 2002. *Gulama cha aani gulam karanaran cha dharm ek nasato* / "Religion of the Slaves and of those who made them Slaves cannot be the same." Trans. Dr. K. Jamanadas. Bombay: Maratha Seva Sangh.

Samarth, Anil. 1975. *Shivaji and the Indian National Movement.* Bombay: Somaiya Publications.

Saptharishi, Kausalya. 2007. "Comic Relief." *India Abroad,* October 26, magazine section.

Sarkar, Jadunath. 1915. "The Passing of Shah Jahan." *Modern Review,* October, 361–68.

Sarkar, Tanika. 1996. "Imagining Hindurashtra: The Hindu and the Muslim in Bankim Chandra's Writings." In David Ludden, ed., *Contesting the Nation: Religion, Community, and the Politics of Democracy in India,* 162–84. Philadelphia: University of Pennsylvania Press.

Savarkar, V. D. 1969 [1923]. *Hindutva: Who Is a Hindu?* Bombay: Veer Savarkar Prakashan.

Sayer, Derek. 1991. "British Reaction to the Amritsar Massacre, 1919–1920." *Past and Present,* no. 131 (May): 130–64.

Schimmel, Annemarie. 1980. *Islam in the Indian Subcontinent.* Leiden: E. J. Brill.

Schodt, Frederik L. 1997. *Manga! Manga! The World of Japanese Comics.* 2d ed. Tokyo and New York: Kodansha International.

Sen, Pulinbihari, ed. 1961. *Abanindranath Tagore: Golden Jubilee Number.* Calcutta: Indian Society of Oriental Art.

Sharma, Ajay. 1994. "Relationship Marketing." *Business Standard,* February 8, A4.

Sharma, Deepak. 2001. "Shivaji Dominates Agra Fort Now." *Pioneer,* February 20, 1.

Sharma, R. C., ed. 1993. *Raja Ravi Varma: New Perspectives.* Exhibition catalog. New Delhi: National Museum.

Sharma, Sri Ram. 1974. "Shivaji's Coronation: Some Reflections." In B. K. Apte, ed., *Chhatrapati Shivaji: Coronation Tercentenary Commemoration Volume,* 1–6. Bombay: University of Bombay.

Shinde, Niyatee. 1998. "Ravi Varma the Painter and Lala Deen Dayal, the Photographer: Contemporaries in Time, Sharing the Horizon." In Ratan Parimoo, ed., *The Legacy of Raja Ravi Varma, the Painter,* 66–69. Baroda: Maharaja Fatesingh Museum Trust.

Shiv Sena Speaks. 1967. Bombay: Shiv Sena Prakashan.

"Shivaji Is My Ideal, Says Vajpayee." 2004. *Mid-Day,* March 20. Online at www.mid-day.com/news/nation/2004/march/79192.htm.

Singh, Mohinder. 2000. "Jallianwala Bagh and Changing Perceptions of the Sikh Past." In V. N. Datta and S. Settar, eds., *Jallianwala Bagh Massacre,* 99–113. Delhi: Indian Council of Historical Research.

Singh, S. R. 2000. "Gandhi and the Jallianwala Bagh Tragedy: A Turning Point in the Indian National Movement." In V. N. Datta and S. Settar, eds., *Jallianwala Bagh Massacre,* 193–209. Delhi: Indian Council of Historical Research.

Siraj-ud-din, Razia, ed. 1970 [1940]. *Chughtai's Paintings.* Lahore: Print Printo Press.

Smith, H. Daniel. 1995. "Impact of 'God Posters' on

Hindus and Their Devotional Traditions." In Lawrence Babb and Susan Wadley, eds., *Media and the Transformation of Religion in South Asia,* 24–50. Philadelphia: University of Pennsylvania Press.

Souchet, Philippe, ed. 1975. *Le Message Politique et Social de la Bande Dessinee.* Toulouse: Privat.

Srivatsan, R. 2000. "Gandhi's Funeral: Event or Statement?" In *Conditions of Visibility: Writings on Photography in Contemporary India,* 107–21. Calcutta: Stree.

Tagore, Rabindranath. 1907. "Sakuntala: Its Inner Meaning." *Modern Review.* Reprinted in Romila Thapar, *Sakuntala: Texts, Readings, Histories,* 242–49. New Delhi: Kali for Women, 1999.

Talbot, Cynthia. 1995a. "Inscribing the Other, Inscribing the Self: Hindu-Muslim Identities in Pre-colonial India." *Comparative Studies in Society and History* 37, no. 4: 692–722.

———. 1995b. "Rudrama-devi, the Female King: Gender and Political Authority in Medieval India." In David Shulman, ed., *Syllables of Sky: Stories in South Indian Civilization in Honour of Velcheru Narayana Rao,* 391–430. New Delhi: Oxford University Press.

Tavernier, J. B. 1925. *Travels in India by Jean-Baptiste Tavernier, Baron of Aubonne,* vol. 1. Trans. V. Ball. 2d ed., ed. William Crooke. London: Oxford University Press.

Thapar, Romila. 1989. "Imagined Religious Communities? Ancient History and the Modern Search for a Hindu Identity." *Modern Asian Studies* 23, no. 2: 209–31.

———. 1999. *Sakuntala: Texts, Readings, Histories.* New Delhi: Kali for Women.

———. 2000. *Narratives and the Making of History.* New Delhi: Oxford University Press.

Tharoor, Shashi. 2004. *Nehru: The Invention of India.* New York: Arcade.

Tharu, Susie. 1990. "Tracing Savitri's Pedigree: Victorian Racism and the Image of Women in Indo-Anglian Literature." In Kumkum Sangari and Sudesh Vaid, eds., *Recasting Women: Essays in Indian Colonial History,* 254–68. New Brunswick: Rutgers University Press.

Trautmann, Thomas R. 1997. *Aryans and British India.* Berkeley: University of California Press.

Trivedi, Lisa N. 2003. "Visually Mapping the 'Nation': Swadeshi Politics in Nationalist India, 1920–1930." *Journal of Asian Studies* 62, no. 1: 11–41.

Uberoi, Patricia. 1990. "Feminine Identity and National Ethos in Indian Calendar Art." *Economic and Political Weekly,* April 28, WS41–WS48.

"Uncle Pai's Fun-Filled Stories Launched on CDs, Cassettes." 2001. *Afternoon Dispatch & Courier,* December 19, 8.

Vajpeyi, Ananya. 2004. "The Past and Its Passions: Writing History in Hard Times." *Studies in History* 20, no. 2: 317–29.

van der Veer, Peter. 1994. *Religious Nationalism: Hindus and Muslims in India.* Berkeley: University of California Press.

Varma, Pavan K. 1999. *The Great Indian Middle Class.* New Delhi: Penguin Books.

Varnum, Robin, and Christina Gibbons, eds. 2001. *The Language of Comics: Word and Image.* Jackson: University Press of Mississippi.

Vasudevan, Ravi, ed. 2001. *Making Meaning in Indian Cinema.* New Delhi: Oxford University Press.

Venniyoor, E. M. J. 1981. *Raja Ravi Varma.* Thiruvananthapuram: Kerala Lalit Kala Akademi, Government of Kerala.

Viswanathan, Gauri. 2001 [1998]. *Outside the Fold: Conversion, Modernity, and Belief.* New Delhi: Oxford University Press.

von Alphons Silbermann, H., and H. D. Dyroff, eds. 1986. *Comics and Visual Culture: Research Studies from Ten Countries.* New York: K. G. Saur.

von Stietencron, Heinrich. 1983. "Die Gottin Durga Mahisasuramardini: Mythos, Darstellung, und geschichtliche Rolle bei der Hinduisierung Indiens." *Visible Religion: Annual for Religious Iconography, vol. 2: Representation of Gods,* 118–66. Leiden: E. J. Brill.

Vora, Rajendra. 1999. "Maharashtra Dharma and the Nationalist Movement in Maharashtra." In N. K. Wagle, ed., *Writers, Editors, and Reformers: Social and Political Transformations of Maharashtra, 1830–1930,* 23–30. New Delhi: Manohar.

Waghorne, Joanna Punzo. 2004. *Diaspora of the Gods: Modern Hindu Temples in an Urban Middle-Class World.* New York: Oxford University Press.

Whitaker, Jarrod. 2000. "Divine Weapons and Tejas in the Two Indian Epics." *Indo-Iranian Journal* 43, no. 2: 87–113.

Williams, Joanna. 1982. *The Art of Gupta India.* Princeton, N.J.: Princeton University Press.

———. 1996. *The Two-Headed Deer: Illustrations of the Ramayana in Orissa.* Berkeley: University of California Press.

Winter, Irene. 1985. "After the Battle Is Over: The Stele of the Vultures and the Beginning of Historical Narrative in the Art of the Ancient Near East." *Studies in the History of Art* 16: 11–31.

Contemporary Indian Studies

Published in association with the American Institute of Indian Studies

The Edward Cameron Dimock, Jr. Prize in the Indian Humanities
Temple to Love: Architecture and Devotion in
Seventeenth-Century Bengal   PIKA GHOSH

Art of the Court of Bijapur   DEBORAH HUTTON

India's Immortal Comic Books:
Gods, Kings, and Other Heroes   KARLINE MCLAIN

Language, Emotion, and Politics:
The Making of a Mother Tongue in Southern India   LISA MITCHELL

The Joseph W. Elder Prize in the Indian Social Sciences
The Regional Roots of Developmental Politics in India:
A Divided Leviathan   ASEEMA SINHA

Wandering with Sadhus:
Ascetics in the Hindu Himalayas   SONDRA L. HAUSNER

Wives, Widows, and Concubines:
The Conjugal Family Ideal in Colonial India   MYTHELI SREENIVAS

Index

Italicized page numbers indicate illustrations.

darśan (seeing the gods), 15–18, 20, 65, 125

Das, Deshbandhu Chittaranjan, 85, 183

Dasaratha, 1, 94

Dassehra, 164

debate: *Amar Chitra Katha* and: 10–11, 21–23, 52, 54–55, 72, 76–77, 79, 82–83, 115, 156–157, 167, 184, 195, 207–209; colonialism and: 62, 77, 83, 166–167, 217n4:2; secularism and: 166–168, 218n5:11

Deccan, 126–127, 135, 138, 144

Delhi, 4, 24–25, 42–43, 81, 132, 149, 151, 154, 172, 178, 189, 191, 193, 209

democracy, 5, 164, 167

demons (*asuras*), 1, 3, 26, 35, 55–56, 87–88, 91, 93, 95, 97, 99, 100–111, 122, 126, 129, 139, 142, 171, 199, 211. *See also individual demon names*

Dennis the Menace, 5

Deshpande, Baji Prabhu, 120

Devaki, 29

Devi (Great Goddess), 15, 88, 91–93, 97–98, 101–113; as Mahamaya, 91; as Yoganidra, 91, 93. *See also* Durga, Kali

Devī Bhāgavata Purāṇa, 90, 105, 108

Devī Māhātmya, 87–88, 90–93, 97, 101, 103–113, 217nn3:4,3:8,3:9

dharma (religion), 126, 128–129, 204

dhoti (loincloth), 19, 73, 176

diaspora, 196, 200–201, 203, 205–206, 209–210, 213. *See also* nonresident Indian

Din Bandhu, 128–129

Din-i-Ilahi, 157–158. *See also* Akbar

Divali (Deepavali), 15, 24, 203

Doordarshan, 46–47, 75, 170, 211–212. *See also* television

Douglas, James, 123–124, 133, 135

Draupadi, 70–72, 78

Dryden, John, 147–148

Durga, 84, 87–93, 89, 95–98, 96, 99, 100, 101–113, 102, 111, 205, 207, 217nn3:3,3:4,3:5,3:7,3:8, *plate 4*. *See also* Devi, Kali

Durga Puja, 105

Durgā Saptaśatī. *See Devī Māhātmya*

Durgesh Nandini, 38–40, 38–39

Durvasa, 57–58

Dushyanta, 53, 55–58, 56–57, 60, 63, 68, 75, 79

Dutt, Batukeshwar, 182

duty, 58, 61–62, 82, 102, 117, 133, 139, 191, 204; woman's duty, 75

Dwivedi, V. P., 43

Dyer, Reginald, 177–178, 182–185, 187, 218n6:5. *See also* Jallianwala Bagh

editor: *Amar Chitra Katha* and, 4, 24, 31, 34, 36–40, 43, 52, 73, 90, 105, 132, 156, 164, 207–208; Indian newspapers and, 124, 126–127, 129, 136; *Tinkle* and, 44

education: religious, 8–9, 15–16, 42, 205–206; secularism and, 8–9, 41, 196

educators, 41, 43, 52, 87, 209. *See also* teachers, principals

efficacy, 17, 215nIntroduction:9

Elephanta, 36

enemy, 1, 114, 116, 121, 131, 137, 141, 144, 172. *See also* foe, villain

English language, 2, 6–9, 21–22, 25, 43–45, 61, 89, 92, 105, 112, 122, 147, 206, 208

epics, 2, 9, 50–51, 53–54, 62–66, 83, 112–113, 122, 215nIntroduction:2, 219nConclusion:4; *Amar Chitra Katha* and, 1–2, 12–13, 15, 46, 50–51, 55, 58, 71–72, 75, 78, 86, 94, 112–113, 117, 119, 133, 143, 171, 199, 204, 206, 212; Greek, 24, 53; visual media other than comics and, 15–16, 46, 62–66, 68, 75, 116, 125, 212; *Vivalok Comics* and, 209. *See also Bhagavad Gītā, Mahābhārata, Rāmāyaṇa*

European comic books, 12, 18, 20

evil, 2, 14, 20, 79, 98, 107, 129, 154, 199, 208

Falk, Lee, 30. *See also The Phantom*

family, 8, 42, 90, 131, 204. *See also* grandparents, parents

Fatehpur Sikri, 158, 218n5:5

Fernandes, Luis, ix

film. *See* cinema

flag, 19, 51, 142, 171, 180

Flash Gordon, 25

foe, 3, 14, 59, 142, 199, 206, 211. *See also* enemy, villain

folktale, 43, 90, 143

fort, 115–117, 125, 131, 138; Agra Fort, 137, 148–150, 152, 170; Chittor Fort, 154, 157–158, 172; Panhalgarh Fort, 120; Pratapgarh Fort, 118, 130, 218n4:13; Raigarh Fort, 124, 126, 131, 138; Red Fort, 51; Sindhudurg Fort, 131

Foster, Hal, 132

freedom fighter, 3, 11, 13, 104, 121, 169, 196, 199, 207–208, 211. *See also* revolutionary

frontality, 16, 18, 20, 69–70. *See also* image

Gandharva, Bal, 68–69, 216n2:11

Gandhi, Indira, 8, 9, 10, 19, 84, 85, 167

Gandhi, Mohandas K. ("Mahatma"), 19, 167, 171–197, 173, 177, 179, 208, 218nn6:1,6:2,6:6, 219nn6:10,6:12,6:13, *plate 10*

Gandhi, Rajiv, 10, 168

Ganesh, Chitra, 209–210

Ganesha (Ganapati), 48, 66, 88; Ganapati festival, 124, 217n4:4

Ganges (Ganga), 16, 88, 116, 182

Garuda, 88

Gaudiya Vaishnavism, 167

gaze, 16–17, 59–61, 68–70, 75, 92, 94, 150, 215nIntroduction:8

gender, 22, 60, 77, 82–83, 190–191, 204; manliness, 131, 171, 196–197, 208. *See also* women

Ghosh, Satyavrata, ix, 187

Gita. *See Bhagavad Gītā*

globalization, 7, 9

Goa, 113, 143

Gobind Singh, Guru, 36, 138, 162, 218n5:7

gods (*devas*), 2, 15, 27, 33, 50, 58, 91, 107–108. *See also individual god names*

god posters, 16–21, 65, 67, 104, 112, 125, 130–132, 134–135, 137, 183, 211, 215nnIntroduction:7,Introduction:9, 217n4:10, 218n4:14, 219n6:11. *See also* lithography

Godse, Nathuram Vinayak, 173, 191–193, 195–196, 219nn6:8,6:10,6:11,6:12, *plate 10*

Gokul, 26, 29, 69

good, 1–2, 14, 77, 80, 154, 156, 158. *See also* evil

gopis (cowgirls), 26

Govardhan Mountain, 27, 29–34, 32, 49, 87, 109, 111, *plate 3*

Government School of Art, 66, 149–150

grandparents, 7, 8, 15, 22, 41–42, 46, 105, 198, 203. *See also* family

Grant Duff, James, 122–123, 133, 135

Great Goddess. *See* Devi

Greek mythology, 24, 53

Hali, Altaf Hussain, 166, 218n5:10

Hamlet, 106–107

Hampi, 36–37

Hanuman, 12, 70, 88, 114, 134, 198–199, 204, 210

Harappa, 198

Harishchandra, Bharatendu, 50, 165

Harivamsa, 25

hartal (strike), 178, 180, 183–184, 189–190

Havell, E. B., 66–67, 150, 160, 218n5:2

Karline McLain is Assistant Professor of Religion at Bucknell University, where she teaches courses on Hinduism, Islam, and media and religion in South Asia. *India's Immortal Comic Books* was awarded the Edward Cameron Dimock, Jr. Book Prize in the Indian Humanities in 2007 by the American Institute of Indian Studies.

CPSIA information can be obtained
at www.ICGtesting.com
Printed in the USA
LVOW02s0825021215
465005LV00010B/140/P